THE
GOLDEN
HAM

A Candid Biography of Jackie Gleason

BY JIM BISHOP

19 — 56

SIMON AND SCHUSTER
New York

FIRST PRINTING
LIBRARY OF CONGRESS CATALOG CARD NUMBER: 56–6680
MANUFACTURED IN THE UNITED STATES OF AMERICA
BY KINGSPORT PRESS, INC., KINGSPORT, TENN.

To
Two Ladies
Elinor Dunning Bishop and Margaret Dunning
—my wife and her mother

Contents

For the Record

THERE ARE several Jackie Gleasons. I know some of them. There is Gleason the comedian. Millions know him, and he's a great talent. Then there is Gleason the serious actor and Gleason the director and Gleason the producer and Gleason the writer. Some people know these Gleasons, and each of these differs from the other Gleasons in substance and size and quality. Then there is Gleason the businessman—second-rate, but he thinks he's good at it—and then there is Gleason the thinker (apt and fast) and Gleason the man (fat, out of shape, but light on his feet and quick on the conversational draw) and Gleason the tenement-house kid from Brooklyn (nervy and not a bit surprised that he's on top) and Gleason the lover, Gleason the musician, Gleason the moody and Gleason the lonely, tormented soul.

Thirteen Gleasons. There are more. But these are the thirteen I have written about. They add up to a complex and fascinating character. Gleason the lonely, tormented soul is the thermostat who heats or chills the remaining twelve. The tormented soul believes in heaven and hell and in divine grace and damnation. Sometimes it does not approve of the other Gleasons. All souls come equipped with built-in consciences. The conscience, in some cases, blackmails the mind of the malefactor, and the sinner finds himself doing all sorts of good deeds for strangers—even giving away large sums of money—to still the whispered indictment.

Gleason, I am convinced, has a king-sized soul. And a loud conscience. These, coupled with a body which was intended to enjoy all of the sensual pleasures, makes for a disparate, sometimes desperate, character. He has a gargantuan appetite for food, women, camaraderie, music and charity. They do not all pull in the same direction.

Is he a genius? I don't know. I've never met a genius. He is brighter mentally than some who are called geniuses. He can, and often does, read two books in one lonely, sleepless night. They may be the wrong books, by intellectual standards, but he reads them and he blots up what they have to tell him. I have never seen Jackie Gleason at a point where he could not understand the subject under discussion. He is a nervous thinker, cocking his head and nodding to the speaker, anticipating what is going to be said and saying it first, or adding to it. Jackie has enormous powers of comprehension plus a sharp assessment of his own weaknesses.

He is as honest and as courageous as an urchin the night before First Holy Communion. In looking over the finished manuscript of this book, for example, he did not ask that anything be omitted or altered, and yet there are parts of this biography that made him wince. He lives by a code which says that a big boy doesn't cry when he's hurt. That probably accounts for the overly callous I-don't-care letter from Jackie, which is printed below. A fighter who is hit hard, and hurt, often grins and dances a little. Gleason is like that too.

In his art, he has the grace and exquisite timing of a Chaplin. He is a good actor because he loves to act and he studies acting. And yet he never immerses himself in a part. Once, after a hilarious scene in The Honeymooners, he came offstage mopping his face, walked up to a stagehand and said: "I was thinking of your problem while I was out there, and I think I have the answer."

Gleason's memory is, in a way, his greatest single asset. He remembers almost everything he ever learned, including the bad things. He remembers that he once had to split a fifty-nine-cent dinner with two other actors because all three were broke, *and so today he overpays all who work for him. Nor do you have to remind him that success is a bubble which can be reduced in a trice to a little mound of suds in the palm of the hand. He is aware of this. He has watched others go to the top and he has seen the day come when some of them were glad to accept a one-night booking as guest stars on his show. For twenty years he had been boasting that some day he would pass them all by, including Milton Berle. When the time came that Berle's sponsors switched to Gleason, the Fat One was the only person in the Gleason office who wasn't jumping for joy. Somewhere, he knew, there was a young unknown, skinny and hungry perhaps, who was feeling his way in the night-club smoke and who would some day come along and pass Gleason by. It had to be.*

In his personal relationships Jackie is as sensitive to affection, or the lack of it, as a schoolgirl. His lawyers, his producers, his agents must not only be good in their chosen fields, but there must also be full confidence in each of them. They must be "pals." It is not necessary that they love one another; in the hurly-burly of show business it sometimes helps if there is a little jostling for position under the star. He delegates practically no authority; Gleason makes the decisions, great and small. His manager cannot promise that Gleason will make an appearance; his executive producer cannot okay a script; his choreographer cannot approve costumes for the chorus of "Stage Show"; his director cannot authorize anyone to build a set. When the new office was completed, and a man arrived with palette, brushes and gold leaf, it was Gleason who paused in his multimillion-dollar industry to tell the man what names to put on each office door and what to hand-letter on the Gleason office: "The Elephant Room."

Jackie claims that he is "hammy" or conceited as an actor. He isn't. He stages a relentless war against hamminess and it shows up in amusing ways. He signs his name in lower case—jackie gleason—and his corporation is listed properly as "jackie gleason enterprises," a sort of uncapital gains. Onstage, he will always give the preferred spot to a subordinate player, and, as Sammy

Birch says, "he'll make you a bigger actor than you are." He is as aware of his stature in his craft as his most suppliant fan, but, now that he is there, he fears the stigma of the swelled head and, to offset it, he insists that his valet take the big car on a day off. It also causes him to be deferential to clerks, doormen and waiters.

And yet, this is overanalyzing, oversimplifying the man. He is real. He is regular. He is sincere. He is possibly one of the great theatrical talents of this century.

JIM BISHOP

Teaneck, New Jersey

Mr. Jackie Gleason
Park Sheraton Hotel
7th Avenue at 55th Street
New York, N. Y.

DEAR JACK:
Here is the manuscript. It's a little bit bulky, but then so are you.
Read it carefully and, if you find any inaccuracies, please draw lines in
the margin and we will discuss them. As an example, three sources
told me that the Cadillac given to you by Frank Sinatra was bottle
green. The Cadillac agency checked its records and says that the car
was black. A small item, Jack, but let's try to catch all the mistakes.
Under the agreement between us, you have no right to change or
omit anything in this book. It is facetious on my part to remind you of
this because, throughout the writing of it, you have been reminding
me that this is Jim Bishop's book, Jim Bishop's idea of Gleason. Thinking backward for a moment, I have seen you only five times in the year
that I've been researching the facts of your life. Almost all of the material you will read came from your friends, your enemies, your teachers,
your neighbors, your childhood friends, your staff, your doctor and
actors.
A good part of the book is unflattering. Some of it would shake a
sinner. It is all here—all on the record. You were, at times, a boaster,
a braggart. There are scenes of drunkenness and despair. Others describe, in some detail, your affinity for blondes. There is one—a heartbreaker to write—of your mother dying while you sat jobless. As a
Roman Catholic, you staggered, skidded, slipped and fell all over the
ecclesiastical landscape. As a husband, you failed, and you failed a
good woman. Later in life you fell in love with a fine girl, but even in
this, with the best of intentions, you were blocked by forces spiritual,
emotional and legal.
There are few men I've met who have tried harder to be "good."
To some, I am sure, it comes easily. Not to you. Everything you have
done—personally and professionally—has been done the hard way.
This, if you can stand one opinion, makes you a bigger and better
man than you think. Conscience and contrition are brothers—and,
brother, you have both in king size!
The over-all portrait shows that your failures were few; your suc-

cesses were many. For example, you did not fail as a father. Geraldine and Linda understand the depths of your affection for them and it is not necessary for anyone else to comprehend it. Also, you have never failed as a friend, although, in not failing, you have often failed yourself. Your loyalty to persons of small talent is adolescent. When you like a man, it is impossible for him to do any wrong.

You have never failed as a performer either, and I think that the book shows this clearly. Even in the old days, you would rather get on a stage for nothing and give fully of your enormous talent than not to get on a stage at all.

This biography—unless I have missed the target entirely—is a complete recitation of the great and awful things in a man's life. It has no "slant," either in your favor or opposed to you. I think that the life of every man is a balance of good and evil, of courage and cowardice, of racing toward the stars while creeping toward the grave.

Good luck in the next forty, my friend. . . .

JIM BISHOP

857 Garrison Avenue
Teaneck, New Jersey

October 17, 1955

Mr. Jim Bishop
Hotel Excelsior
Rome, Italy

DEAR JIM:

Well, I have read the book!

Am I supposed to indignantly shout "libel-fable" in offense, or meekly murmur "circumstance-adversity" in defense?

It is too late in life for me to feign either attitude. I have allowed my egoism to carefully manufacture two luxury items; a dignity opposed to denial, and a pride disturbed by pity.

To admit the truth of most if not all you report gives me no heroic glow. The heroism of confession is satisfying only to a fool. Besides, the clarity and evidence of my indiscretions insulate me from the warmth of any such emotional deceit.

I have no legitimate argument for my conduct. There have been times that I have tried philosophy and liquor to justify my behavior and pacify my conscience. The experiments failed—wisdom and whisky make promises they can't keep.

I have never been a modest man and I have always been suspicious of an actor's modesty. It is usually counterfeit and is actually commercial naïvete. The cause and *effect* contradict the virtue. So, please believe me when I tell you I don't want my success to be admired— just the incongruity of it.

Sincerely,
jackie gleason

P.S. Giving it all one last thought, Jim, it has occurred to me that an actor's security and the eye of a hurricane have a great deal in common.

jg

THE
GOLDEN
HAM

THE PENTHOUSE

THE DOCTOR *was precise and confident. He clipped the tips from four stems of asparagus with one stroke of the knife. He chewed in careful cadence and his conversation was as sharply defined as his hair, which is parted down the middle.*

"To win Gleason's confidence," he said, addressing himself more to the writer's tape recorder than to the writer, "a doctor must be able to defend himself."

"Why?" *the writer said. It's his best word.*

"Jackie knows a lot of medicine."

"Where did he learn medicine?"

"He didn't learn medicine. He has read about medicine." *He glanced at the ceiling, mouth pursed.* "He has a memory. A phenomenal thing at times. If you tell him that this or that is wrong with him, he not only has read about the illness, but he seems to know what's new about it therapeutically." *The doctor's rimless glasses glint yellow in the hotel room.* "A pain in the neck in a way."

The writer looked at his notes. He is a short, slick man who looks as if he is nursing an old grievance. "He told me that he has no fears."

"Gleason is a liar. No, I withdraw that. He's not a liar because that would imply consciousness of fear. Let's put it another way. Jackie Gleason is loaded with fear but doesn't know it."

"Subconscious?"

The doctor nodded. "You've been around. Why do you think he has to be such a good guy all the time?"

"Is he?"

"Is he? Of course he is. You go to any actor, manager, cab driver, hotel maid or television sponsor and they will tell you that Gleason is the greatest man in the world. Well, maybe not the greatest. But surely the most generous, the most sympathetic, the most loyal. Do you think it sounds normal for any man to be one hundred per cent generous, sympathetic and loyal? Of course you don't. Everyone has a little of the rat in him."

"And this has something to do with fear?"

"It has a lot to do with fear. He is afraid of being rejected. His father walked out on him when he was a little kid. Isn't that rejection? His mother died when he was in his teens. Isn't that rejection? He has no family—maybe one or two distant relatives. So he cultivates friends. Hundreds and hundreds and hundreds of them. The best way to make friends is to do things for people. Gleason kills himself being good to everybody."

"Yes," the writer said.

"He puts up with people who have failed him. He cannot fire an employee or refuse to see an old friend. Why? They might go around saying that Gleason is a no-good bum. So he carries people with no talent and he lavishes money and gifts on old buddies who, if he were drowning, would toss him a glass of water.

"That's fear of rejection. He has other fears too."

Central Park, from a penthouse, looks like a hundred acres of spinach. It is a place of bridle paths and lakes and a zoo, quaint bridges and model sailboats and progressive traffic lights. It is a place for airing babies and dogs and it is also a place for mugging and rape. From a distance, it looks like a square-cut emerald with the prongs of spires around it. From close up, it is patchy grass, poplar, oak and elms, and children running with a ball.

It is also a state of mind, a backdrop for success or failure. The people along the north side of the park are poor Negroes and Puerto Ricans. They live on 110th Street and they call it 110th Street. The people along the west side of the park live in beige towers on Eighth Avenue and they call it Central Park West. Those along the southern rim are on Fifty-ninth Street, but the number lacks lilt and so they call it Central Park South. The respectable rich live along the eastern rim, and they are satisfied to call it Fifth Avenue.

The view from Fifth is fundamentally the same as from Eighth or Fifty-ninth or 110th, except that it costs more and the resident

needs front-window draperies to protect him from the afternoon
sun. It is a quiet, elegant street on which money moves on tiptoe.
At a time among the yesterdays, men built mansions here and
they built them of marble and granite and staffed them with the
obsequious Irish. The mansions are gone and the Irish have built
apartment houses here. Still, Fifth Avenue remains an aspiration
for the poor and a mark of security among the rich. To a boy
from Bayonne or Butte or Brooklyn, Fifth Avenue-on-the-Park is
class.

Few make the goal, but the goal is, tantalizingly, only around
the corner from 110th Street. Once achieved, Fifth Avenue can
be taken straight or with an added fillip. The victor can lease an
apartment or, if he wants to gild the goal, he can rent that master-
piece of the roofer's art, a penthouse. The winner then looks
down on other winners. The only possible way that this situation
can be improved is to have a duplex penthouse.

Jackie Gleason leaned on the parapet of his duplex penthouse.
It was a mild spring Sunday afternoon with a Mary blue sky and
three percale white clouds, neatly fluffed. Everything, to Mr.
Gleason, was beautiful. The breeze was beautiful. The park was
beautiful. His Sunday-afternoon guests, loafing on the terrace,
were beautiful, and the food, catered by Donald, was beautiful.
Life was beautiful.

He wore lemon-colored pajamas and saddle-leather slippers.
From the back, as the breeze whipped the cloth, he looked like
an Army weather balloon. For a moment he watched the men and
boys sail their boats in Central Park, far below.

"I told them they could use my pool," he said to Toots Shor,
"if they'd stop throwing the candy wrappers in the water." Shor
made a tired face. A squadron of planes flew up the length of the
park. "Look who I got watering the lawn!" Gleason yelled. None
of this was boastful. It was a wit's echo to outrageous success.
This man, in his fortieth year, was the biggest attraction in the
world of television. About one third of the population of the
United States watched his antics every Saturday night. More people saw him each week than saw a top-rank motion-picture star
in a year. His handsome Irish face, his coal-washed hair, his big
blue eyes, the attitudes of his hands were known almost every-

where. The people loved him. He loved them. He was on top. The biggest. The king. The end.

The Sunday-afternoon tea represented the unveiling of the penthouse. It had been seen, in quick peeks, by a few. Today it was being shown. Gleason moved around easily, graciously among these people because Gleason felt at home with this group. These were his producers, directors, theatrical agents, press agents, assistant directors and recording officials. Each made a good living off Jackie. Each had a degree of talent which added to Gleason's success. Each found that his future was locked irrevocably to the stout man. Each was sure in his heart that if he left Gleason he would have to learn to live on a little less.

The women sat under the green-striped canopy facing Fifth Avenue. They were younger-looking than their men and their dresses looked as rich as their coiffures. They sat, ankles crossed, on summer furniture, and they talked of shows and shoes and shapes. The men were on the other side of the terrace, in a group near the south awning, and they insulted one another with the delight of men who are flexing muscles.

"Where's the raccoon hat?" said one, looking at Gleason's pajamas.

"I have the thing," said Jackie, waving a glass. "Vodka. No hangover."

"Vodka?"

"It's beautiful, pal."

The star finished his drink and went down the curving staircase to the lower deck. In a corner of the living room is a glass-enclosed Seeburg record player. Few nonmusicians have as deep an affinity for jazz as Gleason. His record player pipes it into every room on both floors, and it plays through all of his waking hours. Music does a great deal to him, and for him, but Dixieland jazz mesmerizes him into something akin to bewitched stone.

He selected enough recordings to last the afternoon and evening and then returned to his guests. Music began to seep through the rooms and out onto both the upper and lower porches.

A muted trumpet wept and wailed across the living room and a prissy caterer whispered frantically to red-coated waiters who hurried upstairs with big silver salvers, heavy with food. A guest came downstairs slowly, looked around, and disappeared into the library. He turned a television set on and watched the New York Giants play losing ball while, at his side, he had a small transistor radio tuned into the Dodger game. As a Giant fan, his agony was doubled.

The décor of the apartment is Contemporary Parisian. It comes up almost impure Gleason. This is to say, lavish and rich, but not vulgar. There are six rooms—not counting the two porches—and they are small rooms. The cost of decorating them ("Let's always travel first-class, pal") ran to about $85,000, an average of about $14,000 per room.

The rugs were all especially woven. The rug on the living-room floor, which is the color of a stop light, has a gray blocked edging which follows every turn and corner of the walls. On it rests a paneled color-television set, a grand piano, pale-yellow leather chairs designed with the host's weight in mind, and the glass record player. The walls of this room are flocked gray. Flocking is a kind of suède which is blown on. The recessed ceiling lights turn red or white, dim or bright, at the turn of a rheostat. The effect is modern, although against one wall stands an eight-sided Chinese screen of some antiquity.

"I had to fight," the decorator murmured, "to get that in here."

The dining room is small and square and looks like a large breakfast room. The gold figured wallpaper was imported from Switzerland. Across the foyer is a compact library, done in taste. The shelves are heavy with books on psychic phenomena. There are some popular books, mostly nonfiction, and a four-volume set marked *The Rise and Fall of the Gleason Empire*. These are bound copies of jokes, listed under categories. There is a desk and a telephone and, recessed into the shelves, another television set. Three solid-gold records are pinned to a wall. Each was awarded to the comedian for selling a million copies of a given recording. A slender gold baton is tacked to a board. The legend beneath it says simply that Jackie Gleason was the best band leader of 1954. The walls are flocked in red. Pale-orange draperies cover the front windows.

There is but one bedroom. The big, low, modern bed dominates it. Across the room a television screen is set in a corner of the ceiling. This is controlled by buttons in the headboard of the bed. Around the perimeter of the room are salmon-colored draperies made of panne velvet. These will open or close at the touch of a switch. Black end tables flank the bed. One is a bar. The other is a beer cooler.

There are two bathrooms on the lower floor, one adjoining the master bedroom, one for guests. The master bathroom is half walled with red flocking on gold. The rest of the wall, inside the chased-glass shower, is done in solid-gold leaf. Underfoot, the black and white tiles are set so that they make illusionary squares. No matter how many times they are counted, the total is never the same.

The guest bathroom is papered with large designs of match covers which advertise some of the famous restaurants and bars of the world. Adjoining is a rectangular closet with a built-in bar. The stairway from this floor to the upper deck is in the form of a printed C and leads to a startlingly white room which the decorator calls "cinema white." This is a barroom. The ceiling represents a pale-blue sky with dumpling clouds. This is the only room on the twenty-first floor, and in a wall is a recessed television set. Wrought-iron tables with glass tops enhance the barroom motif, and the man behind the bar wears a red vest with a single brass button. Today the traffic in vodka is heavy.

There is a point in a party which is sometimes referred to as its "height." This one had no such discernible point. The jollity was studied, and the roughhouse horseplay between the men was sporadic and nostalgic. The host, who is a fine wit off stage, lapsed into silences. Downstairs the executive producer, Jack Philbin, sat at the piano hitting soft chords which spelled "I'm Getting Sentimental over You." Upstairs, in the barroom, Gleason's manager and a Capitol Records executive sat talking about a painting by Salvador Dali. A little man with youthful hair, Earl Wilson, crouched behind a small camera and made candid photographs. A few women picked up dinner plates at the buffet and paused indecisively before the caterer's art. A huge horn made of ice spilled whole shrimps and lobster onto the table. A candied ham sat in a silver cradle. There were smoked turkey, Beef Stroganoff, cold cuts, salads, a strawberry cake as big as a coffee table, hot liquids and cold, mints. But little of laughter.

It was as though Jackie Gleason and his team had taken their first long look at the opulence, the grandeur of the penthouse on Central Park and had realized not that they had made the grade but that they had suddenly stopped being a coarse group of buffoons and were now a frock-coated corporation.

At 4:30 P.M. the host was in bed. He sleeps well in the daytime.

Another day, another party. It was 6:40 P.M. and the people outside Track 38 at Grand Central Terminal stared at the Pullman board and at their tickets. DETROITER, the sign said, 7:00 P.M. The conductors studied the stubs and passed the passengers through the gateway. They noted that the train had two new head cars, not normally a part of the train. These were numbered JG-1, JG-2. The orders said that these were to be closed off from the rest of the train.

Gleason arrived, spearheading his own entourage, which spread out behind his presence like a bow wave. His black hair glistened above a turned-up collar. Someone nudged him and grinned at the Pullman board. "See it, Jackie? J.G. one and J.G. two." Jackie looked up and grinned. The party swept on through the gates and people still waiting to present their tickets murmured that this was Jackie Gleason, the big television star.

The actor continued on down the ramp, past the rear coach and its cruiser stern and on by the quiet hum of the glistening Pullman cars. He walked a long way and then he said loudly, "You buy a seat on a train and you get in it. Buy two whole cars and they make you walk to Newark to find them." Up at the front, the Gleason party found cars JG-1 and JG-2 and boarded.

This is the way Jackie Gleason travels to press a button for a worthy cause. He was on his way from New York City to Detroit to press a button which would light a forty-five-foot torch in front of City Hall which, in turn, would signify the opening of the United Foundation Drive for $13,500,000. There was no other reason for the trip.

Some weeks before he had been asked by Myron Kirk to press

the button. The automobile executives of Detroit wanted to have their annual charity drive opened by a star of magnitude. Kirk, a Madison Avenue Homburg whose advertising agency administers the Buick account, asked Gleason. The star, whose code of living is to do anything for a "pal," said yes to pal Kirk. Then, as the date drew near, Jackie's enthusiasm died a little. It would be a long train trip; he didn't like planes; and anyone could press a button. The advertising-agency man, a fiftyish person with big laugh wrinkles around his little eyes, reminded Gleason that he had promised.

That was so. He had. In that case he would do it, but he would want to bring some pals along on the trip—you know, to break up the monotony of it. Two Pullman cars were leased, and Gleason, now in festive mood, got on the phone and invited a group of gentlemen and ladies to come along for the ride. To some he announced, "This is Jackie." To others, with a gay toss of the head, he said, "This is the greatest," and every one of the pals understood. Each was advised to meet at Toots Shor's restaurant two hours before traintime "so that we can get feeling nice."

Now they were feeling nice and they were aboard the train. The first of the two Pullmans was half rooms and berths and half lounge car. The other was roomettes. A Filipino steward made drinks. In the entourage were seven producers and agents, four beautiful girls who had been employed as Portrettes on "The Jackie Gleason Show," three girls from the Gleason chorus, plus Max Kaminsky and his Dixieland Jazz Band.

Gleason sat in a breakfast nook puffing on a cigarette and admiring the chrome and leather appointments of the car. He grinned at a tall Negro drummer and said, "Know what? With any kind of luck we may never get off this train."

"Drink up," he yelled to the six men in the band. "We brought plenty of booze." The band played "Sweet Sue," and it was sheer Dixie to its bass clef. Three girls shared the breakfast nook with Jackie. Beneath the rhythm of the trombone and the cello could be heard the faint castinets of the wheels on the rails. Outside the windows Storm King and West Point and the Catskills slipped by in the dark as the Detroiter raced through the night. A blond girl stood in the aisle, shoes off, and managed to keep her balance and do a Charleston at the same time. The Filipino steward carried trays of drinks through the din of the band, and an old conductor, with forty years of service stripes, plunked tentatively at the strings on a cello he was holding for one of the musicians. The train raced. The band blared. The drinks flowed. Gleason, in a moment of musical silence, said, "Take five miles, fellas."

The producer and the executive producer stood and sang "I Had a Dream, Dear." At midnight two of the musicians donned smoked glasses. Somebody yelled, "Everybody choose partners for the big balloon dance." Jackie, perspiring and with lids half closed, sang while seated. When he finished he said to the band, "You're becoming indistinguishable, boys. Now I can only hear you."

The Detroiter inched into the station at Syracuse and, on other tracks, train crews paused in their labors to gape. They saw the Detroiter come to a stop, and through the broad, soundproofed windows they saw a girl in a car doing a mad dance and they saw, as in a silent motion picture, men blowing furiously into a trumpet, a saxophone and a trombone. They couldn't decipher the tune—it was "Muskrat Ramble"—but they hopped across the tracks and hurried to the side of the car and gaped and grinned and winked at the pretty girls.

In the low-number hours, Jackie Gleason grabbed a trumpet and blew a few notes toward "Ain't Misbehavin'." Two girls sat drinking together. Two others kept to themselves in the back of the car and talked modeling and fees. Two of the men had quit and were in bed. The steward had locked up his New York Central bar, but Jackie had brought his own liquor aboard, and he and the band were engaged in Dixieland conversation. His valet and old friend, Tony Amico, told Gleason where his bed was.

The city of Detroit had a sooty sun. A fleet of Cadillacs waited outside the station and the girls and the men got in. An open truck crossed in front of the procession. Oil drums were lashed to the back. "Look!" said Jackie happily. "They're bringing the booze to our hotel already!"

The star had a hang-over known as "four colors in key." With it one has nervous tension, baby birds pulsing in the temples, a monotonous mental recording sometimes called "the hums," and a feeling of impending doom. Gleason never quits when he doesn't feel good. Sometimes he seems brighter and funnier.

"Well," he said with resignation, "it was a very moral trip anyway. Next time we'll take along three for-sure girls."

He felt like sleeping. The cars drew up to the Cadillac-Sheraton and the Gleason party was given the entire nineteenth floor. This included a group of corner rooms called the Presidential Suite, which had been reserved for Jackie. When he arrived, the star refused a drink, had breakfast, held a press conference, charmed reporters, posed for pictures with a line of dancers showing a few inches of leg while Gleason (little-boy style) made an O of his mouth and popped his eyes, talked to a United Fund official, who irritated Jackie with pompous dicta, made a phone call to New York, made plans for a party in the Presidential Suite that night, told the band to stick around, that they would be paid for their time, ordered plane tickets for the musicians on a next-morning trip to New York, had a conference with Jerry Katz, who represented Music Corporation of America, the Gleason agents, changed his clothes, studied a penciled outline of all the acts that would be part of a benefit show that night, refused an offer of a good pickup, moaned about his hang-over in the privacy of his own "team," and sent everyone out while he took a nap.

In the evening the time came for the button to be pressed. In front of City Hall, 1,400 citizens gathered to see Jackie Gleason in person. There was a wooden reviewing stand and, behind it on the lawn, a gigantic torch to be lighted. A few words were said; Gleason carried a chronically ill child to the front of the stand; the child pressed the button, and nothing happened. The crowd roared, and the child tried again. This time the top of the torch glowed red, and everyone applauded.

Gleason, still sick, was taken to a theater, where the area backstage was cluttered with rolled-up canvas and partly dismantled sets and, in a hurly-burly of misunderstanding between star and orchestra, acted as master of ceremonies for the benefit show. He gave each act a big build-up, told jokes, did his "Away

We Go" bit, sweated in the wings, did a little dance, introduced Miss America, and left just as Eddie Peabody, an old banjo player, arrived, forelock in eye.

The clock was in the morning hours again when Gleason arrived at the Cadillac-Sheraton to do something which he calls "relax." The Dixieland band was tootling; Jackie phoned downstairs for a piano and the manager, Neil Lang, said it was on its way up and if anyone wanted him he would be at the Leland Hotel. Jackie gulped two drinks in a hurry; he took a sheet of paper and a pencil and went among the guests asking what they would like to eat.

The rooms were crowded and Gleason asked his producers where all the people were coming from. No one knew. Most of them were officials of the United Foundation Drive and their wives. More were coming in. Jackie said that they had not been invited. This was repeated at the door by producers Hurdle and Philbin, but the dinner-clothed men and the minked ladies insisted and some forced their way in. Others, turned away at the door, came in through the pantry.

The notes of "Embraceable You" crashed from the horns and caromed off· three walls and fled through the open windows. Jackie was crouching, taking orders for food from people on the floor. He turned to a sad-looking blonde, who said, "I'll take thirty feet of rope."

Gleason nodded solemnly and wrote it. "That's the most sensible order I've heard yet," he said. "You going to hang yourself?"

"Just get the rope."

The order went down, along with orders for steak sandwiches and club sandwiches and platters of spaghetti, and later the chef phoned and asked about the thirty feet of rope. Gleason was called to the phone and said, "Look, pal. The lady wants thirty feet of rope. Just get thirty feet somewhere. It doesn't have to be special rope."

When the waiters brought the food, they also had the rope, on a platter with a napkin. The blonde asked two men to tie her wrists together with the rope. The guests stopped talking. The band stopped playing. Everyone watched the tired blonde and the rope. Her wrists were tied tight and cross-knotted. The blonde asked two men to pull on the rope. They did—hard enough to yank her upright. By some magic, the knots untied themselves and the rope slipped free.

Gleason thought it was a great trick. The band played "Crazy Rhythm" and "You Are My Lucky Star." The people talked or ate. The waiters came and went. The drinks came up to the nine-tenth floor and went down. There were jokes and laughter and bedlam and some serious conversation. Some of the minked women made overtures to the star. Some of the dinner-dressed men had arguments with the minked women.

At 4:45 A.M. Jackie Gleason stood in the doorway and said good night to the last guest.

In the late afternoon Jackie and his team boarded the Detroiter for New York. In most eyes there was remorse. It was the same train with the same car numbers and Jack Hurdle said that the Central must have rerounded the wheels. The band had left in the morning. The two cars were comparatively quiet. There was some therapeutic drinking and everyone got to bed early.

The Detroiter eased into Grand Central Terminal at breakfast time. Jackie got out of bed, shaved, dressed, tried to summon the old Gleason smile as he said farewell to the men and women who had accompanied him, and hurried off with Tony Amico to the Park Sheraton Hotel to change into fresh clothes. He had a 10:00 A.M. engagement to make a recording.

Gleason had kept his word. He had pressed a button.

There are many Jackie Gleasons. The several sides to his character are not always in agreement with the others. Gleason the businessman does not admire Gleason the playboy. Gleason the Catholic is not fond of Gleason the connoisseur of blondes. Gleason the fine actor has little respect for Jackie the drinker. Gleason the lonely brooder has no affection for Gleason the wit.

At the age of forty he was a lonely penitent. The party at the penthouse was a rare thing. When he wasn't doing a show Jackie was alone. He wandered around the penthouse, reading through the predawn hours, making notes on a pad, phoning when he could find someone awake, summoning Tony Amico at 7:00 A.M. ("Come on, pal. I got the coffee made"), making plans for future

shows, discarding many of them, reading books on psychic phenomena in a desperate effort to find proof of a hereafter, having
coffee with a member of his team, sitting on the terrace with
Marilyn Taylor, a woman to whom he is devoted, phoning his
secretary, Lee Reynolds, dressing and running off to Toots Shor's
restaurant to stand around the bar and swap "cracks" with his
friends, hurrying home to jump into bed and hope for the
surcease of unconsciousness.

It wasn't much of a day. For a man whose gross earnings stood
a little bit above $3,000,000 a year, and whose appetite for pleas-
ure was enormous, it was dull. A few years prior, Jackie would
have borrowed "two hundred skins" and gone off with a group of
men and women and said, "Let's go bouncing." The word means
pub crawling, moving from one saloon to another, remaining just
long enough to drain the place of laughter, and moving on to
another place.

Now he did not have to borrow money. He had it. Now he did
not have to worry about a drink of brandy. The hall closet was
full of it. Now his old pals were no longer friendly and insulting;
they stood in awe of him, somewhat subdued, and they laughed
too heartily when he made a feeble jest. Women were no longer
the challenge of contention; their ambitions were open and shame-
less.

Gleason was big business. He owned all the stock in Jackie
Gleason Enterprises Inc., which owns "The Jackie Gleason Show,"
books talent, owns the summer replacement show, controls two
music-publishing corporations, owns a part of a producing oil
well and pays Gleason the actor $10,000 per performance. A sepa-
rate company sells Gleason dolls.

Big business.

Jackie Gleason Enterprises Inc. is also a big penthouse office
at the Park Sheraton Hotel in New York, complete with secretaries, receptionist, executives, writers and agents. It is also a show
composed of high-priced actors, cameramen, musicians, electricians, scenic designers, chorus girls, announcers, directors, producers, technicians, script girls, lighting experts, arrangers, dress-
ers and a seamstress. In all, about 140 persons.

All of it is built around Jackie Gleason, a person. Without Gleason, all of it falls apart at once. Without him, there is no Saturday-night show, no music companies, no dolls, no corporation, no reason for being. With him, all of the bricks and mortar fly into place.

On stage, Jackie is also several persons. He is Jackie Gleason, talented actor of "Studio One" and other dramatic shows. He is Ralph Kramden, bus driver; Loudmouthed Charley Bratton; the pantomiming Poor Soul; Joe the Brooklyn Bartender; Rudy the Repairman; Reggie Van Gleason; Fenwick Babbitt, harassed clerk; Stanley R. Sogg, the television pitchman who sells Mother Fletcher's homely products between reels of Mae Busch in "Should a Girl Tell?" ("For you girls with heavy calves, a cowbell.") He is also J. Gleason, the star who stands in front of the curtain and tells a joke poorly. Most of the time, he is also Jackie Gleason, producer of the show; Jackie Gleason, director of the show; Jackie Gleason, musical arranger and approver of dance routines; Jackie Gleason, script writer; Jackie Gleason, worrier.

As a master of situation comedy, Gleason has been called a genius. This is an exaggeration because it implies a unique and exclusive talent. He comes close to justifying the use of the word inasmuch as his situation comedies seem to be funny to people of all ages and callings. His cosmopolitan reach into all kinds of homes is what makes him a funnier funnyman than any other comedian of mid-century.

In his early years Jackie admired the work of such comedians as Henry Burbig, a dialect comic; Charles Chaplin; W. C. Fields, the master of moist invective; Eddie Gribben; Harold Lloyd, a naive good boy; and Laurel and Hardy—especially the fat and prissy Hardy.

It is almost impossible to invent a comic style. A new comedian is a blend of some old ones plus the addition of his own personality. Any middle-aged student of comedy will find a little bit of the old silent-motion-picture comic, Lloyd Hamilton, in Gleason's "The Poor Soul," and a piece of Eddie Gribben, Keystone Kop, in Jackie's flutter of the arms and "Away We Go!" What Jackie added to these is a natural, unstudied talent for

credible comedy. He was funny almost from the time he learned
to talk. In some of his skits there is even a hint of the Chaplin
pathos.

Physically, this man is a blowfish. His weight bounds from 185
pounds to 285 pounds, and sometimes pauses at 240. He has three
complete wardrobes—one for 185 pounds, one for 240, one for
280. The one for 240 pounds gets the most wear because Gleason
uses it on the way up, and again on the way down.

The weight problem is not glandular. At the table, he is a pig.
Dinner may consist of a dozen oysters, a large platter of spaghetti and meat sauce, a pound or two of roast beef with mashed
potatoes, gravy and a green vegetable, a dessert that looks like
the Canadian Rockies in winter. On the train to Detroit the waiter
watched the big man finish a double sirloin steak, and said, "What
will you have for dessert, Mr. Gleason?"

Jackie raised wounded eyes and murmured, "Another steak, of
course."

When Gleason is slim he is about as handsome an Irishman as
there is. He appears to be about thirty years of age and he loses
some of his funniness. When he gets heavy Jackie works twice as
hard at being amusing and appears to draw more laughs. At the
same time he begins to worry about his weight, and he often
checks himself into Doctors Hospital, where he lives in a room
and counts calories. He does not leave the hospital except for
rehearsals and at showtime. However, a week or ten days of dieting makes him irritable, and late at night he has bribed orderlies
to go outdoors and buy a dozen frankfurters, with sauerkraut, and
he has eaten the twelve in ten minutes.

This problem, obvious to a huge television audience, has led to
joshing by mail and it has led to fanatical suggestions too. One
man wrote:

"I do not use medicines, drugs, injections, etc., but with over
fifty years in this profession my record is I get results when others
try and fail. . . .

"It is not enough just to sweat fat off—to diet it off—pernicious
anemia results—DEATH ALSO IN MANY CASES.

"There is but one way to reduce and stay REDUCED—that is, to adjust the glands so that you can eat all and what you want without adding weight, BUT TAKING IT OFF. . . .

"CALL ME RIGHT NOW—NOT TOMORROW—THAT CAN BE TOO LATE."

Another one, from Bayside, Long Island, said:

"Heard you lost weight again and if any of your suits are too big and you don't care to alter, I'd appreciate it if you'd drop me a line and have me take them off your hands. I'm about your old size and can't afford it. . . ."

There were other problems which confronted this man as he approached his fortieth birthday. Religion is one of the insoluble ones. He was born and bred a Roman Catholic. It won't erase. He seldom attends Mass and he fears the consequence of nonattendance. He has a strong concomitant love and fear of God, and his faith in God and the Catholic Church are intact. For years he made a practice of quitting late parties momentarily to go into his bedroom and drop to his knees in prayer.

Once he petitioned for a favor. He promised that if it was granted he would attend Mass every morning for two years in gratitude. The favor was granted. Jackie almost wrecked his health in the next two years because, as a night-club comedian, he did not get to bed until five and he left a standing call to call him out of bed at 7:30 A.M. so that he could get to eight-o'clock Mass.

A reporter asked him what his greatest fear was and Gleason said, "I'm afraid I'll never make Heaven." Often he stops in at St. Patrick's Cathedral at noon or in the early afternoon for a quick prayer.

He buys gold medallions of St. Genesius, patron of actors, and presents them to his friends, Christian and Jew. He firmly believes that St. Genesius protects "us actors." And yet he was never a blind believer. Gleason was always a questioner. When he grew up he studied all the religions he could find books on before he decided that, as far as he was concerned, his parents had picked the right one in the Holy Roman Catholic Church.

Still, he is in desperate need of fortification, and he studies hundreds of books on psychic phenomena to prove beyond doubt that people who are dead are in communication with this world. That, of course, is not his main problem with religion. The main problem is how to reconcile an addiction to such sins as gluttony, lust and blasphemy with an unquestioning belief that sinners will be punished. These are sins of the flesh, and Jackie the big television star sometimes fights a losing battle against them, while Jackie the poor Catholic kid from Brooklyn weeps.

To atone, he tries to help priests, nuns, rabbis and ministers, either by sending money or by making a personal appearance at a bazaar or parish affair. In these matters, he spurns publicity, and a writer once bet Monsignor LeRoy McWilliams of Jersey City a bent nickel that Jackie Gleason would not show up at 9:00 A.M. on a Sunday morning for a communion breakfast.

"What makes you think he won't?" the monsignor asked.

"He can't," the writer said. "He finishes his show on Saturday night and then he goes out with the boys and relaxes. Now, Monsignor, you ought to know that nobody in the world can relax like Jackie Gleason. Okay. So he gets home at four-thirty or five in the morning. You still think he's going to get out of the hay to come to a small parish he's never even heard of?"

"Yes," the monsignor said. And he was right. Gleason was in the basement of the church at 8:45 A.M. Because of Gleason's presence, the basement was jammed with men in a state of grace.

At almost the same time, Jackie received a letter from Father Casserly of Our Lady of Mount Virgin Church, Garfield, New Jersey:

"I told Father Ferreri to write you a note of thanks for coming all the way over to Garfield for our St. Patrick's night affair," it read. "I don't know if he had all the figures at hand when he thanked you for coming, but I guess you will be glad to know that because of your personal appearance we were able to realize about $1,000 for the Building Fund. I guess I can't do much in return for all your kindnesses, except to offer a remembrance in all my Masses and prayers. We consider you a benefactor of our parish."

A priest in Baltimore asked Jackie for a copy of one of the Joe the Bartender scripts and Gleason, always alert to get closer to Saint Genesius, sent the script and wrote:

"Now I would like to ask you a favor. I am very anxious to get a relic of St. Genesius, the actors' saint. If, in any way, it is possible for you to procure a relic of this kind you cannot possibly imagine how happy it would make me. However, if this cannot be done I will settle for a few Hail Marys and Our Fathers by you for me instead. . . . P.S. Please don't forget the prayers as, when the Guardian Angel says to me, 'Away we go!' I would like to be prepared. Jackie."

Not long afterward he read something nice about himself written by John Lester for *The Sign*, the Passionist magazine, and Gleason wrote:

"I am sending you a St. Genesius medal, who is, as you know, the actors' patron saint. I suggest when you receive it to have it blessed by a priest, as it does wonders for guys like you and me in this racket. . . ."

Eventually Gleason got the relic of St. Genesius. Boston's tall and brilliant Archbishop Cushing unwarily wrote to Jackie and asked him to travel to the capital of Massachusetts to insure the success of an archdiocesan affair. The only condition laid down by the actor was that he had been trying, for a long time, to get a relic of St. Genesius and he would appreciate it if the archbishop would do something about it.

Cushing did. He sent a relic from the person of the saint and a document attesting to its authenticity. It required time and patience and some correspondence with Rome, but it was done, and part of St. Genesius now lives in a penthouse on Fifth Avenue.

And yet the search for truth goes on. Jackie believes, for example, that man uses only a small part of his mentality and that intellectual riches await the mental miner who digs deep enough. The magnitude of the universe inclines him to believe that the secret of it will turn out to be a simple key. A professor of extrasensory perception from Duke University dropped in at the Jackie Gleason Enterprises office one day, and Gleason ordered writers, producers and technicians to leave the room. He and the professor were inside four hours before the door was opened.

"What do you think they were doing?" one writer asked.

The other shrugged. "They probably floated a couple of broads in," he said.

Jackie reads omnivorously, and he can read two books a day and be able to tell all about them in table conversation. His tastes lie in nonfiction and he will read anything he thinks will add to his knowledge. His favorites, though, center around the occult sciences: *Is Another World Watching?*, by Gerald Heard; *The Fifth Dimension*, by Vera Stanley Adler; *Animal Magnetism*, by Gregory; *Huang Ti Nei Ching Su Wen:* The Yellow Emperor's Classic of Internal Medicine; *Plant Autographs and Their Revelations*, by Bose; *Mesmerism True—Mesmerism False:* A Critical Examination; *New World of the Mind*, by Joseph Banks Rhine.

The Haldeman-Julius firm of publishers missed getting a large order for such books when Gleason asked for 425 volumes to be sent C.O.D. The publishers responded by asking for cash, and this was agreeable to the actor, but he bridled when he noted that the letter to him began: "Dear Madam."

This is an understandable error because Jackie writes in a small, feminine script and often signs himself in lower case: "jackie gleason." At other times, if writing to a friend, he signs "The World's Greatest Comedian," or "The World's Greatest." Once, in a note to columnist Ed Sullivan, he signed it: "The World's Greatest—Comedian?"

He enjoys writing formal notes about ridiculous subjects. A few years ago, when he was busy raising a male schnauzer, he learned that Mrs. Earl Wilson, wife of the New York *Post* columnist, had a female schnauzer. Gleason wrote stiffly:

DEAR MRS. WILSON:

I have come into the information that you have in your possession a young, attractive female schnauzer that I understand you are anxious to have meet a reputable, dashing, devil-may-care male schnauzer. This missive is to inform you that I have in my kennel just such an animal. His name is Reginald Van Gleason III. From his actions lately, it is obvious that he has reached the age of puberty. Also, from his clandestine romances with chair legs, gate posts, and trees and several immovable objects, not to mention his several futile attempts to woo my secretary's standard French poodle (which is away above his means) there is every indication that the time has come.

If, as I have learned during a sexy conversation with my secretary, you are interested in having your schnauzer schnauzed, please get in touch with me immediately as there is nothing more disturbing than having a dashing, debonair, devil-may-care, young, attractive male schnauzer twirling his moue in anticipation.

Very truly yours,

jackie gleason

The World's Greatest Comedian

President of Jackie Gleason Enterprises

Star of the Jackie Gleason T.V. Show

Holder of Several Unsigned Movie Contracts

The lady schnauzer, in this case, was too mature and too sedate to be bothered by Gleason's mad monster and so, as a matchmaker for dogs, Jackie failed.

Another facet of this man's character is his lack of appreciation of money. He spent it long before he had it. He pays his valet $100 a week plus board and keep. His secretary averages about $12,000 a year. His directors, producers and assistants are well paid. Five script writers average about $750 a week.

One small shopping spree for suits, slacks, ties and shirts cost $3,000. When he ordered a plaid dinner jacket with white lapels, Gleason's tailor, Mr. Cye Seymour, said that there was no such thing. Jackie, in horror, practically ordered the man to go out and weave one. Seymour made four trips around the eastern part of the United States and finally found the right material in Boston. "I spent twenty-eight bucks on cabs alone," the tailor moaned. When the dinner jacket was made, Jackie decided it wasn't quite right for him. He paid for everything and refused to wear the jacket. He spends $85 on a pair of shoes and, if he likes the model, orders a dozen pairs in brown and a dozen pairs in black.

And yet his charities are enormous. He sends many thousands of dollars to the Boy Scouts, cerebral palsy campaigns, churches, strangers who can write and broken-down actors. In April, 1954, Tom Barnhard, a Greenwich Village janitor, committed suicide in despair and left a sick widow. Gleason read the story, blew his nose, picked up the phone, and called the *News*. "Pal," he said, "I want to pick up the tab for that funeral." He did. A boy studying for the priesthood at St. Benedict's in Brooklyn wrote that "we really desperately need a new set of solemn vestments." Jackie sent a check for $450.

When Arthur Godfrey was sick, Gleason wired that he would be happy to fill in. "Incidentally," he wrote, "it's on the house." Sister Mary Stella wrote her thanks for a check sent to her poor boys of St. Mary's. "May God shower His choicest blessings upon you down through the years."

Gleason makes it, borrows it, and gives it away. Jack Hurdle, his producer, begged him to invest $100,000 in a Madison Avenue building. "You know, Jackie," he warned, "there may come a time when it will be nice to have the rents coming in." Gleason thought about it for a moment. "No," he said quietly. "The hell with it."

An old and dear friend, Mrs. Thomas Dennehy, who often loaned him a dollar or two when he was a youngster, wrote that St. Benedict's Church in Brooklyn needed a new ceiling. Jackie sent $1,000. The boys of the Dukes Baseball Team lacked uniforms, so Gleason sent the money. Flushed with success, they dropped their first two games. A check for a Jewish building fund in Chicago brought a sage reply: "God bless you, but, above all, may He keep you a good boy." In the same mail was a letter from an insurance company asking Gleason for repayment on a loan on his policy. A letter that went out that day thanked Brachman Brothers in Los Angeles for the mink stole for Mrs. Gleason and promised to pay for it "in about ten days."

Very often he sent smaller checks too. One for $100 went to St. Mary of the Angels Orphanage for Boys; $100 to a termite-ridden school in Jamaica, British West Indies; $50 for carfare to New Orleans for an old friend; $60 for newspaper rights to his "life story" was endorsed over to a widow whose letter of thanks began: "My seven children and I want to thank you from the bottom of our hearts for helping us to enjoy a beautiful and bright Christmas." A note from Nils T. Granlund, in response to a check for $500, opened: "I was right down in the bottom of a deep pit when your voice pulled me up and let me live again."

Sometimes, when it is proved to him that he has been a sucker in matters of money, Gleason becomes angry and for the next few weeks he becomes stingy. An old pal wanted $4,000 to put television sets into a Philadelphia hotel. Jackie said no. A schoolmate phoned and said, "Tell Jackie his old friend Tony called. Tell him Tony that was in the play with him in school and used to pal out with him. I need a truck, tell him. [In the summer this man sold watermelons; in the winter he bought junk.] I'm using Mike Torso's truck and I'm paying twenty-five a day and then I gotta buy my watermelons off him and pay him his price and if I got my own truck I could go down south and buy the watermelons maybe three cents apiece. Tell him if he's busy just to send a check it'll be okay."

No answer from Gleason. A few years ago Jackie became thrifty for a few weeks. He ate his meals in his office and remained away from Shor's restaurant. On his program he mentioned certain brand names of whisky so that he would get free liquor sent to him, and he drank at his own bar. Penuriousness made him nervous. He quit one night like a drunk getting off the wagon and plunged into heavy spending. He went out and bought $20,-000 worth of electronics equipment and said that he needed it to take a band to Carlsbad Caverns and record a lonesome echo in music. Two days later he was sitting in the penthouse in a locomotive engineer's cap. On the floor was an expensive set of Lionel electric trains. Jackie sat beaming and pulling switches on slow freights and swift passenger trains. He was happy until someone pointed out that one locomotive was not belching smoke. The trains were sent to an orphanage.

He never had any real money, probably never will. When Jackie earned $35 a week, he was living at a $45-a-week scale. When he earned $3,500 a week, he was living at a rate of $4,500 a week. There were times, in recent months, when he did not have more than $200 in his checking account.

As he reached the top of his profession, it became obvious to Gleason's associates that he could do no real spending at all. From his employers, Jackie Gleason Enterprises, Jackie is paid $10,000 a performance. Here is what happens to that money:

20% goes to his manager, George Durgom.........$2,000.00	
14½% goes to Mrs. Gleason and their daughters........ 1,450.00	
10% goes for agents and deductible business expenses.. 1,000.00	
Total	$4,450.00

Of the original $10,000, Gleason now has	$5,550.00
Of this, New York State wants 7% as income tax	338.50
Of the remainder, the Bureau of Internal Revenue takes 80%	4,161.20
Out of $10,000, Jackie Gleason gets	$1,050.30

The year he signed a big contract with Buick Motor Cars, the newspapers made headlines which said, "GLEASON GETS $11,000,-000." That year, his tax report showed that he earned $350,000 and, after paying all business expenses and taxes, had $45,000 on which to live in his penthouse.

There is other money in Jackie Gleason Enterprises, but it isn't much. The corporation books talent, stages shows, runs two music companies too, but Gleason's habit of doing everything "first class" has kept profits down to $180,000 for the best year it has had. Taxes must be paid out of this too.

He is not, literally, a poor soul in any sense. He will earn large sums of money. But if there is a possible way of spending it, or giving it away, Jackie will find it and do it.

As a drinker, Gleason regards himself as a man among men. Sometimes, in the past, he has drunk prodigious amounts of liquor. At other times, he has had a few and has fallen on his face. He is not, in any sense, an alcoholic. The alcoholic cannot predict when he will have to have that next drink. Gleason can. On show days, he seldom has a drink and sometimes fights off a noisy hang-over with tomato juice and aspirin. Ironically, Gleason's drinking has been cut down since the day he signed a contract with the Buick Division of General Motors. Not long afterward, a friend said to him, "Jackie, let's hoist a few."

Gleason shook his head. The friend clutched his heart in a mock spasm. "Why?" he gasped.

"I don't really know," Jackie said. "Security seems to take all the fun out of drinking."

It is no strain for Gleason to be kind to people because he finds it easy to like whole hosts of people. He has a fear of snobbery and will stop, in the middle of a conversation, to autograph a scrap of paper for a fan, pose for a picture with someone's baby, listen to a guy who wants to tell him how to improve his comedy, discuss women with an oracular cabdriver, be overly patient with telephone operators, maids, stenographers and clerks.

He is funnier off stage than on, and the degree of wit depends upon the size of his audience. Talking to one person, Gleason becomes fidgety in a few minutes. Talking to three or four, he relaxes and, as his searchlight eyes move from face to face, he begins to sparkle. When there are six or eight around him, he is sharp and funny in his conversational asides. When there are more than that, he loses some of his edge and will try to break a small group off the crowd.

Gleason is not a moralist, but he will not tell an off-color story if women are present and he will leave if someone else does. This seems contrary to his earthy admiration of blondes, but it isn't. Jackie has an emotional response to life akin to a fifteen-year-old boy. To his way of thinking, all women are ladies, and when he is introduced he dusts his best knighthood-in-flower manners. He puts the ladies on pedestals and expects them to remain there. If they get off, Gleason becomes basic.

As a performer, he is an artist. It might be that he bills himself correctly when he calls himself "The Greatest." It is beyond argument that he is the greatest situation comedian of his generation. Week after week well-known comedians like Phil Silvers, Jack E. Leonard and Henny Youngman have watched Gleason at rehearsal, laughed as though they had been paid for it, and walked out murmuring, "He *thinks* funny." Others have said that Gleason lives the parts he plays—the bus driver, the bartender, and so forth—but that cannot be true because one night he came off stage mopping his neck and said to a stagehand, "I was thinking about your problem while I was out there and I think I have the answer. . . ."

Some actors achieve near-perfection through long, painful rehearsals. Not Jackie. The almost total lack of rehearsal on the Gleason show is the talk of the entertainment industry. Up until 1956, when his program changed to film, he did not even look at the script for the Saturday-night show until Thursday. He read it in his penthouse, grunted at it, mumbled some lines, made a few pencil changes in the dialogue, and then tossed it aside until Saturday at 2:00 P.M. Six hours before curtain time he would sit on a tall bar stool beneath the footlights and watch the action on stage and also watch it in a television set at his side.

At that hour the personnel ran through the whole show, starting with Ray Bloch's overture and the opening number of the June Taylor Dancers, through the comedy, the commercials, the timing of bits of business down to the second, to the end of the show. When the rehearsal reached the point where Gleason had to go on stage, he would get off the stool, walk up a little flight of steps, and go through the action while Jack Hurdle, producer, watched and Stanley Poss, assistant producer, studied a stop watch and the script. If Gleason missed a line, which happened now and then, Poss would read it aloud to him. Gleason would repeat it aloud and, when showtime came, he did not miss a line.

Those who do not like Gleason the performer argue that he is a broad comic who uses prat falls and pain bits (window slamming on hand) and a flutter of the hands and feet to generate laughter. Others explain that Jackie's artistry probably lies in (1) timing—his audience always understands the situation one full second before he does; (2) credibility—he will not undertake any situation which could not happen to anyone; (3) confidence —on stage he is certain that he is very funny and that he could make people laugh even if the rest of the cast walked off the stage. When he rehearses, even the jaded stagehands and camera crews laugh.

Part of his extreme confidence is shown in Jackie's retention of Arthur Carney. Carney is a fine dramatic actor, a great comedian. In some situations he is greater than Gleason. No star wants to share laughs. And yet Jackie insists, as each new contract comes up, that Art be a part of it, and Carney, who has had offers to star in his own shows, claims that he likes nothing better than playing second man to Gleason.

One of the things Jackie is not is a stand-up comic. Bob Hope and Milton Berle are stand-up comics. They can stand in front of a curtain for eight minutes or more and tell jokes and make people laugh. In this, Gleason is poor. Often his jokes fall flat and the audience laughs more at his plight than in amusement at his story. This is difficult to explain because for a number of years Gleason made his living as a night-club master of ceremonies, which, in essence, is a stand-up comic. But even in those days he wasn't very amusing telling a joke. His biggest laughs came when he traded insults with the customers, his ad libs were at their noisy best when he had a foil to sharpen them on.

It may be that Gleason's rise to the top is nothing more than the result of hardship and a difficult apprenticeship. He worked the amateur hours in third-rate movie houses, held cheap shows together in provincial night clubs, wrote acts which never saw the light of day, took a merciless kicking around in Hollywood, substituted for better-paid comics who were ill, and never tired of telling anyone who would listen, "You wait and see. I'm going to pass them all by. I'm going to be the greatest. . . ."

As a business tycoon, Jackie is schmaltzy. He has offices on the twenty-third and twenty-fourth floors of the Park Sheraton Hotel in New York, and these are plush and modern. Over a Spanish fireplace hangs a huge portrait of Reggie Van Gleason in World War I uniform, complete with puttees and campaign hat. Underneath, in gold, the legend reads: "Our Founder." Phone bells are subdued and here the business end of the show is ironed out until it is wrinkleproof; the music end of the business is primed for millions of copies in retail sales; file cabinets are stuffed with letters and bills and receipts; a tall girl marks debits and credits in big ledgers; visiting actors and band leaders tinkle a piano; kinescopes of earlier shows are run off or are stored in an air-conditioned room; and here Mr. Gleason walks in, fat and sassy, every morning at eight.

He bows an elaborate hello to Miss Patricia Stadelman, the cute blond receptionist; another to Miss Elizabeth Caldwell, his

manager's secretary; a third to Sydell Friedlander, snowy-blond
secretary to the music-publishing business; one to dark Joan
Reichman, in charge of all show scripts; and a curt nod to the
handsome brunette who knows more about his business than he
does—Miss Lee Reynolds, his secretary.

Gleason walks into an office with a huge desk which stands
against a wall. He beams the morning insults at Jack Philbin,
executive producer of the show, a lean, slick-haired man who
at one time was a song plugger. Jackie walks across a tufted
rug to his desk, bowing greetings to Jerry Katz, young Music
Corporation of America agent whom the agency assigns to Gleason; his manager, George Durgom, known as Bullets, a bald,
second-generation Armenian, with the sad, hairless head of an
abandoned infant; and Tony Amico, his valet, a stout, stocky man
who, like taxes, is always with Jackie.

The star sits behind his modernistic desk beaming and rolling
a letter opener across a blotter. Unless there is a conference at
hand, he has little to do. He picks up the phone, happily tells
one and all whom he is going to rib, and puts the phone down
again.

Jackie is nervous, smiling, nodding. He listens to ideas for next
week's show, or the week after. He has a direct line to the Columbia Broadcasting System and, if he has any problems worthy of
their attention, he phones Hubbell Robinson, vice-president. He
talks by phone to Miss Reynolds, who is outside, and he sits
around looking like a man bursting with energy who is waiting for
someone to give him a problem.

If a problem comes, he listens gravely, big eyes on the blotter,
and he often says No. Many times, against the combined advice
of his manager and producers, he says No. Sometimes he cannot
give a logical reason for his decision, but the decision is swift and
beyond appeal. Over the years everyone concedes that his decisions are sound. He has an almost intuitive faculty for seeing trouble where others see smooth sailing and, when he turns out to be
right, he yells, "Well, didn't I tell you? Would you guys listen
to me? No." He is tough and stubborn in business decisions and
will not be persuaded to change his mind.

When the last show is finished for the season—in mid-June—

Gleason writes love letters to the people who have worked with him all year. The following are typical:

To June Taylor and the chorus: "I am just a fresh comic like probably a thousand other guys you have run into and away from during your career as Ladies of the Ensemble and, furthermore, I am a cornball on top of it all, so I do not know how much stock you will place in the gratitude I am about to express. Please believe me, just this once, that in my haphazard career I have never felt so proud of a group of girls. If I thought you would let me, I would hug and kiss every one of you. There is a considered truth in the word that a man can only be in love with one woman. They're nuts. I'm madly in love with seventeen!"

To the technical and camera crew: "I find it impossible to express my gratitude to you guys. . . . Thank you from the bottom of my cornball heart. . . ."

To the stage and lighting crew: "Fellows, there aren't any words that I can use to tell you how grateful I am to you for the co-operation that you have given me. It is overwhelming to know that each of you worked on our show as if you had a personal interest in its success. . . . From the bottom of my hambone heart . . ."

To Ray Bloch and the orchestra: ". . . I don't want to get drippy about this so I am going to close this note, but honestly from the bottom of my E-flat heart . . . I dig musicians the most."

Once he got a letter back. It came from a girl named B. J. Brown:

I'm one of the gals on your show—one of the alternate Portrettres—and I understand that there is a possibility that after this coming Saturday we may be dropped. So, not having had an opportunity to speak to you in person, would like to tell you now, via typewriter, how much I appreciate your kindnesses, and, although I haven't the direct authority to do so, am sure that I am also speaking for the rest of the girls.

It was a terrific boost to the ego, being picked out of such a mass of beautiful gals. It has been an exciting new kind of experience being on your show, and, naturally, the money has been nice too. About the possibility of being dropped—well, that's the fortunes of love, war and modeling, and, having been models for a while, we have all had a chance to get used to the uncertainties of our particular profession. . . .

We all admire you very much, Mr. Gleason. I've never seen anyone work as hard as you do, and with such expert attention to even the smallest detail. I was amazed when I learned that you had even designed the little ruffle that went around my neck (when I was the Mardi Gras Portrette for Snorkel Pen). Needless to say, my somewhat smug, preconceived notions about television stars went crashing down the drain in a hurry.

So, as I have said, we have all come to think a great deal of you, and if it happens that we can't work on the show any longer —again, thank you very much for all you have done. We have enjoyed it tremendously, and wish you the very best of luck, always, in everything you do.

Most sincerely,

B. J. BROWN

Television is the most perpetually baffling invention since the one-way street. It is, in one breath, the savior of actors and their executioner. It creates and it kills. A man may work for months or years to draw up a good animal act. In the days of vaudeville he could tour the country for two years or more, at $125 a week, without ever meeting the same audience twice. Today he puts his act on a television network show and, in six minutes, he has been seen by fifty million persons, has earned $500, and his act is finished. It cannot be shown again. Theatrically, he is dead.

The real winners in the new medium are the writers, not the actors. These gentlemen, like bad little boys, are heard rather than seen. They get an idea, usually based on a format being used by a star, and they reduce the idea to situation dialogue which is mouthed by actors in front of cameras. If the show is good, it has great writers. If it stinks, the star doesn't know how to read lines. The more television opens its opaque mouth, the more material it chews and digests. The more channels, the more stations. The more stations, the more programs. The more programs, the more writers.

Gleason has five. They average about $1,250 a week apiece, and that comes to $3,500 for a script. Jack Philbin, the executive producer, works with the writers, and he has them broken into two teams of two men apiece, with the fifth man, Andrew Russell, as a trouble shooter working with both. On Tuesday of any week team number one has finished next Saturday's show, and team number two begins to work on the following week's show.

Team two, let us say, works out the nub of an idea for "The Honeymooners," in which Alice's mother is coming to visit them on the same evening that Ralph Kramden (Gleason) is to bowl-in a runoff for the club championship. This idea is communicated to Philbin, who calls team two in—with Andy Russell—and they "kick it around." This means to think out loud and to suggest situations and funny lines and bits of business which will lend themselves to mamma's arrival and Jackie's bowling.

If the idea stands up, Philbin sometimes brings it to the attention of Gleason at breakfast in the penthouse. If Jackie has any objection to it, he says so at once and the idea is dropped, and team two goes back into a room to think up a new one. If he likes it, he often has suggestions, and Philbin jots them. In the past year Gleason has discouraged the idea of bringing plot ideas to him because, in effect, this throws the responsibility on him for a possible failure. He forces Philbin and the writers to go ahead with ideas they approve and thus take the chance that Gleason may explode when he sees the script two days before showtime.

Sometimes, after approval by Philbin, the team returns to work and then, after several days, reports back that "the idea we had won't develop." This means that the original premise sounded funny to all hands, but it will not stretch credibly for a half hour or an hour. Philbin's reply is, "Look, fellas. We're in trouble." Everyone starts to think and for hours the office is quiet.

Stanley Poss runs through some old kinescopes of the show in the hope that one of them might inspire the writers to a new and clever idea or the subtle theft of an old one. Writers stand, hands behind back, staring out the terrace windows at Central Park

(they are three blocks south of it at Fifty-sixth Street) and sometimes they mumble aloud in tones like Alice Kramden, and they
reply to themselves like Trixie or Ralph or Ed Norton.

No matter how desperate the trouble, no matter how inexorable
the tick of time, somehow someone eventually comes up with an
acceptable idea and the writers punch out dialogue and rewrite
and revise and eventually "The Jackie Gleason Show" goes on at
exactly the right time on the right day. It does not make the
writers feel better to know that their star feels that, if the time
ever came to go before the cameras without a script, he is sure
that he could be funny for a half hour.

By the time the show goes on the writers are "dead." Sometimes they attend it at the theater (until Gleason switched to
filmed shows) and sometimes they sit in the director's booth and
watch, with exquisite agony, as Jackie Gleason, white carnation
in blue suit, comes on stage between two rows of June Taylor
Dancers and beams at one and all as he tells the people, "Oh,
you're a dan-dan-dandy group!"

In the booth, director Frank Satenstein orders the cameras
around, producer Jack Hurdle clocks the show against a time
sheet he holds in his hand and phones Poss backstage to say,
"We're forty seconds slow," or "We're running a minute ahead,"
or whatever, and backstage the word is passed to all members of
the cast to speed the lines a little, or, if the show is going too
slow, to cut out certain bits of business.

If all goes well, the commercial sales talks should use up exactly six minutes on a one-hour show; Gleason's opening and
closing talks before the curtain, plus the orchestra's opening number, use up four more; the June Taylor Dancers use up five,
leaving 45 minutes for comedy.

When Gleason says, "Good night, everybody!" and waves his
arms, the 140 people connected with "The Jackie Gleason Show"
begin to breathe again. They are off camera and another performance is a matter of theatrical history. Backstage everybody
looks weary. Out front people are leaving the show with comments like "He's great"; "Me, I'm for Carney"; "First time I could
get tickets for this thing and it turns out to be a stinker"; "I'm
telling ya, I'm bustin' out laughing before Gleason opens his

mouth"; "Did you get a load of those babes in the chorus? Wow!"

Backstage Jackie works his way up a flight of stairs rimmed with the distinguished and the not-so-distinguished, each of whom is waiting to shake his hand, tell him a problem, ask a favor, or just sit with the star and kill time. If he doesn't do it, they leave and tell everyone that he's got a swelled head. If he does it, then he's as real and regular as you and I.

In the dressing room Jackie's dresser helps him to get out of his stage clothes and he sits on a busted leather sofa smoking cigarettes and perspiring. He wears an old bathrobe, and he raises solemn, heavy-lidded eyes as Bullets Philbin, Hurdle, Poss, the writers and Jerry Katz come in. They give each other verdicts —usually reassuring verdicts while trying to appear to be very objective. The show was great; you were terrific; I almost died in that bit where Alice hands you the cake; Carney was beautiful, just beautiful; didn't you love the way that Audrey did that little step after she turned the radio on?; and how about that Zamah Cunningham coming through as Reggie's mother—I mean, how about her?; Jackie, you can do no wrong; you act like you invented television.

Gleason sits and nods tiredly, and all of them feel around for the words they hope will find a sympathetic reaction in his breast, because this is what makes a staff look bright. Now and then he says the show was good; now and then he makes a face at it; sometimes, if he feels real good about it, he will smile that big Irish smile, nod happily, and murmur, "Well, we fooled 'em again, didn't we?"

This is the highest accolade of all.

The small hours are almost always lonely. There is a time when the soft sound of an electric refrigerator can be heard. Gleason can pad around his duplex putting the lights on and he can turn the records up loud, but he is alone. Those who applaud are home resting their hands. Tony Amico, his valet, snores behind a closed door. All the television sets wear opaque faces.

These are the difficult hours. A man can take a pill, take a drink, slide into bed. The eyes will shut, but the brain will not. A waxed recording of monotonous trivia runs around the periphery of the mind and sleep will not come. The man sits up, snaps lights on, draws deep draughts from a cigarette. The lights go out, the cigarette too. A fresh pocket is punched in a pillow; the head drops into it.

The record goes on again. It is still spinning when sleep comes. It is a dreamful, fretting state in which many facts, real and imaginary, juxtapose themselves into scenes of frightful credibility. This state endures for hours and days. Then, in a flash, comes wakefulness—super-alert wakefulness, long-overdue wakefulness, the feeling of having slept for days.

Jackie picks up his watch. It is 5:30 A.M. He has been sleeping two hours. There is no point in fighting for it any more. He gets up, yawning and scratching. The foyer is empty. The morning papers have not yet been delivered. Through the windows the park below is blue-gray, formless in a cold dawn. There is no one to talk to.

These are the bad hours. The seconds drip slowly off the face of time. There are telephones with long extension cords, but who is awake at 5:30 A.M.? So he reads. From the library he gets a book called *New World of the Mind*, by Joseph Banks Rhine. He sits behind the library desk, the gold lamp shaded to the book, and bends to the task of immersing his thoughts into the experiences of someone else. The blue eyes move across the lines of type quickly, line after line, page after page. . . .

"Clairvoyance seems simple, however, compared to the kind of experiences that comes next—those involving the future. These are presented next because they appear again to be clairvoyance, different only in being directed toward events ahead in time instead of present or past. It is, in fact, the most bewildering thing about this next type of psychic case that they show no relation to time. In approximately half of the general run of Dr. Louisa E. Rhine's large collection of spontaneous cases, the scene or event connected with the subject's experience has not actually taken place at the time. In other words, if the reporting and interpretation are correct, the perception is prophetic or *precognitive*.

"Again, while it is doubtful if any fair-minded person could read these cases by the hundreds without being profoundly impressed, I repeat that to the investigator in parapsychology such anecdotes are valued not as evidence but for suggestions they give of still undiscovered areas that offer possibilities for further researches. . . ." *

,This, to Jackie, is the most important kind of reading. This is the bold new frontier of the mind, the peek into the future. If God gave to man a conscience and a soul, and denied them to the other animals, then perhaps He gave man latent powers of the mind which man does not yet understand. Jackie would like to find out.

He reads for an hour, finishing 208 pages, and puts a bookmark at the opening of a chapter reading, "Significance of Psi for Human Life." At 6:30 A.M. he fidgets. He wants to call Philbin about a script reading, but the lean dark one would be sleeping. He could phone Bullets—no. He goes out the library door and around the corner. He listens at Amico's door. No sound.

The best way to kill time is to do it a minute at a time. Jackie goes into the kitchen and kills three by filling the percolator, getting two plates, two cups, two saucers, two spoons, two knives, two forks, and plugging in the toaster. He kills one more by going into the hall again to look for the morning newspapers. They have not arrived. In the bedroom he pulls back the salmon draperies and sees the morning edge of sunlight tip the spires on Central Park West.

That is a consolation. At least morning is coming. Soon now alarm clocks will be ringing in scores of thousands of homes all over New York. People will be getting out of bed. The subways will screech under the streets; the cabs will honk; the trucks will rumble; children, in groups, will be yelling as they run to school; busses will whine; the big silvery planes will roar laboriously out of LaGuardia Airport just to the north of the penthouse. Best of all, Tony will be up. There will be someone to talk to.

He waits until the coffee is ready. Then he walks over to Tony's door and raps on it.

"Tone! . . . Tone! You awake? I put the coffee and the toast on."

Inside there is silence. Then the swing of a heavy body on a bed. "Okay, Jackie. Okay."

The coffee is ready by the time the valet emerges, in bathrobe, eyes full of sleep. He yawns. "What time is it?"

"Seven o'clock."

Tony sits hard. Jackie butters some toast. The boss and the valet look at each other and grin. Jackie has chronic insomnia. Tony can sleep anywhere, at any time.

"Take the car today," Gleason says.

"No," says Tony. "I don't rate a big car."

"It's your day off."

"I know."

"Well, take the car."

"You'll need it."

"I can take a cab."

"That ain't right, Jackie."

"Sure it's right. You're getting punchy hanging around here. If I want to go down to Tootsie's, I'll take a cab."

Suddenly Jackie Gleason feels tired. Now, he feels, he can sleep.

THE TENEMENT

THE WRITER *trimmed the broiled fat from around his steak. He was a patient man, the writer; he had spent twenty-six of his forty-seven years trying to locate facts and then to reduce them to words. He wanted a lot of facts from the doctor.*

"Are you the one who checked Gleason into Doctors Hospital?" he asked.

The doctor sipped coffee and nodded. "We had him on eight hundred calories a day." He smiled. "Dropped twenty-five pounds in two weeks."

"Will he stay on a diet?"

"Never. Once we got him down to two hundred and five and we let him go home. I'll bet he was hardly in the door when he ordered Tony Amico to get up a platter of spaghetti and a large pizza. This man can knock off prodigious amounts of food."

"I know." The writer paused. "Is he afraid of death?"

"Abnormally. His mother had an abnormal fear of death— would never see a doctor—and Jackie has it too. He's not as conscious of it as his mother, but he spends a lot of time trying to beat the rap in other ways."

"For instance?"

The doctor looked up. "The more he is convinced that he cannot run away from death, the more he must find an answer to what happens after death. Most of us, to a degree, are exactly the same. He wants the Catholic Church and the Catholic Church wants him, but he cannot accept all of the teachings on faith alone. Who wants total darkness? Nobody. Least of all, Jackie. He wants a good answer now, so he delves into mysticism and psychic phenomena and extrasensory perception. The closer he comes to finding a good answer, the more he worries about the life he's now leading." The doctor described a flat circle with his hand. "If you can find a way out of that one . . ."

"I'm a Catholic. It's common to a lot of Catholics who find themselves boxed between the so-called pleasures of the flesh and certain punishment."

"Oddly enough, Jackie Gleason is a healthy animal."

"Why shouldn't he be?" the writer said.

"With all the stresses and strains on that man, you would hardly expect such soundness. His organs are in good shape, his blood pressure is normal, he has had no known childhood diseases and none in adult life except a ruptured appendix and a few colds."

"Quite a man."

"Better than average. He fatigues slowly. He can outsit, outtalk, outwait, outwalk, outwork and sometimes outthink anybody around him. I don't think he will ever reduce permanently."

"Why?"

"Two reasons. One is that overeating, as you know, is a form of oral aggression—getting even with the world. The other is that if he reduces he will have to compete with the handsome young stars on their own level. If a thin man does a little tap dance—who cares? But if a fat man does it—we marvel. Gleason can get away with much more as a fat character than as a thin one. My guess is that he'll stay fat."

Mae Kelly was tricked the whole forty-nine years of her life. Nothing ever turned out as she expected. She was born with mischievous deviltry in her eyes and she died with her face turned to a wall, the bitterness beyond acceptance. She wanted everything; got nothing. Mae Kelly was a study in despair.

She was the last of five. First there was Victoria, who would save and save and save, who would turn the gas off and sit in the dark to save a penny, who, after she married, paid a minimum electric bill of one dollar a month. Then there was Margaret, who was born to mother her own and everybody else's children. After that came Eddie and Joseph, and finally Mae.

The youngest in any large Irish family is always in danger of being spoiled. Mae was loved and dressed and preened for Sunday Mass, and given spending money refused to the others, and babied by her father, and permitted to go punishment-free.

Her biggest fault lay in the fact that she grew up thinking that this was a fair sample of what life was like. Her father James had a touch of the artist in him and became a sign painter. He made good money in Brooklyn and his family ate well and was well clothed.

When she was fifteen years of age, in 1901, Mae Kelly was short and plump, a girl of stout arms and full figure, a girl lively and witty who dressed her long brown hair with a dripping bow. She had graduated from primary school, she got a weekly allowance, she liked the company of boys and she attended dances and socials and, at fifteen, she married Herbert Gleason.

Married life, to Mae's ways of thinking, would be an improvement over the wonderful life she was leading. It would mean freedom from supervision, which is so important at fifteen, and romance, which is always lovelier in dreams, and a home of her own, which meant that she could have her girl friends as guests every night of the week. It meant new furniture, somewhat classier than the old stuff she had at home, a Morris chair, a pianola, a gas range in the kitchen and a victrola.

Herbert Gleason was a little bit older. He knew better. But he was dizzied by yearning for this laughing Irish colleen and so, even though he knew that marriage was not exactly as Mae had dreamed it, he determined to struggle with all his might to make it so.

He was a tall, thin, nasal kid, born for failure. In time he would learn to accept failure, but not now. Right now he was full of hope. His older brother had a good job with the Mutual Life Insurance Company of New York, and Herb had been hired as a clerk in the Death Claims Department. Others investigated the claims; when they were verified, all Herb had to do was to make out the check, see that his brother signed it, make an entry in a ledger to that effect, and mail it. He had no responsibility other than that.

He had jet hair, ears akimbo, and he loved jokes. When he laughed, he threw his head back, held his emaciated stomach, and yelled, "Har, har!" In the Mutual office down on Nassau Street, in Manhattan, he had a little cage with a sliding door. He earned $25 a week, was paid semimonthly, and after he was married sold candy bars to other employees to augment his salary.

This marriage limped from the start. Mae wanted gaiety and laughter in the little Brooklyn flat; Herb couldn't afford it. They moved from tenement to tenement, always in and around the Bushwick section, always looking for cheaper rent and brighter rooms. There were domestic arguments, as there must be in most families, and most of these arguments were about money. Mae wanted clothes and she wanted to be fashionable; she wanted nice furniture and she wanted to be able to invite her friends in on Friday nights and on Saturday too. Herb tried to underscore the fact that he wanted these things too, but if he didn't have the money, it couldn't be done. Mae's tart answer to this was that Herb's brother was an officer of the company and should see that Herb got a raise in salary. Her in-laws, she said, lived well in Westchester County—like swells—but no one was lifting a finger to accelerate Herb's career.

It wasn't a chronically bad situation. Herb and Mae had many good times together and angry words were often forgotten. Once, when Mae's teeth ached badly, she had to have all of them gold capped, and this cost so much that for months they had no good times at all.

Clemence was born in 1905. He was a long, thin baby, frail enough to keep parents worried most of the time. If Clemence sneezed, both parents felt his skin for temperature. If Clemence cut his finger, it was treated as an emergency. The budget was strained buying bottles of Beef, Wine and Iron in an effort to build a little ruddiness into his white face.

He was a grave, good boy who did as he was told without question. And he was a spectator, rather than a player. He stood on the curb on Herkimer Street and watched the other boys play ball or cattie. He might have liked to play, but his mother had told him not to step off the curb, and he didn't. He was religious in a quiet way, and he seemed to be most relaxed on his knees. In a way, Clemence was ashamed of his height because, whenever he heard his mother talking about him to his Aunt Vickie or his Aunt Maggie, it was a complaint that he was always growing out of his clothes.

The second child was born almost eleven years later, on February 26, 1916. He was christened Herbert John Gleason, and there was a little discussion about this because Herb thought that one of his sons should carry his name, and Mae didn't like the name at all. She like John, and when Mr. Smith, the homeopathic doctor, said that she was well enough to get out of bed and do light household work, Mae fought harder for the name John. In the end it was Herbert John, but she had her way by always calling the baby "Jackie" and insisting that everyone else do the same.

The times in which Jackie Gleason was born were, in an ironic sense, hardly unusual. In February 1916, the United States was trying to keep out of a war. Woodrow Wilson was preparing to run for a second term on the premise "He Kept Us Out of War." The Central Alliance, consisting in the main of Germany and Austria-Hungary, was at war with the *Entente Cordial,* which was Great Britain, France and Russia. In two months' time the Cunard Liner *Lusitania* would be sunk off Ireland and the United States would be much closer to participation in World War I.

The world to which this new baby would belong, in time, was the world of the theater, and the names that made news at the hour of his birth will mean nothing to anyone under middle years. Geraldine Farrar had just married Lou Tellegen and she was starring in *Tosca.* Frieda Hempel was at Carnegie Hall. A new play, called *The Earth,* had opened at the Playhouse starring Grace George. The Dolly Sisters were starring that week at the Palace Theatre.

Maude Adams was at the ornate Empire Theatre in *The Little Minister* and the Cohan Review had picked up, at the Astor Theatre, after a slow start. Ethel Barrymore was tiring after a long run in *Our Mrs. McChesney* and Potash and Perlmutter were in another hilarious play at the Lyric. From Hollywood came a can of film labeled "Mary Pickford in a motion picture called *Poor Little Peppina.*"

At Shanley's in Times Square there was a seven-course luncheon for seventy-five cents, with music. One of the good buys in automobiles was the seven-passenger Abbott-Detroit at $1,195. Franklin Simon was selling men's overcoats for $15, fine worsted suits for $21. For men the collar was Ide, the ale was Bass. A ten-room house with a half acre of property cost $5,500. The favorite cigarettes were Fatima, Sweet Caporal and Piedmont, although only callow weaklings smoked them.

Parades of suffragists demanded the vote for women. Charles Chaplin journeyed across the country from California to stand on the stage of the Hippodrome Theatre and conduct Sousa's Band. The British Under Secretary of War announced that Winston Spencer Churchill had been promoted to Colonel.

The new baby was three when Clemence died. Jackie's consciousness was not such that this death would leave an immutable scar. He did not understand the excitement, nor all of the grownups who came to the flat and wept and prayed and held him in their arms. He was minded by his nine-year-old cousin Renee Wilbert, Aunt Maggie's girl. Everybody remarked that Jackie was his mother "all over again"—the same love of laughter, the same inquisitive alertness, the same moon face. What he had of his father was very black hair.

The funeral day was cold and slushy in Brooklyn. The undertaker, in frock coat, came outdoors with a list of mourners in his hand, and at the curb were the hearse and two horses with black trappings. He was shocked to find Jackie Gleason on the cobblestones between the legs of the near horse. The child was yanked to safety, and when he was asked what he was doing under the horse, he said that he heard a man say that the black horses had white socks and he wanted to put something on them to hold them up. In his little fist he held several rubber bands.

From this age onward Jackie was mischievous. When he had said his night prayers and was put in bed, his mother had to lock the door of his room. If she didn't, he would get out of bed and try to go to "Reen's house." Reen was a cousin who was supposed to be watching him while he was under the horse. At five years of age, when the door to his room was locked, Jackie unlocked the window, climbed out on the fire escape, went up to the roof, crossed two buildings, went down another fire escape into a cellar, and, in night clothing, tried to walk to "Reen's house." Strangely, his mother always waited until morning to pick him up and bring him home.

The first big conscious moment comes to a child when something happens which he remembers with a degree of clarity all his life. To Jackie Gleason, it was his first visit to the Halsey Theatre. His father took him to see a motion picture and five acts of vaudeville on a Saturday afternoon. The child was six. Mae dressed him in a white sailor suit, combed the black, Buster-Brown-cut hair, and sent him off, holding his father's hand.

Next door to the theater was a shop. In the back of it was a speak-easy. Herb crouched before his son and said, "Wait here. I'll be out in a minute. If anyone tries to speak to you, don't answer. Understand?" The big blue eyes stared back. The round head nodded rapidly. "Yes, daddy." The boy waited. In a little while his father came out.

The motion picture made no impression on the child. But the vaudeville actors thrilled him beyond expression. He sat on his father's lap, so that he would be high enough to see over the heads of those in front, and although he did not understand the jokes of the actors he understood the universality of the laughter, and, looking around at the faces distorted with amusement, his nose wrinkled and then he laughed because they were laughing.

Laughter spelled happiness and the little boy was certain that nowhere was there such happiness as he had seen in the Halsey Theatre. He begged to be taken back again. And again. For a while Herb Gleason had a Saturday-afternoon chore. The boy would promise anything in the way of behavior to get back to see the actors, to hear the laughter and applause. Once, as his father took him by the hand and walked him home, Jackie said, "I wouldn't be afraid up there." At home he imitated the funny dances he saw and the funny way the actors fell without hurting themselves. When his parents laughed, he did it again and again until they told him to stop.

Once, when his father disappeared inside the speak-easy, a policeman came along, ruffled his hair, and asked Jackie what his name was. The boy remembered that he was not to speak to anyone, and he looked up in silence. The policeman asked a second time. When he got no answer, he said, "You must be lost," and took Jackie off to the nearest precinct. There a lieutenant sat him on the desk and tried all the wiles of the business to get an answer. The boy, who was not going to miss the show by violating the rules, compressed his lips and turned poor soul eyes from one cop to another. In a half hour he was bailed out by his frantic father, who tried unsuccessfully to explain to the police why the youngster would not speak to strangers.

In time Herbert Gleason worked his salary up to $150 a month —barely $35 a week. This was not enough, and the Gleasons moved from flat to flat—Herkimer Street to Somer Street to Bedford Avenue at Fulton Street to Marion Street. These tenements were always in the same neighborhood, and Jackie attended one school, Public School 73. He played in the schoolyard of another school, Public School 137. The family attended Our Lady of Lourdes Church and the nuns instructed him in catechism and his obligations to God and his church. He received his first Holy Communion there and was later confirmed.

The early instincts for religion were cultivated by Mae, who sat and told him stories of God and His saints and stories of heaven and of hell. Gratuitously, she added stories of her own superstitious beliefs and he quickly learned to fear punishment from forces mightier than his mother and his father.

The newspapers featured a story by a man who predicted the end of the world for a certain day at a certain hour. Mae, who hadn't the slightest doubt that the man was right, called her sister Maggie and Renee, and, with little Jackie, the four sat in the dining room and waited for doom. At the appointed hour, the sky darkened and a wind blew up.

"Here it comes," said Mae tensely and, weeping, she began to pray. The fact that it didn't come diluted the terror only slightly for the little boy.

The disappearance of Herbert Gleason was still on the books of the New York Police Department more than thirty years after it happened. It was never solved; no trace of him was ever found. He walked out on Friday, December 15, 1925. His son was almost nine.

The country was prosperous. Jobs were plentiful. Everyone except Herb seemed to be making money. When he worked overtime, all he got was supper money. He became thinner and more silent. Mae's indictment of him as a failure bit deeply. She brought a boarder into the house to help defray expenses. He was a stout, jolly man named Al Church, but everybody called him "Uncle Fats." Long ago, Uncle Fats had been a bartender, but now he said he was retired, although Herb was sure that he had a horse book on the side.

Uncle Fats always had a few dollars, and he was generous to the Gleasons. He knew that Mae loved nothing better than to have friends in on Saturday nights, so Uncle Fats often agreed to furnish a fifth or two of gin and a pound of ham. On these evenings Mae lived as she wanted to live. She dressed her very best and she looked radiant, even though the supper dishes were lying in the kitchen sink. She loved company and she loved drinks; both made her forget the inner fears which she shared with no one. Herb loved to see her enjoy herself because on these occasions she again became his loving bride, and he liked to stand against the mantel in the parlor and just watch her shine.

Jackie was put to bed in the first bedroom off the dining room. The layout of these flats was identical—railroad rooms. The stairway up to the fourth floor led into the dining room. Behind it was a kitchen with an icebox and a gas range and a table and broom closet. Between kitchen and dining room was a small bathroom. Ahead of the dining room were two bedrooms and then a small parlor, which was often closed off in winter. The boy went to sleep with the sound of laughter in his ears. This sound, more than any other, would relax his tensions throughout his life.

This particular time—1925—was an era of superlatives. Everything that was done right was done more right and bigger than ever. The same applied to everything that was done wrong. Hoodlums, for instance, no longer fought each other with stones and bats. They took each other for a one-way ride in an automobile.

It was an age of exaggeration. Men who had been casual drinkers now had to get drunk. Women were not satisfied with the role of attracting the male to marriage and making a home for him. They had to be his equal on the public forum, in politics and in bed. It was a time of giants too—Dempsey, Jones, Tilden, Ruth, Owney Madden, Dutch Schultz, Capone and Johnny Torrio. A smart man saved his money and acquired $25,000; a clever one played the market and had a million. Cars were being made bigger and faster; trains were running between New York and

Chicago in eighteen hours; men sat in their homes with earphones and heard music come out of the air. In defiance of law, other men made alcohol in cellar distilleries, bottled beer and sold it with an eye against a slot in a door. Young ladies cut their hair, shortened their dresses, drank gin and read Dr. Warner Fabian's *Flaming Youth*. They danced the Charleston and the Black Bottom and they sat under dusty draperies at the Palais d'Or and swayed to the rhythm of B. A. Rolfe's muted trumpet.

There were flagpole sitters, marathon dancers, cross-country walkers, and a loud lady named Texas Guinan saw patrons tip a band leader a hundred dollars to play "Ain't She Sweet." Black Starr & Frost put an advertisement in *The New Yorker* to sell a strand of pearls at $685,000. There were 20,000,000 cars on American roads and the balloon tire was the newest thing in travel comfort. Women played mah-jongg and Junior could play "Poet and Peasant" by pumping the pedals of a player piano. Everyone just had to see Mae Murray and John Gilbert in *The Merry Widow*. An insurance company pamphlet described Moses as "one of the greatest salesmen and real-estate promoters that ever lived." Jesus Christ was called "the founder of modern business."

In the year prior to the disappearance there had been signs that Herbert was ready to quit. On payday he often left the office and, instead of going home, went over to the Hell's Kitchen section of Eleventh Avenue and drank from Friday to Sunday. The speak-easy bartenders knew him well. He caused no trouble and always drank moodily. Double Manhattans were his favorites while the salary held out; beer was the refuge on Sunday when he was nearly broke.

At the office he was always in debt for two or three dollars to Peter J. Schaus or others of his co-workers. He had lost most of his faith in God and in man. He seldom went to Mass, and at the office his august brother seldom spoke to Herbert. At lunchtime he sold his five-cent candy bars from clerk to clerk in almost mute desperation.

Every evening at four he left the big building at 20 Nassau Street and walked to the Brooklyn Bridge. He took a trolley car to Brooklyn and arrived home at about five. If he wasn't in the house at that time, Mae turned off the light under the chops and potatoes, dressed Jackie, and took a trolley to Manhattan. There, on nights of bitter cold, she waited in City Hall Park, looking toward Nassau Street.

Mae was afraid that Herb would go out drinking. So she waited in the cold and the dark with her son, and when Herb came up out of the shadows with two other clerks—often at 10 P.M.—her relief showed itself in anger.

"What's the idea of keeping us waiting in the snow? You have some nerve!"

Herbert's answer was always the same. He would nod good night to his friends and say, "Yes, yes. Well, let's go." At home the argument began. Mae's contention was that he wasn't working overtime; he was out drinking. Herb contended that when claims piled up he had to stay at the office because Mutual wanted to be prompt in its payments. She said that they weren't so prompt in paying him a living wage, and what kind of a brother was Fred anyway? Sometimes, when Herb lost his reserve in a flurry of accusations, he would claim that he had lost her love anyway, that she was paying too much attention to a friend named Al Johnston. This led to hysterics from Mae, who claimed that Al was Herbert's friend, not hers. In bed the little boy heard a lot.

In the office Herb planted little seeds. He said that he was becoming worried about Mae's drinking. After the planting, he went to a loan company and borrowed $150. On a personal loan of this type, he had to get his wife's signature. He copied it and got the money.

On Thursday night he came home with some family pictures that he had kept in the office. Herbert tore them and flushed them in the bathroom. He went through the family album and, to Mae's mystification, picked out all the photos in which he could be seen and tore them up. He told her that he was getting off a little early the next day, and would she meet him in City Hall Park at a quarter of four. She said yes. He said that he would have a few extra dollars, and they would go to Times Square and have dinner and then see a show or stop somewhere and have a few drinks.

Mae looked forward to a night out. She loved the lights and the excitement of Times Square. Sometimes when Herb took her there he could not afford a show, but she was thrilled by the proximity of the lights and the glamour of Broadway anyway.

It snowed on Friday. It came down thick and white and there was enough of it for sleigh riding at Halsey and Saratoga. Jackie was at school, and Mae spent the morning cleaning the flat and putting her hair up. Uncle Fats went out. Mae told him that there would be something in the icebox for him and for Jackie.

At the office the old paymaster came in with envelopes full of cash. He was accompanied by a guard, a retired policeman who carried his gun under two sweaters and an overcoat. The clerks grouped around the paymaster and Herbert signed for his $75 semimonthly salary. He was in a good mood, and he chatted a while outside his cage.

It was 12:10 P.M. when he took his fedora and his overcoat and muffler from a clothes tree and walked out, exactly as he had done every day from 1899 until 1925. He said good-by to no one. At 2:00 P.M. his cage was empty. Someone said, "Where's Herb?" Another clerk looked, then winked. "Probably over on Eleventh Avenue getting a little bun on."

Mae was in City Hall Park at 3:30 P.M. She waited in the cold for an hour, watching toward the World Building for the tall, skinny figure, the slow walk. She phoned the Mutual office and asked for Mr. Herbert Gleason. The man who answered said that everyone had gone home.

Mae boarded a trolley at Brooklyn Bridge and went home. She hurried to the flat, certain that Herb was there. He wasn't. Now she was nervous. Something was wrong, but she didn't know what. Down in the street she saw Jackie sleigh riding. It was dark.

"Be a good boy and go upstairs in a little while."

"Where's Pop?"

"I don't know. I'm going back to New York."

"What happened?"

"Nothing."

Mae went back and stood in the icy slush outside City Hall for hours. What were her thoughts? Who knows? She may have suspected the truth, but it is doubtful. Herb had disappeared on other Fridays, and he had turned up on other Sundays.

She was aching with cold when she got back to the flat at 11:00 P.M. She walked through the familiar dark rooms and in the light from the street she saw that her son was in bed.

"Where's Pop?" he said as she began to undress.

"Are you awake?"

"He didn't come home with you."

"I know."

"Where is he?"

"I don't know."

In the morning Jackie went out to play and pack snowballs. His mother was matter-of-fact as she wound a muffler around his neck and pulled a blue stocking hat down over his ears.

"If your feet get wet," she said, "come right in."

On Monday at breakfast Jackie asked a question.

"Is Pop coming back?"

"I don't know."

A week went by. The men in the Mutual office felt that Herb would hardly be on a bender that long. They wondered why his disappearance had not been mentioned in the newspapers, why no policeman had come to the office to question them about his habits. They chatted about it and a memo came from the office of Herbert's brother advising everyone to "stop talking about my brother's disappearance." Instead of stopping the speculation, this led to more of it. The men gossiped that Charles Fred Gleason must have helped his brother to disappear. This was as unkind and untrue as most gossip. Not long afterward Charles Fred Gleason retired. Some years later he died, and at his wake there was a standing wreath inscribed "From Your Loving Brother."

In time Mae reported the disappearance to the police. They asked many questions. At night they often called for her and took her to Bellevue Morgue. She stood tense as they pulled out a drawer with a body on it.

"This your husband, Mrs. Gleason?"

She turned away in horror. "No," she said. "No. Why don't you leave me alone?"

They did.

A year went by and one day a girl clerk burst into the Mutual office and said, "I just saw Herb Gleason!" The clerks gathered and asked where. "He was in City Hall Park. A lot of men were shoveling snow. You know, in gangs like. It was Herb all right. He's wearing a gray coat with a pin in the collar."

Peter Schaus and others hurried up Nassau Street to the park. A lot of municipal workers were shoveling snow around the walks, but none looked like Herb. They found the foreman and asked him if he had a list of the men who were working. He said he had. They wanted to know if he had a Herbert Gleason working for him. He studied the list. No, he said, no Gleason at all. However, he said, only ten minutes ago we sent fifteen of the men up to Union Square on a truck. Why don't you go up there and look?

They did. Union Square was full of men, mostly down-and-outers, lazily lifting shovels laden with snow and turning it to one side. Schaus and the others searched the faces. There was no Gleason.

Back at the office some said that the girl was nuts. Others said no, they believed that she had seen Herb. If they had found someone who looked faintly like Herb, then they could have written off the girl's statement as a mistake. But there was no one among all the men who looked anything like Herb, and it was the belief of the clerks that the girl had seen Gleason, that Gleason had seen her, and that he had hurried off somewhere.

He was never seen again.

Life had not been good to Mae. Now it was getting worse. In twenty-four years of marriage, she had lost a son, a husband, and most of her illusions. Now her brown hair had wisps of gray, and she was ready to admit that life had defeated her, as it had Herb.

She had to get a job. She had no skill. So, when she was offered a chance to be a subway cashier on the Brooklyn Manhattan Transit Lines, she took it. The pay was small, the job was lonely, and she had to sit in a booth at the Lorimer Avenue station and make change for people in a hurry. She reported for work at 8:00 A.M. rain or shine, sleet or heat. At 4:00 P.M. she was relieved by another woman, as tired as she. Sometimes her legs became so cold that she wore Jackie's Boy Scout leggings to work. She complained incessantly that her teeth hurt her "something awful."

Twice she was held up. On both occasions she did not argue with the man with the gun. She gave him all the money she had and burst into tears. When the gold-capped teeth ached badly, Mae bought a pint of gin, drank it, and went to bed. Jackie slept on a cot in her room and he laid in bed many nights and watched her toss and moan. When he asked her what the trouble was, she said that the pain in her teeth was bad, but that the medicine the dentist gave her was worse.

The misery of these two—mother and son—brought them infinitely closer. Each was all the other had left. As Jackie grew old enough to join the street gangs, the one game he would not play was "skip the subway." In this game, everyone waits until a train is in the station. As the doors are about to close, the boys jump over the turnstiles and, before the cashier can stop them, they are on the train, the doors are closed, and they have a free ride. Because of his mother's job, young Gleason always paid his nickel.

This is not to say that he was angelic. On Saturday afternoons, when he went to confession at Our Lady of Lourdes, there was enough to tell to keep a priest listening for some minutes. Jackie had a strong sense of absolute honesty, and this, now and then, led to trouble. At confession one day he came bounding out red of face and frightened. Inside, Father Berlin could be heard growling to himself. One of the boys waiting asked Jackie what had happened.

"He asked me how many times I disobeyed my mother," Jackie said in bewilderment, "and I said 'exactly four hundred and thirty-nine times.' "

On Saturday afternoons Mae Gleason got a pillow from the bedroom and set it on the front window ledge for her elbows. There she crouched, graying, aging, watching. What she watched was the stairs to the elevated railroad down at the corner. Soon her friend Sarah Leeman would be coming down those stairs. Much would depend on which way Sarah turned when she reached the bottom step. Sarah always carried a big black handbag. In it were two house dresses. Although she arrived on Saturdays ostensibly for a short visit, Mae always coaxed her to stay over until Sunday or Monday and Sarah usually surrendered to the coaxing. Sarah was single, an unhappy piano teacher.

In the black handbag also was a bottle of gin—that is, most of the time. Sometimes, when Mae's teeth were hurting the most, the bottle was not in Sarah's bag. Lately Mae had got in the habit of looking out the window. If, at the bottom step, Sarah turned to the left, that meant that she had the gin and was stopping at the fruit store for oranges. If she didn't have the gin, she walked straight to the Gleason flat, in which case, sometimes, Mae turned to Jackie, held a finger to her lips and said, "When the bell rings, don't answer it."

They never discussed the disappearance of his father, and this, on Mae's part, was a mistake because it built up fears and confusion in Jackie's mind. At play with other boys in his neighborhood, Gleason was the only one who could contribute nothing when the talk got around to fathers. Some said that their fathers were great guys; others said that their fathers got drunk and beat up the old lady; one or two said that their fathers were dead. Only Jackie said, "I don't know where my father is. I don't know whether he's dead or alive. He just walked out one day. That's all."

After his father's disappearance, the boy began to wolf his meals. He ate more than Mae could afford to have him eat, and yet he did not get any heavier. He could eat at almost any time of day or night and he wasn't particular about what he ate. There was a new self-reliance in his attitude too. He was more certain in his attitudes at home and at school. With it, he took on a certain sentimentality. At his confirmation in June of 1928 he took the name of Clemence. He formed till-death alliances with boys he liked and respected. He would give or lend whatever he had to a friend; he had a spitting contempt for boys who did not "belong." His first club was called The Four Original Eagles, and its members sawed a fifty-cent piece four ways. Each member got one and they pledged secret and eternal allegiance.

Mae Gleason never brought the matter of Herb's disappearance to the attention of church authorities or civil courts. When her friends asked if there was any news about Herbert, she froze in silence. When they expressed the opinion that he must have been killed in an accident, Mrs. Gleason smiled to herself. She knew better.

There was some talk that, after seven years, the Mutual Life Insurance Company paid her a sum of money on Herbert's insurance. This is not true. Herbert Gleason, who worked in the Death Claims division of an insurance company, had no insurance.

For a short while Mae had an admirer. His name was Ralph and he had a waxed mustache and he called for her now and then to go out for an evening. Mae lost him because she couldn't manufacture an interest in Ralph.

She concentrated on her work on the subway, her cooking and her son. She liked to cook "fancy," and her mashed potatoes always had marshmallows in them. When she left the house, even to go to the corner grocery store, Mae dressed with pride and held her chin a little bit higher than was necessary.

The first important day Jackie had—all to himself—was graduation night, 1930, at P.S. 73. After the ceremonies there was going to be a play. The theme was to be a peep into the future, when people would be able to see pictures come into their home from the sky outside, just as, at that time, they could hear music and voices on radio. The title of the play was *Audio, Video and Radio*. The cast would read its lines from inside a huge frame on the stage. This would give the illusion of that unnamed medium, television.

Everything about the play was fine, except that Gleason was not in it. He ached to be in it, probably more than any other youngster in the graduating class, but the teachers didn't want him. He was a school pest. He had been a trial to Miss Pappen, Mr. Sonnenfeld, Miss Caulfield, Miss Huelein, the music teacher, Miss Miller, and Mr. Ambrose Cort, the school principal.

Jackie had never been expelled. His trouble was not along the lines that cause sudden dismissal. He was an arguer. He would wait until the teacher had committed himself on a subject, then raise his hand for permission to speak and, while the class giggled, would argue that, just by coincidence, Gleason happened to be reading up on this very subject last night, and what the book said did not agree with what the teacher said.

"And what," the teacher would say with asperity, "did *your* book say?"

Jackie would tell him. There was just enough distorted truth in the Gleason version of the subject to drive the teacher crazy. The debate would move back and forth. The teacher would start to shout. Jackie, under control, would accuse the teacher of losing his temper. The teacher would shout that he most certainly was not losing his temper, but as long as the New York school system was paying him to teach this subject, he was going to teach it his way regardless of what junk Jackie Gleason read at night.

The kid could argue almost any subject that was taught. He read at home and he had a phenomenal memory for things that he read, so that he was able to quote his sources almost word for word. He argued his way through school, and he won many of the arguments, but he never achieved high marks. He was always the disloyal opposition.

So, when it came time to pick a cast for the graduation play, no teacher wanted Gleason in it. Jackie knew it, and he wanted more than anything in life to be a part of that play. Ever since the Saturday matinees at the Halsey Theatre he had felt a kinship for the stage. Now, because he had been a fresh kid, they were going to keep him from showing his mother that he had talent.

Jackie did something that he despised in others. He begged. He went to see the principal and he pleaded for a chance. The principal said no. This seemed final, but in the last week the boy heard that there was a conference of teachers going on in the principal's office so he stood before all of them and asked again.

"What will you do," one said, "if we let you in it?"

At the time there was a dialect comic named Henry Burbig who was popular on radio. Gleason, with no coaxing, did an impersonation of Burbig telling the story of Little Red Riding Hood in a Jewish dialect. The teachers and the principal, in spite of animosity, laughed so hard that they waved him away.

"All right, all right," they said. "You're in, Gleason."

On graduation night Mae Gleason came alone to see her Jackie.

She sat far back, but her son was playing to her all the way. He upset the cast by ad libbing; he hammed up the production and acted all over the place. He knocked a microphone stand off the stage and the audience was in an uproar. The principal picked it up and sat it back on the stage. Gleason knocked it off again. Again the principal put it back.

Gleason waited for quiet. Then he shouted, "That's the first time you ever did anything for us kids." The parents roared with laughter and applauded. Jackie Gleason had won his first laugh.

He went home and asked his mother how she liked him in the show. She said that he had been pretty good, and pretty fresh too. He was going to be an actor, he said. Mae Gleason laughed.

Jackie wanted no more of school. Under the law, he was sent to Bushwick High School, but after two weeks he quit. He was sent to John Adams High School to learn a trade. A few weeks later he arranged to have Renee's new husband, a man named Wilson, appear before the principal and explain that this poor boy could no longer attend school because he was the sole support of his mother, who was very sick.

Gleason never attended school again. For a while he was a well-dressed bum. It would have been helpful if he had hurried out each morning to look for a job, but he didn't. He wanted to be an actor, nothing but an actor, and anything that was not a part of the theater was distasteful. He hung out in poolrooms, and it is doubtful that there were many youngsters anywhere in the United States who became so expert with the cue in so short a time. He was so clever that after the first few weeks he no longer needed money. Neighborhood boys would "stake" him to a game and then bet on him.

Al Church quit as the family boarder, and Mae had to move again. This time she found a unique flat at 358 Chauncey Street where the rent was cheap and the neighbors had a heart. It was a neighborly neighborhood in the old-time sense that everyone knew everybody else's business and most of the women were on sugar-borrowing terms. The whole row was called Dennehy's flats, although neither Tom Dennehy nor Anna Kelleher Dennehy owned them.

They managed them. And kept them clean. And collected the rents. And sweated it out with the poor tenants who didn't have the rent. The Dennehys came from County Kerry, Ireland, and both tried to make their neighbors understand that the name is pronounced *Dunn-a-hee*. Tom was forty, a squat man of muscles who worked as a stationary engineer and who admired young men who worked with their hands. Mrs. Dennehy had a big heart and a mouth that matched it. When she greeted a friend, window glass rattled.

Mae Gleason and Anna Dennehy became friends at once. Mae lived on the third floor right, and, two houses away, Anna lived on the fourth floor. They learned from their children—the Dennehys had two growing daughters and a son—that it was simpler and shorter to walk up to the roof and across and down when visiting than to go down to the street and up. In the summertime, Pop Dennehy worried about the boys taking girls up on the roofs of his houses, and he used to stand on the opposite sidewalk and roar, "Hey, you kids! Get off the roof!" He found it easy to dislike Jackie. Any boy who dressed like a dude and cared for nothing but making up jokes "anneyed" him. The boys evened the score by inventing libels against Pop. They said that when he slipped off the water wagon, he used to prop a small cask of whisky between the head of the bed and the wall, then get into bed and run an enema-bag tube from the cask to his mouth.

Nobody believed it.

The neighborhood was poor Italian and poor Irish. Nobody had much of anything, but they shared what they had and they had an enormous amount of fun. The men were often souses and sentimentalists; the ladies were dreamers. Practically everyone attended Our Lady of Lourdes or St. Benedict's. There was a park, a whole square block of park and trees, but none of the youngsters could play in it because the old lady who owned it died and left it explicitly for old people to sit in the sun.

In almost every direction there were four-story tenements, broken, here and there, with rows of two-story private homes which leaned against each other. Down the block was P.S. 137, which accommodated students up to the sixth year of primary school, and which had a schoolyard designed for Gleason and his

friends. There they played stickball and basketball, and when it
rained they forced the door to the school after hours and played
downstairs in the gymnasium.

All of the neighborhood streets—Chauncey, Herkimer, Saratoga—branched off Broadway like feathers off an arrow. The
noise of the elevated trains tempered the wail of babies on summer nights and drowned some of the language of the Ralphs and
Alices of the neighborhood.

It was an earthy, gutsy place, a place where snobs were quar-
antined like lepers; one of a score of villages inside Brooklyn
where loyalties were jingoistic; where a boy had to fight to belong; where short Anglo-Saxon words were used, not so much in
blasphemy but as a means of punctuation; a place where the
dumb-waiter and a code ring of the downstairs bell were part of
the daily life; where petty theft was not regarded as real stealing;
a place where, at sixteen, a girl could become known to one and
all as a lady or as a tramp; at the same age, a boy who was well
dressed, had a dollar in his pocket and no job was quite a guy. A
man, almost.

In this neighborhood, the gang to belong to was the Nomads.
It was composed of teen-age boys. They had sweaters and they
fielded a baseball team, and, now and then, they met in a guy's
house on Sumter Street. Here they argued, made plans, paid
dues, plotted against their rivals, the Alpines, on Marion Street,
indulged in horseplay, voted secretly on the admission of new
members, told stories about grownups in the neighborhood, and
talked about broads. One kid who ached to join entreated his
mother to permit the Nomads to meet in her house and to bake
a cake and serve coffee. Against her better judgment the woman
did it. Her son was blackballed.

They had their brand of chivalry. One member of the club was
a skinny kid named Orange. When he laughed, he coughed.
When he coughed, he couldn't stop. The Nomads always gentled
him a little and took turns protecting him from the usual rough-
housing. When he moved out of the neighborhood, they remembered him and inquired about his health. On infrequent occasions
when they saw him, they all agreed that it was impossible for
Orange to look any worse than he used to, but he looked worse.

Gleason was permitted to join the Nomads and he fell into the spirit of the gang as though he had invented it. He loved to hang out on the street corners at night and make cracks about the passing girls, and he had the guys in stitches. They leaned against the wall of Schuman's Candy Store and sobbed at Jackie's line.

Soon he got to know all of them. There was Joe Tolle, tall and slender, who always told a story dead-pan; John Cocoman, who later became a singer in the Firemen's Glee Club; Tom Robinson, who was destined to become one of New York University's better teachers; Charlie Cretter, whom Jackie claimed was the only man in the world bowlegged in the opposite direction; Jimmy Proce, whose father owned a couple of buildings and was therefore regarded as rich; Marty Dyer, who became a detective; Tom Healy, John Healy; Jimmy O'Hare; Billy and Jim Kiernan; Harold Kroell; Diji Dennehy; Buster Sands; Teddy Gilanza, who would stand in the cool of Gleason's shadow for the next twenty-five years; John Heinz, known as Heinzy; Shorty Skrobel; Primo Ippolito; Vincent Chatfield; Adolf Signorelli; and Sonny Gould.

On the average day, this gang met in the schoolyard of P.S. 137 and played basketball until supper. If the weather was warm, they would walk a mile, a straggling group of loud kids who blocked the sidewalks with their wrestling and fake punching, out to Island Park. There they would play baseball. If they found no opponents, they would play against each other. First they played for nothing or, at most, some coins. Later they played for beers and the losers had to buy beer for the winners in the winners' tavern. Gleason pitched on the baseball team and he was good. As a hitter he wasn't much, but once he hit a home run and fell down between third base and home and was tagged out.

When it rained, the Nomads met in Lennie Ippolito's house. Lennie was born blind. He shot craps with the gang in his cellar and trusted the boys to read the numbers correctly. Lennie studied piano hard. Years later he played piano at the Blue Terrace in Brooklyn. Vincent Chatfield also became a pianist of note.

The nighttime activities of the Nomads depended upon the

weather and the mood. They played Johnny-on-a-Pony (a back-breaking version of leapfrog, in which the weight of all is placed on one) against the wall of the candy store. They played cards and, having no money, made the losers do the bidding of the winners. One night Teddy Gilanza and Vinnie Cann had to run around the block in their underwear.

Later the boys became interested in girls, and they dressed brightly and combed their hair and shined their shoes and attended dances at Arcadia Hall and stood around nudging each other and making lipless comments as new girls showed up. Often they met in the Dennehy flat because Tom and Anna Dennehy believed that it was healthy for their daughters to invite the boys indoors where everybody could have a look at them. The Nomads chipped in, on these occasions, and bought a keg of beer and pumped the player piano and played kissing games and had buns and coffee. One night Pop Dennehy came into the parlor and announced an election result, and, in ecstasy, the gang threw his parlor furniture out the fourth floor window and started a bonfire in the middle of the street.

If there were excesses, they were sexual in character. Like most tenement-house kids, the boys acted as though they had a copyright on biological discoveries. One evening at ten a mother came home and found four boys and four girls sitting around her dining-room table playing poker. All were in varying stages of undress, which, she was assured, was part of the game.

When the boys had money, they went to the Myrtle Burlesque Theatre, which featured Izzy Pickle and his Cucumbers. Jackie didn't care much for this. He had a small radio at home, and his favorite program was "Uncle Don." His favorite screen actor was John Barrymore.

The Nomads came close to breaking up when Red Avery was elected manager. They had a meeting in Elmer Lane's house, and after the dues were collected someone extinguished the lights. When they went on, Red said that some of the money was missing. "Okay, wise guys," he said. "I'm gonna put the lights out again, and when they go on I wanna see the missing dough on the table." He put the lights out. When they went on again, all of the money was missing.

In the early 1930s the Masked Marvel was a fixture around Brooklyn poolrooms. Only the manager knew his identity; the guest would show up in a short black eye mask and, as the local boys gaped, would offer to play anyone in the place, for money. If no one would bet, he would stage a short exhibition match.

Jackie was intrigued by these Masked Marvels and, after watching several of them, assured the gang that he could beat them without a struggle. Some of the kids believed him; some didn't. They knew that Gleason was clever with a pool cue—he had already trounced the best men in the neighborhood—but the Masked Marvel was something else. Still, Orange had faith in Jackie. Orange only.

His father was a guard in the Raymond Street jail and he wore his uniform day and night all week long. The only time the man donned a civilian suit was on Sunday. So Orange took his father's suit to a pawnbroker and hocked it for four dollars. Then he bet the four that Gleason would beat the Masked Marvel.

It turned out to be a tight match, and Orange perspired in the cold poolroom. When the last fifteen balls were racked up, it was Jackie's turn to shoot and he needed one ball to win. The Masked Marvel needed eight. The strategy, on Gleason's part, would have been to play it "safe"—that is, to tap the cue ball lightly against the rack of fifteen balls, hit two cushions, and bring the cue ball back in front of the rack, where the Masked Marvel would find it impossible to make a shot.

Instead, the young man decided to break the rack wide-open on a win-all or lose-all shot. He chalked his cue, nodded toward the rack, and said, "Seven in the corner." Orange held his hand over his eyes. If Gleason missed the shot, the balls would be all over the table and the Masked Marvel would run off eight balls easily. Gleason's driving shot hit the apex of the rack a little bit on the right side and the balls flew all over the table. The seven edged between the skittering spheres and dropped in the corner pocket.

Jackie seemed to be the only person unsurprised at the result. He set his cue back, shook hands with the Masked Marvel, and walked out. Orange began to breathe again. He collected eight dollars, walked down the street, bailed his father's suit out, went home and hung it in a closet.

One of the kids Jackie enjoyed beating at pool was Killer Healy. He was a good boy and a serious boy. He was also a top-flight pool player, but he had a glaring weakness—anger. When the Killer was teased, he took it in silence for a long time, grinding his teeth and pretending not to notice, but when he blew up, it was like a conflagration at a fireworks-manufacturing plant on the third of July.

Gleason could beat the Killer any time. He knew that Healy was good. All Jackie had to do was to wait until it was the Killer's turn to shoot and make a few remarks in an aside. In ten minutes Gleason could reduce his opponent to a stage where he was whispering to himself and couldn't sink a hanger.

One day Jackie said patronizingly, "You can't shoot pool and I'll prove it to you. I'll play you fifty points, spot you forty-five, and beat you." The Killer took the bet, and lost. In silence, he took his cue, walked over to a high wooden stool, and rammed the cue through the seat and down into the floor. He walked over to Gleason, paid him off, and smiled at Jackie. The Killer rubbed his right fist into the palm of his left hand.

"One of these days, Jackie," he said softly. *"One of these days—* Pow! Right in the kisser!"

On another occasion Jackie heard that a Masked Marvel was to put on an exhibition at a local poolroom at 3:00 P.M. At 2:00 P.M. Gleason, in mask, walked into the place, bowed to the applause, and showed the customers some fancy shooting. He was still at it when the real Masked Marvel arrived. The manager of the place almost killed Gleason.

He was fourteen years old when he first fell in love. Her name was Julie Dennehy and she was dark and plump and appeared to be older than the twelve years on her baptismal certificate. In any case, Julie (or Jool, as she was called) knew more about love at twelve than Jackie knew at fourteen.

The first meeting occurred outside Schuman's Candy Store. Jackie was playing the spoons, a minor musical accomplishment in which two teaspoons are held back to back between the

fingers, and, by causing the backs to touch each other in synco-
pated rhythm, a musical effect is achieved. They can be bounced
against a knee, on the sidewalk, against a wall or a friendly
skull—also against teeth. The gang stood around watching Gleason; Julie,,on her way home from the store, stopped to watch.

Jackie spoke to her, asked her if she was interested in spoons.
She said that indeed she was—a lie of a particularly crude order.
That evening he walked her back to the house. Gravely, he said
that he'd like to call for her the next night, to show her how to
play the spoons. Julie smiled shyly and said that she would await
the lesson.

After that Jackie became a fixture at the Dennehy flat. Pop
Dennehy, who was not noted for tact, almost spat in the kitchen
every time Gleason came in, tall, slender, slick, well-groomed
and unsoiled. "He's a bum!" Pop said to anyone who would
listen. "And you can't make anything else out of him."

Julie was still going to primary school, and every day Jackie
called for her and walked her home, a distance of about four
hundred feet. He was in love with Julie; she wasn't sure about
him except that he was "cute." She saw a great deal of him and
learned much about him, but she never learned how to play
the spoons.

The acid test of love came, as far as Julie was concerned,
when she played a prank in school and the teacher said, "Do not
report in tomorrow, Miss Dennehy, without bringing your
mother with you." Julie was in a panic, a very real panic, because
she did not dare to break the news to her mother. She talked
it over with Jackie.

"Don't worry about it," he said, with the same assurance that
he used to drop the seven ball in the corner pocket. "Tell her
your mother is sick but your big brother will be there."

In the morning Julie felt so much better that it became impossible to keep the secret. With pride, she told every girl in the
class how her "boy friend" was about to pose as her big brother.
The class was in session when Gleason arrived. The teacher
took him out in the hall to explain what a villain Julie was.
Inside, half the class was in hysterics. Outside, Jackie listened
quietly, clucked sympathetically, and said, "Wait till my mother

hears this. Jool is going to get the fanning of her life." The teacher begged that the Dennehys not be too harsh, that after all Julie was a young girl full of animal spirits and a good sense of humor. Jackie promised.

When the teacher returned to the room, she announced to the class that young Mr. Dennehy was polite and mannerly, "such a lovely boy."

There came a day when Jackie did not show up to carry Julie's books and she worried all the way home. She was sure he was ill so, instead of going directly to her flat, she walked up the stoop to his. Inside the vestibule, she shrieked. There stood Jackie Gleason, the sides of his head shaven. He looked like a Heidelberg student who had dueled once too often. He explained apologetically that he wanted to look like Conrad Nagel, a matinee idol. Mr. Nagel had a severe widow's peak and Jackie had tried to shave the sides of his head to form one, but somehow it had come out crooked. For weeks he wore Mr. Dennehy's spare cap to hide his hair.

He was fifteen when his cousin Renee told him the facts of life. She was his only known relative, and she was six years older than he, and married. Renee was pretty sure that Aunt Mae wouldn't assume the job, so she took him aside and tried to get him to listen. Jackie, however, was an inquisitive extrovert, and he could hardly wait for her to finish the speech so that he could start asking questions. He had learned so much from the talented Nomads that, in the end, all Renee did was to make it official, and counsel caution.

On the street corner Charlie Cretter and Jackie teamed up as an "act" and entertained the gang and such pedestrians as might want to stop and laugh. Most of the comments centered around "You guys are a scream. You ought to be on the stage." This was exactly what Jackie wanted to hear and, when the chorus was unanimous, he entered himself and Charlie Cretter in the amateur-night show.

This was a Wednesday-night feature at the Halsey Theatre, and local talent went on stage immediately after the last vaudeville act and before the feature picture. The prizes were five dollars and two dollars, and the winners were ascertained by coming on stage for a reprise while a master of ceremonies—in this case a youngster named Sammy Birch who looked like a solemn Harold Lloyd—held his hand over each head and listened to the volume of applause.

Then as later Gleason could not stand failure; in fact, he feared anything less than perfection, so for a week ahead of time he worked on the act. Cretter was a high Irish tenor, and Jackie had him dress as a girl. Gleason played the man. They wisecracked, sang a song, and did a little dance. To insure the matter, the word was passed to all Nomads to be at the Halsey Theatre on Wednesday night and to spread the word among their families and friends. The idea was to pack the theater with friends of the Gleason-Cretter act.

They did well. There were other acts—a solemn boy who recited, a nine-year-old girl who was taking ballet lessons, a twin-boy soft-shoe dancing act, a sixteen-year-old magician who was almost hooted off the stage because the flowers popped out of the vase before he was ready—and then Gleason. The master of ceremonies, Sammy Birch, put Gleason on last because, in the early interview, he was impressed with this youngster's self-assurance.

Jackie came on, in flannels, sports shoes and a straw hat, and introduced Charlie as La Belle Marie. Charlie sang "Humming to Myself," to tremendous applause. Jackie then came on and cracked jokes. After that they did a little dance. When they finished, the theater rocked with applause. Most of the mothers and fathers had attended out of loyalty to two neighborhood youngsters, but the two were so amusing, so sure of themselves, that the people applauded and stomped and whistled because the boys were that good. They won first prize *and* second.

Instead of seven dollars, Jackie got a dollar and a conversation with the theater manager. He said that he was very much impressed with Jackie's stage presence. Sammy Birch, he explained, was booked to play theaters in Harlem and Staten Island and, if Jackie wanted, he could be the regular amateur-night master of ceremonies at four dollars a night.

Gleason accepted. He also got a card of introduction to a

booking agent on Broadway named Solly Shaw. He gave fifty cents to Cretter and said, in a tone that showed a consciousness of history in the making, "Charlie, we're on our way."

"I don't know," Charlie said. "My old man is death on actors."

"We are definitely on our way," Jackie said, ignoring any adverse comment. "What we need is a good act, well written, with some· new material. After that, we need a break. One good break and we're in."

Mae Gleason did not think much of Jackie's first stage appearance. She sat and watched it, and she was pleased to see so many of the people from around Chauncey Street applauding for her son, but she did not believe that Jackie would ever amount to anything on the stage. Experience had proved to her that life was tough and callous, that there was no real joy in it, and that the main fight was for a dollar. The dollar could be best secured by working long hours at a dismal job.

Nothing could stop Jackie now. He had had a swallow of success, and it had tasted good. He bought a handful of old theatrical booklets full of acts and dialogue and he salvaged enough from these to write one full act called "The Sardonic Spectator." The format was hardly new. Charlie Cretter, in a tuxedo ("We need tuxedos to look the part of money"), was to come on stage and announce that he was impelled to proceed alone because his partner had been unavoidably detained. Gleason, in a tuxedo, would be in the audience and, at the right moment, would begin to heckle Charlie's act. The thing would close with both of them on stage in patter and a final song.

The act was held up because of lack of tuxedos. Buster Sands, a member of the gang, heard about it and said to Gleason, "You guys don't have to worry. My old man belongs to a lodge. He has two tuxedos—an old one and a new one." The boys went over to Buster's house to try them on.

Cretter got the new one. Except for the fact that the cuffs were a third of the way up to the elbows, it fit fine. Gleason drew the old one, an ancient dress suit with brocaded vest and trousers that were so tight on the legs that Jackie had to remove his shoes to put them on. He told Buster that the suits were great.

Then he went out and got a booking at the Brooklyn Masonic

Lodge for five dollars. When Buster heard the date, he became frightened and said, "My old man goes to his lodge the very next night. Those suits better be back right after the show."

The people were dancing at the Masonic Club when there was a roll of drums and the announcer asked for quiet. Couples left the floor and Charlie Cretter, in a tight tux, said that he was sorry that his partner had not shown up, but that he would proceed without him. He turned to the band leader and said, "If you'll play something, I'll pick up the air." From the crowd, Gleason yelled, in Yiddish dialect, "You sing, and don't worry, you'll *get* the air!" He walked onto the deserted floor in the ancient tuxedo, and everyone laughed. He started up the steps to the bandstand and fell three times. He had practiced this, and it drew automatic amusement. The rest of the act consisted of jokes, with Cretter playing the straight man.

It was hokum, but it was a hit. A Jewish manufacter liked the Gleason dialect so much that he hired Jackie, for five dollars, to play at a Saturday-night party at his house. They played several of these dates and earned a few dollars here and there, but Gleason was impatient.

"We're not getting anywhere, Charlie," he said. "Nowhere at all. Somehow, we got to meet a big star; you know, somebody who can tell us what the next step is."

They learned that George K. Stone, a fine motion-picture actor, was about to make a personal appearance at a Brooklyn theater. This was their man. Jack and Charlie waited in the theater alley, with autograph pads, for the great star to come out. When he did, he was surrounded by friends. Jackie asked for an autograph, please, and Mr. Stone obliged. As the star signed, Jackie said, "My friend and I have an act, a little act and not much of an act, but we would sure appreciate a few tips on how to hit the big time, Mr. Stone."

Stone stopped smiling. His friends closed in around him. The big party moved on out of the alley. Gleason was depressed after that. Cretter wanted to quit. In a short time he did.

At the Halsey Theatre, Jackie wasn't satisfied to do a four-dollar job. As master of cermonies for the amateur group, he came on stage after the final professional act. Whatever this act was, jugglers or a band, they left their equipment on stage and Gleason used it to do a burlesque of their work. Once he came on stage flying, with a rope tied around his waist, and he flew across the stage and back.

He was kindly and encouraging to all the amateur acts. He made jokes, but they were not the kind that would hurt. He gave them friendly build-ups, and often begged the audience to "give the kid a chance." Now and then he augmented the show by having Vincent Chatfield and Charles Allen, old pals who could play a piano and sing, show up for a short recital. He would introduce them as old friends "who just dropped in from the Paradise Club on Broadway." Neither had ever been on stage, and neither had ever seen the Paradise Club.

At the same time Jackie acquired his first two writers. Both were ushers at Loew's Metropolitan and both were stage-struck and had a dance act. They were Elwood Halliday and Eddie Mullen and, on their own time, they wrote material for Gleason— jokes and bits of stage business. Gleason loved it and thanked them with all his heart, because the material was always good. It should have been. Elwood and Eddie stole it from the best acts playing Loew's Metropolitan. Whenever a headliner comedian got to the theater, both Eddies used flashlights and pencils to copy his best lines. They forgot to tell Jackie that the material was borrowed. Sometimes this led to a painful situation in which a star was accused of stealing material from a kid amateur.

Suddenly the whole neighborhood had theatrical fever and a man named Gilbert—his first name is lost to posterity—came into Bushwick and began to cast for an amateur show to be called "The Halsey Follies." It would play at the Halsey Theatre for three days, and there would be four shows a day. Nobody would be paid, of course, except Mr. Gilbert and the manager of the Halsey, but no one wanted money anyway. The youngsters wanted fame, a chance to get on the stage and be a second Douglas Fairbanks or a Dolores Del Rio, or perhaps a Pat Rooney.

Gleason applied for the job of introducing the acts, but Gilbert seemed to have no time. He was busy listening to singers and watching dancers. Now and then Gilbert would look at Gleason

and say, "In good time, my friend. In good time." Jackie followed
him around, backstage and front, but the man was always busy.

Two days before the show was to open Mr. Gilbert told the
boy that he was to be master of ceremonies. Jackie took the sum
of his newly acquired theatrical knowledge and poured it into this
show. He was fast and he was clever. His mother came to see
"The Halsey Follies" several times in three days but, once more,
she did not think her son was funny. She laughed uproariously,
but not at Jackie's antics. To her way of thinking, the funniest
bit in the show was the twelve chorus girls. They had been
taught to drop to one knee as a local boy sang, "Swanee, Swanee,
how I love ya, how I love ya, my dear old Swanee." The costumes had been furnished by Mr. Gilbert and the girls wore short
green-satin skirts with matching panties. All except Julie Dennehy. She wore white ones because Mrs. Dennehy wouldn't permit her to wear the ones furnished by the impresario. This had
Mae Gleason laughing long after the chorus line had kicked its
way off stage.

After that Gleason did some work for Gilbert's other shows and
received five dollars a night. There was a Mrs. Kelly, who lived in
Greenwich Village, and she also staged some local talent shows
in which Jackie appeared. At one of these shows Mrs. Kelly introduced him to her two nieces, Genevieve and Geraldine. They
were ballet dancers and lived in Astoria. Sometimes they were
billed as twins and, looking them over, Jackie decided that they
might be twins. Both were blond, both had pretty faces and
figures, both wore look-alike dresses. Perhaps, close up, Geraldine
might have been a bit prettier than Genevieve.

Jackie Gleason fell in love with Genevieve almost at once. Julie
Dennehy and a whole world of women went out of his mind. He
had a few dates with Genevieve and he found out that she was
cool and objective and suspicious of hand-holding. She refused to
listen to his jokes, was horrified at the use of bad language, went
to Mass and the sacraments regularly, said her rosary for the poor
souls in purgatory, and Jackie sometimes wondered why she
bothered to go out with him at all.

He hurried to Renee's house one night and, spinning in circles,
said, "I'm going with a girl serious."

"What happened to Julie?"

"Julie's fine. Good friend of mine. I may marry this other girl."

"What's her name?"

"Gen—Genevieve Halford. Isn't that a beautiful name?"

"Well, I'm still on my feet, Jackie. But she sounds nice."

"A lady, Reen. A real lady to her toes."

"Take it easy, my boy."

He took her home to mother. Mae looked her over, woman to woman, and liked her. What she saw was a good, solid, sensible girl—exactly what her harebrained son needed. Mae and Gen liked each other and got along well. But the romance, such as it was, ran like a local bus—many stops, many starts. Between times Jackie returned to Julie Dennehy, who was not idle either. She had dates with a Nomad in good standing, Adolph Signorelli, and one night while she stood on the roof she saw Gleason and Signorelli, far below in the street, fight over her. The words were loud and awful to listen to, but not a blow was struck.

Jackie's career, at this time, was also stopping and starting. In the summer he worked at Cypress Pool as a comic diver and swimmer. He also M.C.'d a "professional" amateur show produced by Ernie Glucksman, who, some years later, would produce shows for Dean Martin and Jerry Lewis. Jackie was a talker in a speeding car at daredevil track races. He put on an act for home parties. For a while he thought seriously of becoming an artist. His drawings were good and the neighbors urged him to forsake the stage for the drawing board.

He wanted to make people laugh. Nothing else. Just that. The momentous question, to Jackie, was: "How?" He had been an amateur, or professional amateur, for two years. How does a man break away from that category and move up a step into the thoroughly professional ranks? There had to be an answer; thousands of actors had started in the amateurs, but now they were on Keith Albee time, or Gus Sun time, or Pantages time. They were making sleeper jumps all over the United States and playing split weeks in Peoria or Pocatello or Penobscot. If a man could make that one step, the rest of his success would be a matter of talent plus material plus breaks. Jackie didn't worry about that part. He was certain that he would reach the top of his profession someday, and he told the gang that he would be the funniest man in the country, but the question remained the same: How could he break out of the amateur ranks?

Mae too had a problem. Hers was not a question of how to get to the peak; rather, it was a question of how to keep out of the pit. She was forty-nine years of age in the spring of 1935; her son was nineteen. She was defeated, lonely, afraid. For years she had secretly hoped that Herb would come back; she had permitted herself to live on that hope. When mail had come, her aging, calloused hands had riffled through the envelopes quickly, her blue eyes fixed on the handwriting.

He had not come back. There was no clue. She did not know whether he was alive or dead. She had worked hard on the BMT, and she had long ago sickened of it. The one thing Mae Gleason had left was front—she had continued to dress smartly and had continued to hold her chin a little high.

Now the façade cracked. She spent more time in bed. She dreamed at a back window, looking at clotheslines. She tired of cleaning and dusting and for weeks she would not allow anyone in her kitchen. The parlor and the front bedroom were stacked with old dusty furniture and sugar barrels. The yellowing keys of an old upright piano shone in the gloom.

Only the second bedroom and the dining room were open. A kerosene stove heated these and, if the gas oven was turned on, the kitchen could be heated on cold days. Recklessly, she had gone to a time-payment store and bought a studio couch and a sideboard for the dining room. Mae slept on the couch in the dining room; Jackie had the bedroom.

He could have helped her if he had tried to get a salaried job. He was tall, thin, good-looking, strong. But there was a deep depression out of which the country struggled slowly, and jobs were hard to find. Besides, Jackie had his eye on a bigger goal—a goal that would insure a life of ease for his mother. They had struggled a long time; a little bit more wouldn't hurt. That's what he told himself. That, probably, is what he really believed.

But Mae was giving up. She was quitting. She saw few people outside of Mrs. Dennehy, who stopped in for a chat and a cup of tea. When Mae was broke, she borrowed a dollar or two from

Mrs. Dennehy, and the Dennehys knew Mae was "a good payer."
When she got home with her salary, Mae always paid the neighbors at once and got money orders for whatever time payments
were due on the studio couch and the sideboard.

Once in a while, when she had an extra dollar or two, she would
ask Jack to have Julie in for dinner. The boy and the girl sat at
the dining-room table. Mrs. Gleason worked in the kitchen and,
when she came in with a platter of meat, she'd holler, "Grab it,
Julie!" and Julie would take enough for herself, put some on Mrs.
Gleason's plate and then hand it to Jackie, who would finish everything. Mae had warned Julie that Jackie would "eat everything
on the platter" if it was given to him first. She also, quite paren-
thetically, begged Julie not to become serious with Jackie.

Jackie borrowed from the Dennehys too. When he needed two
dollars, he would hop across the roof and down to the Dennehy
kitchen. There he would stand talking about nothing in particular, until Pop Dennehy had his back turned. Then Jackie stood
behind Pop and silently held two upraised fingers behind Pop's
head. To Mrs. Dennehy, at the kitchen sink, the two fingers
looked like Indian feathers over her husband's Irish face. If she
had it to lend, she would nod curtly. If she hadn't, she would
shake her head. Jackie, too, always paid his debts promptly and,
when he hugged Mrs. Dennehy, he referred to himself as "your
number two son."

The years did not soften Mr. Dennehy's attitude toward young
Gleason. He still admired boys who learned a trade and had no
use for well-dressed bums. He was strict and fierce with his own
family, although he showed a soft side when he hung nicknames
on his children. Young Tommy was always "Diji" to him; daughter
Catherine, for no known reason, was "Gotzie"; and Julie was
"Jewel Gotz." In time the neighborhood forgot the Christian
names of the Dennehys and used "Diji" and "Gotzie" and "Jewel
Gotz."

In the early part of 1935 Mrs. Gleason had a boil, or carbuncle,
on the back of her neck. She did nothing about it except to try to
squeeze it. For two years she had been subject to sudden and
violent nosebleeds. Sometimes while shopping she would press

her hand to her face and, in a smear of blood, would fall to the sidewalk in a faint. She did nothing about this either.

Sometimes passers-by phoned for an ambulance. When it arrived, Mrs. Gleason would be sitting on a store step with a small crowd standing around. She always refused attention, wiped her face, and hurried home. Tension increased her nervousness and her fears. She could no longer abide noise. She became ashamed of her flat and dreaded to hear the bell ring.

Jackie asked for permission to go on the road with a show unit, and she shouted no, that he was wasting his time. All this stage business was nonsense; if he was any kind of a boy he would go out and get a decent job. Then, exhausted, she threw herself on the studio couch and dozed.

Mae Gleason began to take days off from work. The carbuncle grew bigger and the pain was steady and intense. She spent more and more time on the studio couch. She moaned awake, and she moaned sleeping, so that Jackie was afraid to ask how she felt in fear that he might be disturbing her rest.

His was the inner fear, for she represented all that he had left in life. Outwardly, he was cocky and careless. Inwardly, he worried about this woman who, to him, represented all that was pure and good, all that was unselfish and suffering.

He commiserated with her. He begged her to please call a doctor. She said no, that she had feared doctors all of her life and that Smith, the homeopathic doctor, was the only one she trusted. Now she couldn't find him, and she'd get along without a doctor.

Jackie tried to be a doctor. He ran to the druggist, begging for something to cure a carbuncle. He returned with black salves and with unguents and with pills. His mother submitted to all of them, and after six weeks of intermittent torment she began to feel that nothing would cure it.

April tenth was chill and damp. In the afternoon Mrs. Dennehy, under a woolen shawl, hurried across the roofs and down the skylight to Mae's flat. She tiptoed into the dining room. Mae was dozing on the couch.

"Mae," said Mrs. Dennehy. "Mae, are you awake?"

Mrs. Gleason turned slowly from the wall. Her eyes were puffed with sleep. Her face was swollen. The skin was saffron. She looked almost oriental.

"Sit down," she said. "I'm just taking it easy."

The women chatted. Mrs. Dennehy had brought some hot soup. Mae said she didn't feel hungry. Mrs. Dennehy, with Irish tenacity, said that Mae was out of her mind if she didn't get a doctor. Mae shook her head slowly. No doctor. She wouldn't change now.

Mrs. Dennehy excused herself. "I'll be right back," she said. "I've got something on the stove." The neighbor was frightened. She went back to her flat and phoned for an ambulance. She said that there was a woman named Mrs. Mae Gleason, desperately sick, who needed attention at once. She gave the address, third floor left in the eight-family building.

Then she hurried back to sit with Mae. They chatted about small matters and Mae sat up on the studio couch and tried to fix her hair.

The bell rang. "Now who could that be at this hour?" Mae said. Mrs. Dennehy opened the door. A hospital intern, a thin young man with a toothbrush mustache, stood in the frame.

"Mrs. Mae Gleason?" he said, looking at a card in his hand.

Mae stood. "I'm Mrs. Gleason," she said. He said he was an ambulance doctor. At once her face flattened in hard lines. "Who sent for you?" she said shrilly.

The man stared through the darkness of the dining room. "Somebody phoned," he said. "Said it was an emergency. A Mrs. Mae Gleason."

"If anybody sent for you," she said, "it wasn't me and I'm Mrs. Mae Gleason. Thanks for coming." She moved toward the door and the doctor backed away.

"Just a minute," he said. "If you'd just sign this sheet right here, it will show I made the call." He held it against the door. Mae scribbled her signature. The door closed.

"Now who do you suppose would play a dirty trick like that?" Mrs. Gleason said. "You don't think the kids—"

Mrs. Dennehy shook her head. "They wouldn't do a thing like that."

Mae sat. She couldn't imagine who would do a thing like this to her. She guessed almost every name in the neighborhood. Late in the afternoon when Jackie came in with Julie she gave up guessing.

He was all bounce and joy until his eyes became accustomed to the dimness. "Your face is all swollen, Mom," he said.

"You can see it in the mirror," Julie said.

Mae nodded. "I've seen it," she murmured.

Jackie fidgeted. "It's the core that's causing it," he said hesitantly. "If you'd sit in the kitchen, where the light is, we can try to get it out, can't we, Julie?" Sure we could, Julie said. Mrs. Gleason was too spent to resist. She sat on a kitchen chair, in the midst of unwashed dishes and stale bread, and bowed her head.

Jackie got a needle and washed it in the sink. He handed some paper napkins to Julie. "If the stuff comes out," he said to Julie, "you wipe it with the napkins." Julie was scared. So was Jackie. Mae wasn't. A little more pain didn't bother her.

Mrs. Gleason kept her head bowed, and the moans seemed to come from her soul. "I can see the core, Mom," the boy said hopefully. "It's a long white thing. If I can only get a hold of it, I'll pull the whole thing out." Julie felt sick. Jackie perspired. He worked and worked and worked as though his mother's life depended on his efforts.

"If I could only pinch it in a bobby pin," he said. "Or something. It keeps slipping out of my fingers."

A half hour later he gave up. Mrs. Gleason thanked both children. She staggered back into the dining room and onto the couch. "I couldn't take it any more," she whimpered. "I just couldn't." She saw Julie's snowy, frightened face and she tried to make a joke. "You know what I told you, Jewel Gotz. I'm scared of dead people and I'm scared of death, so if I die, I swear I'm coming back and haunt you."

Nobody laughed. Mae Gleason fell on the couch exhausted.

The face continued to swell, slowly, perceptibly, steadily. By the evening of April twelfth, Mrs. Gleason no longer looked like Mrs. Gleason. Jackie wanted to go out; he changed his mind. He and Julie and Shorty Skrobel sat at the dining-room table in the evening hours playing cards. Mrs. Gleason slept with her face to the wall.

At first the card game was an uneasy thing. The three young-sters spent more time looking at the figure on the couch than at the cards. Then the natural ebullience of youth won out, and they began to laugh and kid each other and bluff their hands. Infrequently Mrs. Gleason moaned mightily, and each time Jackie put his cards on the table and got up and walked over to the couch.

"You all right, Mom?" he would say.

If Mae was awake, she would turn to look up at him through slitted eyes. "I'm all right, Jackie," she would say. "I'm all right." If she was sleeping, she seemed to sigh in answer. He would bend low over his mother and listen to her breathing. The fear would go away and he would straighten up and shrug. "She's all right. Dreaming, probably."

After midnight there was very little moaning. Julie was tired and wanted to go home. Shortie was shuffling cards. Jackie said, "Oh, sit for a little while." They played a few more hands. The room was quiet. Conversation was down to the irreducible. Then they heard a loud sigh, almost an explosion of breath.

Jackie got up. "You all right, Mom?" he said. He listened. There was no breathing. He straightened up and looked at the others. Then he listened again. Mae Kelly Gleason was dead at the age of 49 years and 363 days. Jackie started to walk back and forth quickly and silently in the dining room. He wrung his hands, partly in fear, partly in entreaty.

He went back to his mother and touched her lightly on the shoulder. He coughed and tried to sound casual. "Better call a doctor," he said to Shorty. The boy got up quickly, closed the dining-room door softly behind him, and got down the stairs, three at a time. Abruptly, Jackie went into the bedroom and sat on the edge of the bed. Julie, mouth hanging open, watched him go. He sat in silence, fingers drumming on knees. His eyes were on the dark wall in front of him. Julie came to the doorway and looked at him. He seemed to be swallowing. Then he shook con-vulsively and the tears came. He started to sob, and in the gloom she could see his face distort and twist. Suddenly, he stopped. He took a deep breath and for a moment had control. Then the sobbing started again and she turned away.

Jackie was alone.

She heard a rhythmic noise and she looked back. He was punching his knee with his fist. Julie started to cry. "There's a terrible smell, Jackie," she said softly. He got up and walked into the dining room. He looked down at his mother. She seemed to be exactly as he had seen her so many times in these weeks—sleeping quietly with her face to the wall. He went out to the kitchen and opened the windows. He opened the door to the hall. Cold blasts swept through the rooms. But the odor remained.

"Let's go downstairs, kid," he said. "We can wait downstairs."

The intern arrived. He was thin and he had a toothbrush mustache. "It's my mother," said Jackie. "Mrs. Mae Gleason, third floor left." By the time the intern had come back downstairs, the Dennehys had arrived and so had Reen. The doctor was matter-of-fact.

"Your mother died of erysipelas," he said, writing on a card. "You will have to burn all her clothing and anything she used around the house."

There is a time when no words are right. This was the time. The street was quiet. The Dennehys and Renee stood on the stoop with Jackie, trying to think of the right words. It is difficult for any human being to adjust his thinking to death in a loved one. He must constantly remind himself, again and again. Jackie could hear their sympathetic words, but he could hear his mother's last words better. "I'm all right, Jackie. I'm all right."

She hadn't been all right at all. She had been dying all the time, and he had not known it. He had been certain, as she had been, that she would recover from this thing on her neck. It was mean to have her go like this, to hide behind a pain-free mask for ever and ever, without giving him a chance to tell her how much she had meant to him, how much he appreciated all that she had put up with, of how he had planned, when he got his big break, to see that her teeth were fixed so that they would never hurt, and of the beautiful dresses he saw in the windows of the big shops designed just for her, and of how they were going to have a flat of their own, with a maid to cook the meals and wash the dishes, and of how she would have nothing to do but wait for Mrs. Dennehy and Sarah Leeman to come visiting.

He had been robbed. No one had warned him that this could happen coldly, undramatically, while his mother dozed. He was not prepared for this, and it seemed vicious to have it happen to a boy who would always need people who loved him.

Someone got Feeney, the undertaker. Jackie stood, dry-eyed and attentive, and answered the questions which had to be answered. He wanted the best for his mother, he said, but when he was asked about insurance he said that there was none. He was asked if he had any money and he said no. Where, the man asked, would he like to have his mother buried from?

"From our house," he said.

Some men carried Mae Gleason out of the house and down the short stoop. Dawn was coming. Jackie watched the hearse move down the street toward Pop Proce's saloon, and Mrs. Dennehy said that he should come up to her flat and have some coffee. Her number two son smiled briefly and said okay. It felt good to be told what to do by an older woman.

Jackie spent the rest of the day making the flat presentable. The parlor had to be cleaned of the old furniture and the sugar barrels. The front bedroom had to be cleaned too. The Dennehys and Renee cleaned up the kitchen. That evening Mrs. Mae Gleason came home, dressed richer than she had ever been dressed, a rosary in her hand and an ice bag under her head.

The neighbors came in quietly. They shook hands solemnly with Jackie and mumbled, "I'm sorry for your trouble, Jackie." They shuffled through the rooms and nodded to other neighbors on camp chairs and then they knelt and said a prayer. Behind the casket was a huge red velvet drape. Before it was a big gold crucifix with a red vigil light flickering at the feet of Our Saviour.

Flowers came from the neighbors and flowers came from the Nomads and the Alpines. Aunt Maggie gave Jackie five dollars and told him to go out and get some flowers for his mother. He got a spray of gladioli and placed them on the casket. Inside was a card that read: "From your loving son, Jackie." In the morning a messenger brought a check for $250 from the BMT. The subway people had heard that there was no insurance, and this was to bury Mae. Jackie turned it over to the funeral director.

Mrs. Gleason was buried on a rainy morning. There was a Low

Mass at Our Lady of Lourdes Church, and a cortege of three cars followed the hearse to Gate of Heaven Cemetery.

A few laborers leaned on shovels. The newly turned clay, heavy with rain, kept slipping back into the grave in small chunks. The men, solemn and expressionless, carried the casket out, and Jackie stood, hat off, beside the grave with the Dennehys and Jimmy Proce and some of the Nomads who had come in Jimmy Proce's father's car, and they watched the casket slip inside the raw pine box, saw the screws turn, watched the canvas belts holding the box over the grave, and then someone blessed himself and then they all did and, after a moment, Jackie took a last long look and burst into tears.

Mae Kelly Gleason slid down slowly to rest beside her sister Vickie. This was her fiftieth birthday.

That evening Jackie was in a cleaner's shop.

"Look, kid," the tailor said patiently, "you owe me two bucks right now."

"Who the hell said I didn't?" Jackie said. "All I said was I need the suit. I got a job in the Folly Theatre. You don't want me to show up in this rag, do you?"

The man shook his head. "Jackie," he said solemnly, "I feel like a heel, believe me. But I ain't rich and two bucks is two bucks. You just buried your mother—may she rest in peace—and now you wanna run off with a pressed suit and who knows when you're coming back?"

"Coming back!" Gleason snarled. "I ain't going no place. I got a house full of furniture upstairs, right? Who's running away?"

"Yeah," the tailor said, brightening. "Yeah. You got furniture up there. You'll be around a while. You can have the suit."

He went upstairs and Mamma Dennehy asked him to come and live with them until he got straightened out. He said no, thanks. He was going to New York. He'd be back from time to time. While he was changing the suit a man came from the furniture company. Mrs. Gleason had made five payments on the furniture and, if Jackie wanted, he could keep the furniture and make the payments himself.

Gleason shook his head no. Julie told the man that the doctor

said the studio couch would have to be burned. The man said
that the stuff had to be repossessed, that's all he knew. Jackie
said, "Take it, will ya?"

That night he started his new job, as master of ceremonies for
the amateur hour at the Folly Theatre. His salary jumped from
four dollars to six dollars. In the wings Vincent Chatfield and
Charlie Allen stood watching. Jackie heard his cue, took a hitch
in his tie, smoothed the lapels of his jacket, and moved onto the
stage with a silly dance step. In a few minutes Vinnie and Charlie
heard gales of laughter from out front. They almost wept.

After the show each Wednesday night, Julie waited for Jackie
and he walked her home to Chauncey Street. As they strolled
from Broadway and Graham Street, they talked animatedly about
show business and Jackie's great future, and while they talked he
guided her to the opposite side of the street and then, after a
block or two, back to the original side. This was done four or
five times before they got to Chauncey Street. Julie puzzled about
it. Then she remembered that Mae Gleason had owed a dollar or
two at several stores.

THE FURNISHED

ROOM

"IT TOOK me a little while," the doctor said, "to see Jackie as a complex patient." He reached for the sugar for his coffee. "Now here is a bright boy," he said earnestly. "I mean really bright. And yet, when he is thin he gets cramps on the morning of the show. When he is fat he doesn't get cramps. Somehow there is an emotional connection between a thin Gleason having a pain in the belly and a fat Gleason not having them."

"Did he have the cramps after the show?" the writer asked.

"Never," the doctor said. "And yet, to make sure, I took several series of G-I pictures. Nothing. So I had a talk with Jackie and I suggested a psychiatrist."

"Did he go?"

"Wait till I finish." The doctor sipped his coffee. "Jackie didn't think much of the idea. I asked him why and he said that he was a Catholic and that Catholics didn't have much respect for *psychiatry; secondly, a man in his position couldn't afford to be seen walking into a psychiatrist's office.*

"I phoned the psychiatrist, a friend of mine, and I explained the situation. He didn't like it. He said, and with some validity, that it was wrong to start a doctor-patient relationship off on the wrong foot by having him go to Gleason. Well, to cut it short, the doctor went to see Jackie as a favor to me."

"I know," the writer said. "Gleason analyzed him."

"You're anticipating," the doctor said. "The doctor made about ten—I don't know, maybe eleven—visits to Gleason. As fast as he threw questions at Jackie, Jackie threw questions at the psychiatrist. The doctor was getting nowhere. After three months, or whatever, he was about ready to quit when Jackie said to him, 'You're not psychoanalyzing me, I'm psychoanalyzing you. I don't see any reason why we should see each other any more.' He beat the doctor to the punch. Fired him before he could quit."

"Did the doctor learn anything?"

"A little. He is convinced that Gleason has slight paranoid overtones with a disposition toward suicide. He also told me that Jackie has deep fears about his own ability as a comedian, and this accounts for the stomach pains. The gluttonous appetite, of course, is a means of getting even with the world which had rejected him long ago."

"I don't know," the writer said, half to himself. "I always think of Jackie as a lonely man. A man who can't find anybody to talk to."

The doctor nodded. "Yes, yes," he said. "You're right. Lonely is the word. He's up so high now that his pals are afraid to disagree with him and that takes a lot of fun out of success."

"I'd be lonely for that kind of dough."

"No, you wouldn't. You don't know what you're saying."

Six dollars a week was not enough. Jackie had to have more, and he had to have it quickly. He worked one night a week at the Folly Theatre, and there were six other nights and seven days. Something had to be done with that time. He was frightened, of course. Death had flipped him into cold economic seas. There was no time to ask for lessons in swimming; Gleason had to swim at once or drown.

A sensible boy would have gone to see the nearest politician and asked for a job on a WPA project at $25 a week. Or he might have gone to a grocery store and offered to work days for $20 a week. But Jackie Gleason was not sensible economically; he would never understand or appreciate money.

He went to New York to see Sammy Birch. Jackie remembered that Sammy, as Gleason's predecessor at the Halsey Theatre, had been kind to him and had explained the basic tricks of running an amateur show. Now Jackie sat on a bed in a six-dollar-a-week room at the Hotel Markwell, on West Forty-ninth Street, and, with the aplomb of a Barrymore, told Sammy that he could no

longer afford to wait for the "big break." He had to make his own
big break right now.

If Gleason had little economic sense, then Sammy Birch was
also short of attributes. He had no ambition for greatness, no
envy, no great talent. When Gleason told him that someday the
name Jackie Gleason would be bigger than that of Milton Berle
and Henny Youngman and all the others, Sammy smiled and believed him. This boy was nothing right now, but if he said he was
going to be great, then he was going to be great. Sammy gen-
erated enthusiasm just listening to it.

"I need a job, Sammy," said Gleason. "I need a job bad. I also
need a place to stay. I'm broke."

Birch, who was booked by Solly Shaw to act as master of ceremonies at six dollars a night in vaudeville houses in and around
New York, had very little money. He said that he shared his bed
with Walter Wayne, another local M.C. If Jackie could squeeze
three-in-a-bed and if it was all right with Walter, Gleason could
stay in the room with them and pay two dollars a week. Sammy
would see the bookers about getting a job for Jackie.

It was all right with Walter. All three slept late so that they did
not have to worry about breakfast. Lunch could be a few pieces
of cheese or ham and a loaf of bread and a glass of water. Dinner
was somewhat of a trial, but they got around this by discovering
a blue-plate special at Kellogg's Cafeteria. The blue plate cost
fifty-nine cents and consisted of soup, an entree with rolls and
butter, and dessert and coffee. The member of the trio who had
the fifty-nine cents had his choice, and he usually chose the entree.
The remaining two tossed a coin to see which one would get the
soup and rolls, the third member getting the pie and coffee.

A few weeks later Sammy came into the room, saw Jackie and
said, "Would you work in Reading?"

"Why not? It's no different than anywhere else."

"I can get you a spot in Reading. It's called Tiny's Château.
Twenty-five clams. You go on twice a night."

"Okay," Jackie said. He could have mustered more enthusiasm,
but now that he had found the thing he hunted, he was afraid.
Jackie knew he was funny. The people in Brooklyn knew he was
funny. Would the people in Reading, Pennsylvania, laugh? Who

knew? He might be big. He might be a bust. The one thing he could not afford was to be a bust. In that case, it would be proved beyond argument that Jackie Gleason was not an actor, not a comedian, that he had betrayed his mother by waiting, hoping, praying for the one big break instead of taking any job to help her out. So he said okay to Sammy, and he built a small smile in front of his fright and said, "When do I go?" Sammy said that Solly Shaw would handle the booking.

Reading, to Jackie, was an alien town. No one met him at the station, no one on the street said, "There's Jackie Gleason," no one at the Tiny Château did any more than lean on a mop and say, "The manager's office is back there."

When the show went on, the manager stood in the back of the smoky club watching. He had watched a lot of these kids in his time. Wise guys, girl crazy, drinkers, moochers—youngsters with a fast line of patter stolen from God knows where, bouncing from one tank town to another, dry-cleaning the jokes between stops, hoping that some other wise guy had not preceded them and told the same stories.

Jackie heard the opening bars of music and jumped on stage. There was considerable gymnastics to his style—in fact, for a while he was billed as Jumping Jack Gleason. He bounced all over the stage, laughing at the band and at himself before he made the people laugh. Most of his routine was a matter of trading insults with customers and it worked fine in Brooklyn, but he was afraid of it here. So there were no ripostes. He told clean, quick jokes and a few women giggled. The men stared at him and watched him sweat. The snowy spotlight followed him around the stage, his blue suit looked neat and well creased, his white kerchief had enough careless flow to it, his blue striped tie was smart and arresting, and his small, almost dainty feet twinkled.

But his face was floury. He left the stage and the sound from the audience was as though someone dropped a dozen walnuts. The manager beckoned him over to the phone near the bar.

"Stay here," he said. "I'm calling New York." When he got Solly Shaw, the manager said, "This man is fired. He hasn't got an act. Get the bum out of here."

There was no real rancor in these words. The man felt that he
was the aggrieved party, not Gleason. He had paid out money to
a booking agent to get him a young and funny M.C. and he could
not hope to hold the customers with a nineteen-year-old boy who
was scared to death.

Gleason said nothing. He walked into the bar and asked for a
drink. He tossed it down and asked for another. His fingers
drummed on the bar and, in the dim light, he saw the fellows
and the girls on stools looking at him. He had another. He could
not believe that he was an amateur-night comic and nothing else.
It wasn't palatable; it wouldn't go down. Was it possible that he
had overestimated his talent? No, he thought, I'm better than
this. Either I'm better or these yokels are deaf and dumb. He had
another drink.

When he went on for the second show, he knew that it was his
last. He'd be heading home on the train in the morning and now,
before he left, he would leave something for these people to remember him by. He hit the center of the spotlight relaxed and
cool. His brain started to think funny and he said whatever came
into it. The people began to laugh a little. He went into a series
of impersonations of famous people which were more than impersonations—they were deadly satires. He sang a song, kidded
the customers down front, traded oral darts with the waiters,
made fun of the service and the management. He left the stage to
deafening applause and whistling.

Outside the spotlight the manager met him. He took a cigarette
from his mouth and squinted into his own smoke. "Why didn't
you do that the first time?" he said.

Gleason lasted two weeks, a pretty good run for a kid with
home-made material. Solly Shaw booked him into other small
clubs. He got experience; acquired seasoning. He learned the
hard way why one joke would make people laugh until they wept,
and why another would make them shrug. He learned that a little
flutter of the hands, a two-bar step, made the difference between
dead time and live time. An elaborate double take, old as it is, a
prat fall, older still, were both good for laughs if executed with a
sense of timing. At 2:00 A.M. a nostalgic song, delivered with

more sentiment than musical talent, reaches the heart and holds it.

He spent the whole summer at the Oasis, in Budd Lake, New Jersey. Sometimes he got $25 a week, sometimes $18, but always he ate as much food as the chef would give him, drank as much free liquor as he could mooch. As soon as the customers began to yawn he packed his valise and headed for another town, another club.

Between engagements he was often back in New York, living at the Markwell with Sammy and Walter. Sometimes now they had enough money for three fifty-nine-cent blue plates at Kellogg's Cafeteria. Sometimes they didn't. Often they sat through the dawn hours over a cup of coffee and a morning *News* talking about their profession. Now that Gleason had proved that he could be funny anywhere, he would always be superconfident; he would exude an aura of egocentricity; he would make people laugh for money or for nothing; in time, some people would call him the funniest man in the world.

Only he and Mae shared the fear that he wasn't funny.

Mr. Shaw phoned the Hotel Markwell. He spoke to Gleason. "Can you come right over?" he asked. "All right. I'll wait." He hung up. "This boy will be right over," he said. He glanced at the two customers and went back to studying his mail. Cabdrivers yet. Well, who knew what the night-club business was coming to? Repeal was still new and if characters like Big Frenchy de Mange and Owney Madden could make a success of clubs in New York, maybe two hack drivers from Newark could do better. Who can tell about these things?

They had a place called the Club Miami, a roughhouse joint on Parkhurst Street in Newark, New Jersey. On one side of it was the Hotel Riviera. On the other was Schary Manor, a place administered by a Mrs. Schary and her son Isadore. The Club Miami was loud and legal until 3:00 A.M. Then it was closed, but, as the neighbors learned, customers were being tossed into the gutter as late as 6:00 A.M.

Of the two who sat waiting to look at Gleason, the one on the

left with the big muscles and the chesty voice was Al Siegel. He
was a bouncer with a dress suit. On Fridays, Saturdays and
Sundays, when customers might become boisterous on booze,
Siegel always stood at the door of the Club Miami to show people
to their tables and to show them out, if necessary, with hands at
neck and crotch.

The other man, short, squat, silent, was George Sossin, the
owner of the club. He made friends and enemies quickly and irrevocably. He and Al Siegel had been pals for years, on cabs and
off. He had worked with sand hogs in Newark and, in a way, had
backed into the saloon business. A man had offered him a half
interest in a gin mill if he would prevent his sand hogs from
wrecking the place every day.

In oral argument, Siegel and Sossin found that they usually
thought of a bright reply long after the other party to the dispute
had left, so they got into the habit of closing arguments with
hairy fist to the mouth.

Their floor show was as weak as their whisky, but they felt
proud that regular customers had acquired the habit of referring
to the Club Miami as the Bucket of Blood. All waiters in the
place had to have three qualifications: how to carry food and
drinks on a tray; how to sing; how to fight. It would also help if
they could add, but this was not a requirement because about
a third of the customers were newspapermen and politicians in on
a cuff. The best waiter they had was a broad-beamed second-
generation Italian kid named Tony Amico. He was a grinning,
happy young man from Pittston, Pennsylvania, a youth with
beautiful teeth, dimples and a fist about the size of a calais ham.

"We're looking for a good M.C." said Siegel to Shaw. "Socko."

"This kid is coming," said Shaw. "A good kid, but when he gets
the wrinkles out of his belly he might run out on you."

"He won't run," said Siegel softly, "because I'll break his head
for him."

· Jackie walked in. His hair was growing down over his collar.
The pencil-striped blue suit was cut sharp and Broadwayish. The
two men from Newark looked him over.

"You're an M.C.?" said Sossin.

"Yes," said Jackie. He looked very young, very thin and somewhat seedy.

"You want to go to work in Newark?" said Al Siegel, the bouncer.

"Sure. What's the place?"

"Club Miami."

"How much?"

"It's only a week-end job," said Sossin. "Eight bucks."

"It's not enough."

"We'll feed you," said Siegel.

"If you're any good," said Sossin, "we can fix the dough a little."

"Okay."

"Here's the score," said Sossin. "We'll give you a tryout. If you're any good, you stay on. If you're no good, you get chased."

Mr. Shaw wrote out a ticket for the booking. Gleason reached into his jacket pocket and drew out a pair of socks. He was packed and ready.

The three men got into a car. On the way out they told him about the club, its clientele, the fact that it seated 260 persons, had a small stage, a band, a bar, a kitchen and lavatories upstairs. They did not tell him that business was poor, that the Bucket of Blood needed a transfusion.

When they arrived in Newark, Sossin staked Jackie to a haircut and got him a room down the street from the club. The rooming house was managed by Mother Mutzenbacher, a middle-aged woman who wore a constantly harassed look and had a conviction that there must be an easier way to make a dollar.

It was a cool September day in 1935 when Jackie Gleason arrived. The best part of his theatrical education lay just ahead.

Gleason was a smash hit at once. He was so good that Sossin and Siegel decided not to tell him. "He's so sensational," said Sossin, "that he's terrific." The kid had a snotty, take-it-or-leave-it attitude, and the customers took him to their bandaged hearts. Business boomed over the week end. The word spread around Newark and within a week actors from the Branford and the

Paramount were coming over to "catch" the kid and to find out what all the talking was about.

"Never mind the week-end stuff," Sossin said to Jackie. "You stay on regular until I tell you to stop. How's thirty-five a week?"

Gleason said okay.

The first night he went on stage he held a sheaf of music in his hand. "I just found out," he said brightly, "that nobody in the band can read music, so we won't need this." He tore it and tossed it at the audience. "And I have no routine, so we're even."

Introductions, so far as Jackie was concerned, were always brief. "Good evening ladies and gentlemen. I got a broad here direct from the Chez Paree named Alma Ross." He would fling one arm back toward the curtain and yell, "And here she is!" A dark and pretty girl would come on stage, smiling nervously, the band would hit a few introductory bars, and she would be off on a torch song. Jackie would disappear in the direction of the bar, timing the recess so that he would get back on stage at the exact moment the girl was taking a bow. At the bar he asked for beer, and because Jackie was so young the bartender thought that he knew nothing about potables. He was often given an eight-ounce glass with an ounce of gin, an ounce of Scotch, an ounce of bourbon and five ounces of beer. Jackie gulped it, said thanks, and returned to work.

He told a few jokes—this was his weak suit—traded cutting wit with the customers and the waiters, and sometimes he would sing an off-color parody on such as "Brother, Can You Spare a Dime?" He would introduce other acts, rib the band, and blow a riff on a trumpet while Leon Easton, the band leader, stood behind him holding the proper valves down.

Sometimes he donned a bartender's apron, wearing it high like Pop Proce, and sang "Frivolous Sal" out of the side of his mouth. He liked Tony Amico at once and he would call Tony up on stage and the two would execute a short challenge step. Once, when a customer tossed a penny on stage, Gleason yelped, "There's only one kind of animal throws a scent!"

After hours he was fed by Walter Struck, the chef, and Mr. Struck watched this thin boy finish a roast of beef, a side of turkey, half a loaf of bread and whatever desserts were around.

Struck always listened to the applause as the show closed. Some-times when it wasn't heavy he would say, "You didn't do a good show, Jackie. No eats."

In that case, Gleason and Tony went down the street to a cafeteria at 4:30 A.M. and ordered a pot of beef stew. Sometimes Jackie asked the waitress to drop a ball of ice cream into it. There was another place, called The Ideal Restaurant, which was a hang-out for vegetarians. The M.C. did not patronize the place until he saw a sign outside: "All you can eat for fifty-five cents." He and Tony went inside and ate triple portions of every vege-table on the counter (Gleason alone finished two baskets of seeded rolls). When they walked out, the sign came down.

There was a camaraderie between Tony and Jackie because both of them believed in Gleason's future. Jackie proposed that they get a room together, and they shared the one at Mother Mutzenbacher's. This cut expenses—it cost them three dollars apiece—but it led to complications.

Sometimes, when they got into the room at 5:00 A.M., there were arguments. They slept in a big double bed and each com-plained that the other was using more than his half. So, whenever Mrs. Mutzenbacher put a clean sheet on the bed, the boys drew a pencil line down the center. The one light in the room came from a ceiling fixture in dead center with a pull cord and, after they had finished reading the *News* and the *Mirror*, an argument started about whose turn it was to get up and put the light out.

"Put the light out, Tone," said Jack.

"Nuts to you," Tony said. "It's your turn."

"Aw, come on. Put the light out."

"Jackie, I'm telling ya serious. No power on earth can get me out of bed to douse that light."

Gleason thought about it. "I'll bet I can make you get out of bed."

"You're out of your mind," said Tony.

"Watch."

Tony sat up sleepily. Gleason took a final puff on his cigarette and touched it to a book of matches. The matches flared up. With expert nonchalance, Jackie flipped the flaming matches across the room and into a waste basket. When the first flames began to flicker over the top of the basket, Gleason folded his arms, leaned against the headboard and grinned. Tony Amico watched in horror. In a moment the flames had engulfed the basket and were crawling up the side of the wall.

"Jackie! For God's sake!"

"Pal," said Gleason calmly. "I'm not moving."

Tony jumped out of bed, grabbed a pitcher of water from a stand, and doused the flames. Smoke and steam filled the room. The wallpaper had been burned two thirds of the way to the ceiling. They heard a pounding on the door, and when Tony opened it Mrs. Mutzenbacher stood outside in a bathrobe, her braided hair hanging down her back.

She looked at the room and clasped her hands in anguish.

"Out!" she said. "This is enough. Out!"

"I didn't do nothing, Mrs. Mutzenbacher," Tony said.

"Both of you!" she said. "I should call the police. By morning, out!"

"If we go out in the morning," Gleason said, "you owe us a buck and a half rebate."

"Look at that wall!" the lady roared. "Out in the morning!"

She slammed the door. Gleason reached down beside the bed and came up with a pair of dirty socks as Tony shook his head in bewilderment. Jackie threw the socks. One caught around the light cord and yanked it sufficiently to put the light out.

"You couldn't do that again in a hundred years," Tony said in the dark.

"I know it," Jackie said sleepily.

In the morning, they found that Mrs. Mutzenbacher had not changed her mind. At 1:00 P.M. she was still demanding that they leave at once. Jackie went out and got a room a block away. He came back and told Tony to pack the valises and wait for him on the curb. Amico assumed that his friend had gone out to get a cab. How much can a taxi cost for a one-block ride?

But no. Gleason had decided that, if they had to travel 500 feet, they would do it in "class." He walked into the Club Miami and saw the early workers getting the place ready. George Sossin was making out a check for the iceman. His fiancée, Henrietta Moore, a pretty dancer who worked the hat check concession between engagements, was filing her nails. Walter Struck was in the

kitchen carving a side of beef. An act was complaining to Al
Siegel about the music. Bozzi was polishing glasses behind the
bar.

"Hey, Boz," Jackie said. "You got a car?"

Bozzi looked up from his work. "You know I got a car."

"Where is it?"

He jerked a thumb.

"I want to use it for a minute. Tony and I are moving down to
the Frenchwoman's."

"Who drives?"

"I do."

"You gotta license?"

"Sure."

Bozzi tossed the keys onto the bar. "Be careful, Jackie," he
said. "And watch them doors."

The car was at the curb. Some of the windows had glass, some
did not. Two heavy ropes held the four doors closed. Tony saw
Jackie untieing the doors and he walked down with the bags.

"You drive?" Tony said.

"Of course I drive."

Jackie got one rope off and one door open. "Come on," he said.
"Get in." They tossed the grips into the back seat and Tony
climbed in after them. Gleason sat in front, pressing buttons and
turning things until the engine caught on. The gear shift was in
the floor, and when he pulled it, it sounded like a cross-cut saw
going through a gross of elephant tusks. The boys took off in a
cloud of blue smoke, and halfway up Clinton Avenue Jackie tried
to make a U turn. The car almost made it. Then it stalled.

Gleason gave the car a decent chance to do something. When
it didn't, he yelled to Tony, "Wait here!" and ran. Traffic piled up
behind the car and the din was loud, even for Newark. Amico
climbed into the front seat, pushed a few things and jiggled some
others. Nothing happened, so he took off and left the car and
luggage in the middle of Clinton Avenue.

Tony mopped his brow at the bar in the Club Miami.

"You move your stuff okay?" Bozzi asked.

"Hell, no," Tony said. "Your car is out in the middle of Clinton
Avenue."

Bozzi hopped the bar, apron and all. Traffic was tied up in both

directions. Two policemen were trying to push the car. Bozzi
helped. When traffic was straightened out, Bozzi told the truth
and the cops laughed and told him to forget it.

The scene closed with Tony carrying the luggage to the Frenchwoman's boarding house. Gleason hung an enema bag outside the
door and told the Frenchwoman that it was his family coat of
arms. In two weeks they were dispossessed and, by the grace of
Jackie's charm, were back in Mrs. Mutzenbacher's place. She
gave them a larger room with twin beds and the boys were so
grateful that they behaved themselves for a week.

The Miami Club often grossed between $700 and $1,000 a night
after Gleason's arrival, but Sossin and Siegel were afraid to give
the boy wrong ideas, so, when he hollered for more money, they
got him a job as second comic in the Empire burlesque house.
Besides this, he still traveled to Brooklyn once a week to M.C. an
amateur-night show, and, with the $40 he got from burlesque, he
was earning about $80 a week. At one time he succeeded Henny
Youngman at the Adams-Paramount theater in Newark and did
well until Mr. Adams caught him pulling on the stage draperies in
imitation of a strip tease. For this Jackie was fired.

On the side he also played house parties and *bar mizvahs* and,
in the company of Sossin, he would visit other clubs around
Newark and be introduced from the floor for some sharp repartee
with the local master of ceremonies.

At Jack Schwartz's Clothing Store, Gleason bought apparel on
the time-payment plan. He got suits, slacks, fancy shoes, white tie
and tails, complete with high hat. Above all, he loved shoes, and
most of his extra money went for footgear, although at one stage
Henrietta Moore persuaded him to save five dollars a week until
he had thirty-five. He took the money and bought baseball equipment, played one game of ball with Tony, and gave it away.

After a few months of steady work the young man became more
self-assured. The Miami was a rough place requiring rough
humor. When a knife-throwing act called Tanya and LaRosa
failed to win approval, Gleason lay down on the big board while
LaRosa, an Italian with a low boiling point, flipped knives with
his teeth. The patrons loved it.

Sometimes the kidding between M.C. and customers got out of hand and then Gleason had to walk off stage with the customer, back into an alley, and slug it out. One of the remarks which got him into trouble was, "Is that your face or did your pants fall down?" When someone hissed his work, Jackie wagged his head elaborately and said, "There's a snake that hasn't got a pit to hiss in."

Once in a while a group of patrons would rush on stage swinging, and just before the battle broke Gleason would yell, "And now, ladies and gentlemen, the floor show!" and the band would swing into "I Can't Give You Anything But Love, Baby" as the fists flew. Sometimes the ladies got into it too, and handbags, loaded with splits of ginger ale, cracked heads.

Jackie usually won his fights, although in free-for-alls Sossin and Amico and Siegel tried to keep him away from the front lines, not for love, but because he represented the bread and butter of each of them. One night a fat, balding Italian heckled Gleason and Jackie took him apart, bone by bone, from the stage. The customer invited the M.C. out into the back alley and Sossin followed, begging Jackie not to fight. Gleason got his fists up and at once soft satiny darkness closed in around him. Sossin forced whisky down his throat and slapped his face until he sat up.

"I told you not to do it," said George. "That was Tony Galento."

"Who's he?"

"A pro. He stopped in the club after knocking out Unknown Winston tonight."

By day Jackie and Amico dreamed about Jackie's future. Often Gleason murmured, "Someday, Tony, I'll be bigger than Berle. Bigger than any of the guys I'm impersonating."

Tony believed it as though it came out of scripture. One afternoon he told Al Siegel about Jackie's great future.

"He'll never get anywhere," Siegel said.

"You'll see," Tony said.

"I'll see? Tell me something—if he's going places why is he here so long?"

Jackie was now certain that the difference between him and such top-ranking stars as Berle, Hope and Youngman was just a matter of becoming known to the public, and he began to concentrate on publicity. He dogged Sossin every day for more and more mentions in the advertising columns and in the amusement-section stories.

To appease him George hired a press agent named Henry Okun to place Gleason's name before the public. Okun was a top-flight man stuck in a small town. To make a living, he hired himself out to several night clubs at, say, $15 a week apiece. The Club Miami was one of his clients. Whatever editorial magic Okun was able to conjure, it worked with Gleason. Jackie hardly ever picked up the Newark *Star*, or the *Ledger*, or the Newark *News*, or Jerry Nussbaum's column, without finding his name somewhere in the lists. He kept a meticulous scrapbook and he learned to appreciate the value of publicity because he found that more and more people, heretofore unknown to him, were aware of Jackie Gleason. For a while, Sossin even had a small scooter car running up and down Broad Street and across High and down Market with big signs announcing "Jumping Jack Gleason, exclusively at the Club Miami."

At Mutzenbacher's, an elderly widow took the room next to the Gleason-Amico zoo, and she complained that they were killing her with sleepless nights. They told Mrs. Mutzenbacher, as politely as possible, that the old bag was cracked.

Jackie was in the middle of his act when he heard the fire engines go by. Tony ran out on the street and saw the firemen running into Mrs. Mutzenbacher's boarding house. He hurried backstage and waited in agonizing silence for Gleason to come off stage. Then he told him.

The M.C. heard the news, clutched his forehead, and gasped, "Run over, Tone, and get my scrapbook."

The damage was slight, but Jackie and Tony solemnly assured Mrs. Mutzenbacher that the old lady had started the fire to get them out of the house.

In all, Gleason spent two and a half years at the Club Miami, and these were the years of primary education. He was a tough kid pitted against a tough audience. No one gave him anything free—applause or money. When he borrowed against his salary, he was given no salary at the end of the week. No one soothed him when he ached; no one mothered him; few, except Tony and the Dennehys of Brooklyn, had any real affection for him. At the Empire Burlesque house he learned the ropes of even tougher comedy because here he was the house comic. A new show arrived each week with a new cast. Gleason and the men in the orchestra pit were the only holdovers. Most burlesque stars do not like a house comic and will devote considerable time to devising means of making him look bad. At the old Halsey Theatre, once a week he saw new and frightened youngsters come on stage, and, watching, he could see the broad chasm between the Jackie Gleason of only three years ago and Jackie Gleason now. There had been no books to consult; no written fundamentals of the trade. Like every actor before and after his time, he had to go out on a stage and learn, by negation, the slippery substance of comedy. At the same time he was learning, skit by little skit, how to become an actor.

Gleason's aspiration was not money. It was fame. At any stage of his career, he would have traded the money for the music of the applause. He wanted to please people. He wanted them to like him. He missed his mother more than he realized.

He has always been partial to policemen. In his early days Jackie Gleason was the recipient of two favors from cops. In the later years he repaid those favors again and again—through appearances at police communion breakfasts and charity affairs— without ever mentioning the reason.

He was at the Club Miami when Tony Amico took a few days off and went home to Pittston, Pennsylvania. It was summertime, and on the following Sunday the club was closed. Jackie borrowed a car and decided to drive to Pittston to say hello to Tony and his family. With him, as guests, went three other masters of ceremonies—Neil Laferra, Monroe Seton and Vic Bruce. They worked at near-by clubs.

The only one who could drive was Laferra, but he was so nearsighted that he couldn't see the radiator cap. Jackie said that this was nothing to worry about because he would sit up front with Neil and advise him of road conditions as they went along. It is a pessimistic commentary on comedians in general that the others thought that this was a sensible arrangement.

They piled into an old Pierce Arrow and rolled out of Newark. Jackie's commentary consisted of: "A little more to the right, pal. You're on the left side of the road and a gravel truck is coming up. . . . That's better. . . . Now straighten out because you're on the shoulder of the road and you're clipping the branches of the trees. . . . A little less gas and a little more brake, please. . . . That's nice, Neil. You missed that lousy Sunday driver by a foot. . . ."

They got to Paterson, New Jersey, before the police got to them. In a town outside Paterson, the four wits were thrown into jail. Late that evening word reached George Sossin that his star was in the jug. He phoned Monroe Seton to ask for help and was surprised to find that he too was in jail somewhere. When he called Neil Laferra, and when the word came back that Neil was in prison somewhere, Sossin began to believe that this must be Can-the-Comics day.

Sossin's first impulse was to let Gleason spend a night in jail. After a chat with Henrietta, however, it was decided that Sossin and Siegel should begin to pull political wires at once to free Jackie. Siegel had worked for Colonel Kelly, of the Essex County Democratic party, and had once been named as a possibility for warden of a jail of his own, so the two men found plenty of wires and began to pull them.

At midnight Sossin showed up at the jail prepared to sue out a writ of habeas corpus, but when he got inside he found that the chief of police and most of the department were standing in various attitudes of helplessness holding their sides. Gleason, with three other comedians to back him up, was telling all the jokes that could not be told in night clubs. The other three were shouting variations of last lines for each joke Jackie told.

"How much is bail for these men?" Sossin demanded.

The chief looked hurt. "There is no bail," he said, "because there is no charge against these gentlemen. They can leave whenever they want to."

The other occasion involved Inspector John Brady of the Newark Police Department. Brady was not only a good cop, he was a good promoter as well. In the depression years he insured the success of many benefit shows for the poor, for orphans, and for Patrolmen's Benevolent Association affairs. He was wise enough to know that he could close any number of small night clubs for minor infractions. He chose instead to keep the owners indebted to him while, at the same time, sacrificing none of his prestige as a first-rate policeman.

Brady could produce a show out of Newark on forty-eight hours notice. All he had to do was to make a few phone calls, or beckon. The acts, great and small, came a-smiling. He used Gleason so often that Sossin's favorite remark was to ask whether Jackie was working for Brady or for the Club Miami.

Once, when the inspector decided to stage a so-called "Monster Benefit" for crippled children, he did not beckon to Gleason. This show was to be staged at the Mosque, Newark's showplace. This one was to be big. There would be no room for small-time masters of ceremonies. Stars would appear on invitation only—no volunteers allowed—and among those to grace the stage that night were Mr. Milton Berle and Mr. Henny Youngman.

Sossin was hurt. He looked the inspector in the eye and said, "Look. You used Gleason in every little rathole in this town. He never turned you down. Now you got a really big show and you don't want him."

"The kid will be out of his league," the inspector said. "Let me think about it."

"Do me a favor," Sossin said. "Put him in, even if he has to open it."

"Let me think about it."

A few days before the big show the invitation arrived. Jackie Gleason would open the show; his function would be to warm the audience for the big stars. When the boy left the stage, the men would take over.

Gleason is restrained in the presence of unexpected happiness. He does not jig or throw hats into the air. He sits, if a chair is handy, and he begins to think. He and George and Henrietta—known as Hank—sat and thought. They were not satisfied for Gleason to make an appearance and to be listed among the stars. They wanted him to make a big hit and at the same time kill the competition. Hank, who later married George Sossin, had been following Milton Berle and had made notes of his best jokes and

bits of business. These she handed to Jackie with the offhand remark "This is a little bit of material I picked up. Maybe you can
use some of it." They talked over Jackie's various bits of business,
and they culled the sure-fire stuff and decided to use it, discarding other material. Sossin reminded Jackie that the musicians
who would be playing in the pit were regular customers at the
Club Miami and knew everything in his repertoire. The band
might run into trouble with the big stars, but the boys knew
Jackie without music.

Before showtime Inspector Brady said, "We're going to put him
on, but we don't know when."

This caused Mr. Sossin to throw a slight sweat because everything that he and Jackie had plotted was predicated upon opening
the show and using enough Berle and Youngman material *first*
so that it could not be used later.

"Inspector," said Sossin, "if Jackie doesn't get on early, he'll
be killed. When Berle and Youngman get through, do you think
anybody is going to listen to my boy?" The inspector did not
answer. "When these big stars are through, they're going right
back to New York. You'll never see them again. But Jackie will be
right here in Newark and I'm telling you here and now that if he
doesn't get on early, he'll never do a police benefit again."

"Okay, George. When do you want the kid on?"

"Third would be nice. You got a tap-dancing team to open and
a magician for your number two spot. Let Jackie warm them up
for laughs."

Backstage, Gleason was quiet and polite. He did not press himself on the big stars; he is a coward in the face of a rebuff. So he
stood silently and watched them move about, munching on sandwiches, drinking hot coffee, slapping each other on the back, talking shop. If one looked his way, Jackie gambled with a smile and
a nod. Sometimes they nodded and smiled back, although it is
pretty certain that none knew him by name or reputation.

Once he went on stage, however, his attitude changed. He
walked on with swagger. He played to the people as though they
were kept relatives. For openers he did his whole Club Miami
act. One of the funniest bits seen was when he impersonated a

strip teaser, and the pit band played "A Pretty Girl Is Like a Melody." The audience roared. The moment Jackie felt that he had the audience with him, he decided to stick around.

He had been told to do his bit quickly, and to get off. He was Newark's own, but tonight Newark's own wasn't good enough. Gleason decided to let the audience decide whether he was good enough or not. He told every joke he remembered. Then he began to tell the ones that Hank gave him. Milton Berle, standing in the wings in a tan topcoat, knew that these were Milton Berle jokes and they were being told well. Then Gleason finished with Henny Youngman's violin bit. It required forty-three minutes to get him off stage. Jackie took five bows to thundrous applause and came off perspiring and beaming.

Milton Berle buttonholed the police inspector. He shrugged. "There's nothing left for anybody to do," he murmured, and walked out.

After that show Gleason was a smash hit in Newark. He had bested the top comics from New York and, to Newark's way of thinking, Jackie Gleason was a local boy. Jackie never forgot that it was a cop who gave him a big break.

A day or two later Al Siegel and Tony Amico were still talking about Jackie's success at the Mosque Theatre.

"I think what hits me most," said Tony, "is the difference between Gleason on stage and off stage."

"In what way?" asked Siegel.

"There's a lot nobody knows about this kid."

"For instance?"

"Well, he has a quiet side."

"He gets tired."

"Not that. He gets on his knees every night and prays, for instance."

"So do millions."

"He prays ten minutes. One night I asked him about the junk he had on the bed while he prays. I never got close enough to see it. Turns out one thing is a crucifix. The back opens up and inside he has a little piece of a shinbone from one saint and a rag from another."

"Yeah? Well, that's something."

"That's what I mean. He's a couple of different guys."

Gleason went on stage one night, put on his happy Irish grin, and looked over the audience carefully. He choked in the middle of a line when he noticed, at a side table, Genevieve Halford. This was the good girl, the pious blonde whom he had introduced to his mother. This was not the kind of girl for gaiety, for laughter, for love-making, for kicks. This was the kind for whom a young man might build a shrine. This girl was *different*.

What shocked Jackie was that, at the moment, she wasn't being very different at all. She was sitting with a tall, good-looking aviator, who seemed to find it no strain at all to ignore Gleason while staring at Genevieve. As quickly as he could get off stage, Jackie sauntered to the table, said, "Hello, Gen," and sat. He was introduced to the aviator, and Jackie gushed charm and hospitality.

He had neglected Genevieve in his chase for sudden success. Now she had made the correct move, consciously or unconsciously, to jog him. She had casually dropped in, and she had brought a good-looking man of accomplishment with her. Gleason learned that she was working in a chorus line at a place called the Half Moon, in Yorkville. She asked how he was doing; did he ever get back to Brooklyn; did he have a Mass said for his mother; was he still living with Tony; did he ever get to New York; how's things?

Jackie was back on stage when the aviator paid the check and took Gen's arm. She waved casually to him and Gleason fumbled in his lines. It took concentration to be funny the rest of that night. He was stunned to learn that the good little mouse would go out with a well-dressed rat. Jackie had gone out with other girls—had dates with shockproof "broads," in fact—but that was different. This aviator might turn out to be one of those clever characters who literally soothe good girls into bad situations.

Gleason brooded. He sat and sulked. He thought for five days. Then he buttonholed Sossin and said, "There's a joint in Yorkville

called the Half Moon. I'm going over after the show. Wanna
come?"

George didn't particularly wanna. But he went. The two men
got a table and Sossin sat sourly over a drink watching a soubrette
named Mickey Andrews. It was a late summer night and Gleason,
in a pale ice-cream suit and dirty white sports shoes, sat watching
the show. A small line of chorus girls came out. Gen was at the
end of the line and now George knew why the kid had to get to
this little joint in a hurry. The baby-blue spotlight framed the face
of Johnny Morgan as he sang "You Do Something to Me," but
George could see the girls dimly and he could see Jackie watching.

After the show Gen came to their table and George studied her
anew, as he did every time he saw her in Jackie's company. A
fair, pleasant-looking blonde, with a sweet, almost restrained manner of speaking, and a world of sincerity in her blue eyes. She was
about as far from beauty as she was from ugliness.

When she sat, Jackie pounded the table, glared at the Half
Moon and growled, "We're going to be married tonight! Now!"
Genevieve tried to pacify him. He wasn't having any. He kept
staring at the patrons as though he had exclusive knowledge of
what they were thinking about Gen, and they were wrong. His
voice became louder. Sossin tried to shush him. It didn't work.
Genevieve looked around in helpless embarrassment.

"I'll drop over to Newark tomorrow," she whispered.

"You gotta quit here!" Jackie said, eyes bulging. He took another look at the tables and his fingers drummed nervously on
the tablecloth. "You gotta quit. You gotta quit. You gotta quit."

"We'll talk about it tomorrow," Gen said.

"We'll talk about it right now."

On the way home Jackie said to George, "You know what these
joints do to a kid."

"Sure," said Sossin.

The next night Genevieve Halford arrived at the Club Miami
with her sister Geraldine. Marriage was discussed, and George, a
Jew, said that he would arrange matters with a priest.

Gleason said to Tony, "I'm going to marry her."

"Jackie," said Tony, "I'm all for it."

"Tony, I don't know anybody I'd rather have for best man."

It was settled quickly and irrevocably in one session. Genevieve would quit the Half Moon at once. The aviator, by indirection, would not be mentioned again. She would come to Newark, be married in Newark, and Jackie would have a talk with Mrs. Mutzenbacher to see if he and Gen could have the room he now occupied with Tony, and perhaps Tony could be moved into a smaller room.

At the moment Gleason was earning $64 a week at three jobs, and that seemed sufficient, except, as Sossin pointed out, the kid never got a salary because he was always borrowed up to the hilt. Gen set a condition that, from now on, Jackie was not to sign tabs for anyone without her okay. This was agreed to, and Sossin said he had a further idea, if the contending parties would like to kick it around, and that was that the club should have some kind of a chorus line—maybe four girls—and if Gen wanted to work in the same club with Jackie, she could earn a little money that way, and George's girl, Hank Moore, would make a second girl, and they could find two more somewhere around. This was agreeable to Gleason, who felt that it would be all right for his girl to dance in a club where he worked, while, by the same token, it would be ruinous for her to work in any other club.

Womanlike, Gen saved the clincher for the last. "You know, George," she said, "Jackie isn't really making enough money to get married on." Sossin shrugged and surrendered. "Okay, I'll give him ten more. Anything else?"

"Yes," Gen said, reaching into her handbag. She drew a quarter and shoved it toward Jackie. "Here," she said. "Now make me laugh twice." Beaming, he reached over and cupped his hand around her ear and whispered. She laughed until she gasped. The others laughed without knowing the joke. Jackie placed the quarter in his pocket.

Sossin made the arrangements. He talked to Father Stone at Saint Columbia Church and arranged for a Nuptial Mass. He helped Tony Amico rent a tuxedo. Then he went out and met a man fresh out of prison who needed money and, for $60, George bough a hot engagement ring and a wedding ring. Invitations were sent to Genevieve's family and Jackie's friends. He had no relatives except Renee. The members of the band, the waiters, Bozzi and Walter Struck and Al Siegel were invited from the club. Sylvia Smith, a *Ledger* columnist, was also invited. Hank Okun ordered the flowers.

On September twentieth, 1936, Genevieve Halford was married to Herbert John Gleason. He was twenty. She was nineteen. When the ceremony was over, George invited everyone back to the club and yelled that this was "open house. Today nobody pays." He also put up a wedding breakfast which could reasonably have graced the tables at the Waldorf. There was chilled wine, and the tables were colorful with cornflowers and chrysanthemums. Jackie sat, chin cupped in hand, staring at his girl. He refused a drink, even a wedding toast. Afterward he put on a show which, all hands agreed, was better than his best.

If there was a flat note in the proceedings it was that Walter Struck, the chef, refused to cook the turkeys because he had heard Jackie tell the patrons the night before the ceremony that whatever gravy wasn't used would be bottled and sold for wallpaper paste. "That does it!" Struck had shouted from the kitchen. "I'm cooking no dinner for that bum!"

On his wedding night Gleason did his regular show. There was no honeymoon. They went, arm in arm, to Mrs. Mutzenbacher's furnished room. Tony moved into a smaller room and, like everyone else around the club, he waited quietly to see what kind of a girl Gen really was, and what effect she would have on the star of the show.

She turned out to be good, not only for Gleason, but for the Club Miami. For one so young, she had a practical approach to all problems. She felt that the show could be clean and still be funny. She kept her bridegroom away from the bar. She won the respect of battlers like Sossin and Siegel. Gen and Hank Moore formed a dancing duo which added another act to the show. The bride made her own clothes and, after a quick look in the windows of the stylish shops of New York, could sit in the room at Mother Mutzenbacher's and perform minor miracles with a bolt of cheap cloth and a needle. She made her own hats too, and she fashioned all of the costumes for the chorus line. This line con-

sisted of Genevieve Gleason, Henrietta Moore, who would later
marry George Sossin, a girl named Joanne, who married Tony
Amico, and an attractive kid named Jerry Dimond, who was engaged to a dancing waiter named Bob White.

On the surface it was an ideal marriage—the clown and the
good woman, the spendthrift and the economizer, the emotional
boy and the practical girl, the idolizer and the idolized. He
wanted a woman he could respect and enshrine—and he got her.
She wanted a man who would stay home with her and save for
the future—and didn't get him.

They were happy. A combination of youth and health and
hope and ardent affection will not be stayed by the weighing of
practical values. At least, not for a time. In the early days of
marriage the only failure was Gen's campaign to get Jackie to
cut down his spending. He had to be the big sport; he had to pay
the check for everyone at the bar; he had to pick up dinner checks
for strangers; he had to tip lavishly wherever he went. Mrs.
Gleason began to learn what it is to "travel first class."

Finances skidded down and down until, in a very short time,
the newlyweds were broke. A furniture store passed out huge tin
coins with Good Luck etched on them and a real penny in the
center. Someone gave Gleason a pocketful of them and he hurried
to the store and asked for more. "I'll pass them out among my
friends at the club," he said. Jackie took a bagful to his room, and
he and Gen sat and punched the pennies out and bought sandwiches and coffee with the proceeds.

It was spring according to the 1937 calendar. It was wintry on
the streets of Newark, and there was a sherbet slush in the gutter
when the Gleasons decided that Jackie would not get any closer
to the top of his profession by remaining at the Club Miami.
George Sossin agreed that there was nothing further to be gained
by remaining. So did Al Siegel. Tony Amico said that he would
stay on at the club.

Jackie said that someday, when he got to the top, he would
need a valet and friend, or a dresser and man Friday. Would Tony
like a job like that?

Amico nodded. "Sure, Jack. You know I'll go anywhere you go."

Gleason patted his friend's shoulder. "Someday," he said. "Someday, Tone. You'll see . . ."

What happened to the Club Miami after Jackie left was to happen to other clubs when he quit. It died. Business dropped off. Old customers said that the joint didn't seem the same without the nutty kid up there driving everybody crazy. George Sossin kept it going for a while, but it was a losing fight. Al Siegel left and opened a little place across the street called the Purple Box. The Miami tried a dozen masters of ceremonies in about as many weeks, but the customers sat in silence and shook their heads dolefully.

The first stop for the Gleasons was Frank Donato's Colonial Inn at Singac, New Jersey. This was a good suburban night club with a good reputation. Jackie was given $65 a week and had to quit his burlesque job and his amateur-night work. He had a little following now, and some of his friends from Newark traveled up to Singac to see him.

Donato, the owner, permitted Jackie to borrow on his salary and to sign checks for friends. After one week he called the comedian into his office and said, "If anybody ever needed a manager, kid, you're it."

"Who would take me on, Nick?"

"I know a guy. Let me make a phone call."

Nick Donato phoned a man in the Bond Building on Broadway. This was Willie Webber, a small, inoffensive manager of comedians. Willie was a bald worrier, with lemon skin, and Willie Webber had rules. He would manage only comedians, and then only as long as they remained small time. If they prospered and became nationally known, Willie sold them to the big agencies.

"Willie," said Nick, "if you will come over here I have a kid that I think you can help a whole lot. He shapes up as a good comedian and I proved it to myself over the week end."

"I can't make it until next Friday, Nick," said Willie. "I'll stop by then. And, Nick—thanks."

Webber arrived at Colonial Inn, took a small back table and watched. He saw Gleason as a handsome Irish type, very young and beginning to pick up weight. He had an ultra-wise delivery and he could trade wit with the customers and the other members of the cast. He sang poorly, but he did a fair soft-shoe break, and his impersonations of noted people were deadly.

The Broadway manager liked the boy and stayed to see the rest of the show. Immediately after Gleason an Italian kid from Hoboken came on to sing. His name was Frankie Sinatra, and Willie asked a few questions of the headwaiter and was appalled to learn that Sinatra was singing for nothing.

Back in Donato's office, Nick said, "Well, what do you think of the boy?"

"I like him. I think I can do something with him."

"How about the Sinatra kid? He's a good boy, Willie."

"Singers never interested me, Nick."

"Well, will you handle Gleason?"

"I'll be back tomorrow night."

He was. And he saw the show again on Sunday night. By that time Willie was convinced that Gleason was exceedingly funny and that there was no hint of the troublemaker about him. Willie did not want to manage drunks, wife-beaters, or agitators.

Webber signed Jackie to a personal-management contract. This meant that he would get jobs for Jackie, argue salary for him and transportation too, and, in general, represent the Gleason interests to the best of his managerial ability. The contract guaranteed Jackie a minimum of twenty-six weeks of work in the first year at an average of $75 a week, and $100 a week for twenty-six weeks in the second year. In return, Gleason agreed to give Willie 15 per cent of all his earnings during the life of the contract. As a matter of practice, Webber never deducted more than 10 per cent.

The acts in the show changed, but Gleason lasted for several months. He got to know the regular customers and could spot a stranger after the first glance around the club. One night he spotted a man alone at a ringside table chewing gum.

"Now there's something," Jackie said to the audience. "Chiclets instead of booze. Got an extra one, pal?"

The man at the table grinned. "Sure," he said. He reached
into his pocket and flipped a piece of gum to the comedian. Gleason studied him. The man inspired amusement. He had a babyish
face, bald head, and the friendly pathos of a Charlie Chaplin.
When the show was over, Jackie dropped by.

"You in show business?" he said.

"No."

"Want to get in the act?"

"No, thanks."

"You'd make a good stooge, pal."

"I'm here to look at a singer."

"Oh."

"I'm working for Glenn Miller."

"Who's the singer?"

"Connie Haines."

"Swell dame."

"Miller asked me to take a look and report back."

"Great singer. I mean, really."

They shook hands. The bald man introduced himself as George
Durgom. That was all. The stranger popped another chiclet in
his mouth, got his hat, and left. Gleason watched him go, and
murmured, "What a natural as a stooge!"

In the summer Jackie was booked into Wanamassa Gardens in
Asbury Park. Genevieve spent part of the summer with her
mother in Jackson Heights and Jackie stayed at a local boarding
house near the beach and spent so much of his salary that he was
behind in his board bill. One noontime he lowered his luggage
out a back window to a friend waiting below and then walked
through the lobby in his bathrobe.

"Going for a little dip," he said brightly. "They say it's wonderful for the appetite." When he got outside, he hopped into his
friend's car, got in the back seat, and put his clothes on while
they drove to New York. Three years later he went back to the
boarding house to pay the overdue board bill. The landlady took
a long look at Jackie and burst into tears. "We thought you
drownded!" she moaned.

He was bouncing from club to club, making more money than
before, saving nothing. He worked at a place in Cranberry Lake,

New Jersey, the Rathskeller in Philadelphia, back to the Club Miami in Newark, over to the Bally Club, back again to Colonial Inn, at a small club in Irvington, and once all the way out in Michigan. When there was no work, Gleason was a comic diver at Cypress Pool in Long Island. For a while he was a spieler in a racing car with B. Ward Beam's International Congress of Daredevils. He did a little more rowdy comedy in burlesque and he did guest shots on local Jersey radio stations.

Gleason was learning all the time. The International Congress of Daredevils job is of some interest because it did not fall into the pattern of comedy. It was, rather, a display of maniacal frenzy on motorcycles and it seems doubly strange to imagine Gleason as a part of this type of show because, for a number of years, Jackie wouldn't trust himself in a funeral cortege if someone else was at the wheel.

The show played such places as Reading, Bangor, Centerville, Michigan, and Alpina, Michigan. Two free shows were given in front of a grandstand as a come-on attraction. Jackie's job was to give the signal at the proper psychological moment for the motorcycles to start their engines. The ear-splitting roar inside the motordrome influenced the crowd to come inside. Jackie would then shout, "And now we will witness the death-defying ride for life by Madame Olga, the women's champion of Sweden, who has raced before the crowned heads of Europe."

At the afternoon show he introduced the Hell Drivers, a group of men in crash helmets who drove skidding cars on a cinder track. He got in a car, grabbed a microphone as the vehicle raced down the front of the grandstand and skidded at exactly the point where the grandstand ended and the railbirds were watching the show free, and Jackie would yell, "These pebbles are traveling at the speed of a forty-five-caliber bullet, ladies and gentlemen. You stand there at the risk of your lives. Please get into the grandstand where it is safe." When a sufficient number had purchased tickets and were in the grandstand, Jackie would stand behind a lectern and announce the day's events: the ride through the fire wall, the slide for life, T-bone crashes, head-on collisions, and all the thrills, chills and spills that he could work into the copy.

Gleason was working hard, perhaps harder than ever, but he did not work steadily, and Gen was worried. She was pregnant and what she wanted was a normal life with a normal husband and a weekly pay check. Now and then the subject came up and Jackie blazed.

"I only started four years ago. You think I'm doing bad?"

"I didn't say that. What I said was wouldn't it be nice to have a little apartment instead of bouncing all over the country, and wouldn't it be nice to have a small steady income every week instead of owing everybody we know."

"Give me a break, Gen. I can hit the top in this racket, but I need a little time."

"No one wants to see you make it more than I, but we're going to have a family. Think of this thing from my side for a change."

Nothing was decided; nothing altered. She might, if she wished, have said that she was tiring of his running off with "the boys" after the last show and coming home drunk at dawn. There had been scenes about that too, but nothing had been agreed upon between them. The early schism between the two is traceable to Jackie's desire for roughhouse fun with the boys; his late-hour dates with show girls; and his unshakable feeling that Genevieve was a saint who should remain enshrined at home and who should not—to put it in Jackie's words—"be around where fellows curse."

The other side of the coin was that Genevieve Gleason was a normal woman who was capable of giving love and capable of accepting it. She did not suspect that she was replacing Mae Gleason, even when Jackie came home to be mothered after a double cross, or loss of a contract, or pay, or whatever. She figuratively cradled him in her arms and soothed him, and, when in trouble, he would run always to her. Still, she wanted to be a wife—a full-time wife. When she heard from friends that he was out drinking in the early hours, she demanded to be taken along. She could not become reconciled to Jackie's image of Gen.

Geraldine Gleason was born on July 31, 1939. She was a healthy infant who looked like her mother. Jackie grinned at his first-born and looked at Genevieve. "Give me until I'm twenty-five," he begged. "If I don't make Hollywood by that time, I'll quit." He went back to the infant. "Two years, honey," he said. "Say a prayer that I get a break."

Christmas week of that year Gleason was booked into Queen's Terrace. This was a substantial break. It wasn't Broadway, but it was around the corner, symbolically, from Times Square. Jackie didn't get a lot of money—$75 a week—but it was Willie Webber's notion that, if he could get Gleason into Queen's Terrace, he could get a Broadway night-club owner to stop over and look at Jackie. This, in track parlance, is a two-horse parlay. Willie waited to make certain that Gleason was a smash hit. In the middle of the second week this was a certainty. All over town club habitués were talking about a "new" comedian at Queen's Terrace.

The next move on Willie's part was to try to get Fred Lamb, part owner of the Club 18, to journey out to Queen's Terrace to "catch" Gleason. This was not easy because Mr. Lamb was importuned every day to look at new comics. He had seen too many of them. He was laughproof. Besides, his own Club 18, at 18 West Fifty-second Street, had the funniest men in New York—Pat Harrington, Jack White and Frankie Hyers. These men were so funny that some customers were sure that they were insane. They had no script as such, and the sharp crack of their collective wits varied from performance to performance and was quoted daily in the Broadway columns. Harrington, a product of Griffith Park, Canada, looked like a gentle, wavy-haired Irishman. Even the hair was spurious. White, a pinched-faced man of about fifty, was the chief actor at the club, owned a part of the place, and hung the score on the front door every time the New York Giants won. When they lost, he flipped the sign over, and it read, "No game today." Hyers, a young comedian with features which forgot to stop, was the third member of the unholy triumvirate. He grinned constantly, displaying quite a formidable headful of teeth, and gave the impression that he was never certain why he had been cast with buffoons.

The 18 was an actors' night club, a late hang-out for Broadway-wise people, a place where the stars relaxed in oral bedlam. Many a manager would have hesitated before consigning a young man to the calculated cruelties of the barbed wits at the 18. Willie Webber wasn't one of them, however.

He phoned Fred Lamb and said, "Freddie, I'm over at Queen's Terrace. I've got a fat kid over here called Jackie Gleason. Believe it or not, Freddie, the people won't leave him off the floor. He does a tremendous job." Mr. Lamb could hardly have been less impressed. He thanked Willie and said that he was busy, but that he'd be sure to catch Gleason later.

Willie phoned again. And again. Willie's grammar did not glitter, but his mind did. He knew that now and then one of the three top comics at the 18 became ill, or took a vacation, or took a part in a Broadway show, and at those times Fred Lamb needed a funnyman in a hurry. Occasionally Vince Curran had been used with success, but the field was wide-open for a new face.

"All right," said Lamb. "I'll make a date with you."

Webber picked Lamb up in a car, drove him out to Queen's Terrace. Nothing was said to Jackie, because Willie did not want him to strain to be funny in front of a visiting celebrity. Gleason went through his regular routine, wrestled with the customers, sang a bit, told some new stories, and the applause was deafening.

Lamb sat up through the entire act. When Gleason had taken his last bow and disappeared, Fred Lamb said in some wonderment, "Willie, this is the boy for me." Jackie Gleason was booked to open at the Club 18 on January 20, 1940, at $75 a week. He asked if there would be any objection if he continued his work at the Queen's Terrace and Lamb said no. Jackie arranged with his old Brooklyn friends, Jimmy Proce and Paddy Noto, to drive him from Queens into Manhattan nightly and, immediately after the Club 18 show, back to the Queens Terrace for the late show. He now earned $150 a week, less the 10 per cent he paid to Willie Webber.

It was a big break. In retrospect, an enormous break.

At his home on Long Island Willie Webber talked shop with Mrs. Webber. "This Gleason kid is great," he said. "It's just a question of how long it's going to take to get him the great big break. As it turns out, mamma, he's not easy. He has to be a big sport. It's in him and he's gotta be the big sport. Money means nothing and if I'm not careful he's going to borrow me blind. But he's funny, and he's got a heart like a house."

No one has ever summed up Jackie Gleason as succinctly.

The Club 18 was in the basement of a brownstone front. There was a small green door in an areaway and a turn to the right, and there was the club. A bar with indirect lighting leaned against the right-hand wall. Behind the left-hand wall was the kitchen and Willy Grogan, the tomato-faced waiter. Up ahead were small tables with snowy cloths and, beyond them, one of the smallest stages ever to hold a band plus three comics. Ladies had to cross the stage to get behind it to the ladies' room, and when this happened the band stopped playing and the remarks from the Messrs. White, Hyers and Harrington were outrageous. Mr. Grogan, the waiter, would wait until the patrons were cutting their steaks. Then he would come out of the kitchen with a greasy garbage pail on his shoulder and yell up to Jack White, "Where'll I take this?"

"Take it across the street to the 21 Club."

Ten minutes later he would be back in the club with the same pail of garbage.

"What's the matter?" White would yell from the stage.

"Twenty-One refused it."

Another device of Mr. Grogan's was to wait until everyone was eating; then, from the kitchen, would come the sound of a loud snap. He would appear innocently in the doorway and yell to White, "A whole week we've been trying to catch him." He would hold his hands apart to show the proportions of a rat. "Just got him. Thought you'd like to know."

It was that kind of a place. That is why, when Jackie Gleason showed up the first night for the first performance, he should not have been surprised to find that the others in the cast had double-crossed him. Harrington, at the time, was out. White and Hyers, instead of joining him in the opening number, were sitting downstage with their backs to the audience looking at Jackie. They defied him to be funny, to make the people laugh.

He did. He sneered at the two, called them heels, turned to the customers and went into a monologue. He impressed the wise ones as a fresh Irish kid with the manners of a Brooklyn bartender. He had scorn enough to go around and he poured it thickly. He chopped White and Hyers into small pieces and then began to take the celebrities apart. The audience laughed so hard that White and Hyers gave up. They got to their feet and started to walk off stage. Gleason paused in his routine.

"Come on back, you cowards!" Jackie shouted. "Come on back and watch The Greatest."

Backstage, White looked at Hyers and pursed his mouth. "I guess the kid will do," he said.

The engagement lasted only two weeks, but Gleason made such a profound impression that a month later when Frankie Hyers had to go to the Coast, Jackie was rehired at $100 a week. This was his first meeting with the usually gentle Pat Harrington, but Pat had heard that the youngster was pretty sharp, so he was prepared to kill the kid at once. It was an easy thing to do. Harrington remained quiet until Jackie opened his mouth. Then Pat said something loudly—anything at all—and literally walked across Gleason's line. Result: no one heard the kid.

Jackie Gleason was not a whiner. He was in the big leagues and he had to expect big-league tricks. So he went backstage and asked a lot of questions about Pat Harrington. The colored boy in the men's room—Jackson—said that Mr. Harrington had a queasy stomach.

The next night, just before showtime, Gleason sent the boy out to a restaurant for a container of beef stew. When it arrived, he jammed the stopper into the men's room sink and poured the beef stew in. Then he sent for Harrington. When Pat stuck his head in the door, Gleason was grasping the sink with both hands. His eyeballs were stuck out, and his mouth hung open. "Pat," he gasped, "am I sick!"

Harrington took one look and turned as white as talcum. He slammed his hand against his mouth and began to retch. When he was sick, Gleason tapped him on the shoulder. "Pat," he said, "that's nothing to what I can think up the next time you try to louse me up." After that he and Harrington became friends.

This time Gleason remained at the Club 18 for two months. He got an offer to go to work at Leon & Eddie's night club at $300 a week, and he took it. His name and his brand of comedy were becoming known and he was given a part in an unremembered play called *Keep Off the Grass*.

It starred Jimmy Durante and Jane Froman. Everyone was cordial to the new comic, but Jane Froman was extra sweet. Jackie was rough and inclined to ad lib, or to play to a pal in the audience, and Miss Froman sat with him and talked show business and gentled him into smoothing some of the rough spots in his performance.

The show closed quickly. Gleason told Miss Froman he would not forget her kindness.

Three months before the United States got into the second World War, Jackie was back at Frank Donato's Colonial Inn. Genevieve was waiting for their second child. Late one night a phone call came in announcing that Gen had been rushed to Physicians Hospital in Jackson Heights. A Doctor Cagney, brother of James, had placed her in the labor room.

Gleason was distressed. It was 1:00 A.M. "I got to get all the way out to Jackson Heights in a hurry," he said to Nick. "But how?"

"Follow me," said Nick. He shoved Jackie into a car, ordered a waiter to drive them through North Jersey to the George Washington Bridge, thence into New York and across to Jackson Heights. The waiter poured the coal on and the car raced through the night.

At the bridge a motorcycle cop caught them. Gleason explained the rush.

The policeman glared. "I've heard that one many, many times," he said. "I'll tell you what I'll do. I'll escort you to the hospital myself. If your wife isn't in there, my friend, you'll wish *you* were."

At the hospital the four men found Mrs. Gleason sitting up in bed, pretty in a bed jacket and entirely at her ease. Jackie mopped his brow and wanted to know what had happened. The answer was: false alarm. The policeman said that he was sorry that he had doubted Gleason's word. However, to make up for it, he would escort them all the way back to Singac. He did.

On September sixteenth, 1941, Linda Gleason stepped out on the stage. She was a chubby, black-haired doll, the "spittin' image," as cousin Renee said, of Jackie Gleason. Renee was right. This youngster not only looked like her father, but she also had the same mischievous twinkle in her eyes.

There would be no more children after Linda, and it might be expected that two lovely daughters would tend to draw the skeins of family life closer.

In the case of the Jackie Gleasons, the goals of husband and wife were too divergent for harmony. She wanted modest success, peace and lots of home life. He wanted huge doses of fame, adulation and plenty of freedom from domestic responsibility. These goals are beyond reconciliation.

The marriage might have cracked long before it finally did if it had not been for the inherent Catholicity of the couple. Both were certain that marriage was a sacrament, and one can violate a sacrament only at the risk of one's immortal soul. Secondly, the priest had said, "Till death do you part," and those words had locked the door to divorce.

At the time of Linda's birth there was no thought of an eventual split between the parents. It wasn't an ecstatic union, but from what Jack and Gen could see of other marriages around them theirs was fairly normal. There were arguments, there were threats, and sometimes there were shouted feminine orders to "Get out and stay out!" But there were many moments of happiness too. There were times for tears and contrition and promise and hope.

Genevieve's major complaints were: (1) Jackie's running around with other women; (2) Jackie's drinking; (3) Jackie's spending; (4) Jackie's neglect of his wife. His complaints against Genevieve were two: (1) too much nagging; (2) too much religion.

There is some validity to each of these complaints. Gleason made late-hour dates with beautiful girls. He was known at this time as a sucker for any beautiful blonde, and New York was full of them. He was not an alcoholic, but when he drank he

drank as he ate—too much. He was never known to excuse his
drinking on the ground that he did it to relieve the tensions of his
profession. He did it for fun. So far as money was concerned,
Gleason seemed to have developed a habit of living slightly above
his means at all times. He owed money all over town, but here
his strong conscience came into play anew, because, when money
came to him, he raced all over New York paying back the tens
and twenties he owed. His neglect of Genevieve was something
that Jackie could not understand. He did not consciously propose
to neglect her. It just developed that his idea of fun was too low
for participation by his wife. She was, in effect, too good for his
playmates.

His charges against Genevieve, while minor in character compared to her indictments against him, were valid in his eyes.
She did not appreciate the kind of life her husband was leading,
and she complained about it fairly constantly. This is nagging.
Nagging acts as sandpaper on a sore. It broadens the irritated
surface until the contending parties can no longer remember the
original focus of infection.

Gen believed, without question. Jackie believed, and ques-
tioned everything. That was the basic difference between them.
Genevieve Halford was born with the grace of complete faith—if
the church said it was so, it was so. Gleason, on the other hand,
was not a doubter—he was a prober. He wanted to know why.

And so, when he reached adulthood, he spent some of his time
at home studying the religions of the world. He was always a
bright reader (and a fast one) and he assimilated facts and di-
gested them quickly. To Mrs. Gleason, this kind of reading bor-
dered on heresy. She did not want to know about the other religions of the world. Roman Catholicity was the one church, the
true church, the only church.

She told him that it was a sin to be reading about others. He
wanted to know why. She reminded him that priests often ad-
monished their parishioners not to go to churches of other faiths.
Jackie nodded, and said, "I'm not going to any other church. I'm
just reading."

He reminded her that more than half the people of the world
did not subscribe to Christianity, and he believed that these peo-

ple—the Buddhists, the Shinotoists, the Jews, the Mohammedans, the Taoists—were sincere in their own beliefs. He could not believe that God would punish people for misguided sincerity. All right, Gen said, but if you have discovered the truth, why not stand by it? Why try to find out why others are in error?

Ironically, the more Gleason hunted, the more he became convinced that the Catholic Church is the repository of truth. The more he read, the deeper went his faith. If his so-called "alien" reading changed his thinking at all, it made him more sympathetic, more understanding toward people of other faiths. It also taught him that greater minds than his had searched the mysteries of eternity for thousands of years and had come to the conclusion that God wants man to believe without seeing.

When he finished reading the major religions of the world, Jackie read Butler's *Lives of the Saints* and other Catholic works. This pleased Genevieve, and the more he read about the trials and mistakes of the sanctified ones, the more he realized that the mistakes he was making had been made before by millions of tiny beings who had reached toward the stars as they crept toward the grave.

After a while he ran out of Catholic books and saints and, still reaching for an understanding of the future beyond the grave, he turned to reading psychic phenomena. This, to Genevieve's way of thinking, was unmitigated quackery, and the arguments started all over again.

THE HOTEL

THE WRITER *sipped his coffee and listened.*

"There is a thing," said the doctor, wiping his mouth with the napkin, "called a pain threshold."

"I've heard of it," the writer said. "They're trying to measure it, like decibels for sound."

"Exactly. Well, Jackie has a low pain threshold. Any pain to him is one hell of a pain. In all his life he never had a little bellyache or a small toothache. Whenever anything happens to him that can be called painful, he must have someone he can call for help. Someone he trusts."

"I see."

"No, you don't. Right now, when it comes to physical pain, it's me. He will call me at any hour of the day or night, and if he is in pain he expects me to perform a miracle. If the pain is emotional, the person he used to run to was Gen. She babied him and patted him and made it all better. Now that they've split up, who's going to do it? I don't know, but I know that he needs somebody."

"He doesn't go anywhere any more. Sticks to the penthouse."

"That is not related to the problem. Gleason likes people to come to him. Remember the psychiatrist? Everybody has to come to Jackie. This isn't snobbishness, you know. Oh, no. He just feels safer when you come to him. Less likely to be hurt. Underneath that cocky front is a shy man. He is shy and sensitive."

"Maybe we're not talking about the same guy."

"Oh, yes we are. The reason he refers to himself as The Greatest is a form of left-handed mockery. This man, great as he is, bruises easily."

"He always loved to be insulted, Doctor."

"No, he didn't. He loved to clown at being insulted. He loved to trade barbs with less gifted people. As long as Jackie felt that it was nothing but good clean fun, he enjoyed himself. The moment he felt that the remarks hit home, he was hurt."

"He goes to Toots Shor's place."

"Practically lives there. I realize that. That proves to me that he must trust Shor enormously—first, because Jackie goes there instead of waiting for Shor to come to him; secondly, because he accepts insolence from Shor and loves Toots for it."

"Do you think he'll remain in love with the girl he has?"

The doctor laughed. He removed his glasses to wipe them. "Who knows? I'm an internist. I know less about affairs of the heart than Jackie. As an outsider, I would suggest that his record shows a pattern of falling in love for periods of time ranging from a few months up to—well, maybe two or three years at the most."

"You haven't answered the question, doctor."

"Ask Jackie. I don't think he knows either."

By the time Jackie Gleason reached his twenty-fifth birthday, he was in Hollywood. This triumph in no way compares with that of Shirley Temple, but he had set the deadline and he had made it. Jack Warner, in New York on a visit, had stopped in at the Club 18 to witness the rowdyism and had had a talk with Fred Lamb about the fat new comic. The result: Jackie was signed to a contract, with the customary options, at $250 a week. Warner was that impressed.

Jackie was happy and Gen was happy and they saw stardom in Hollywood and perhaps, someday, an Oscar. He had been well received on Broadway, where every scrub lady is an astute critic, and Hollywood seemed to be a natural evolution in the spawning of success. In time there would be a Gleason estate up in the hills or out in San Fernando Valley, and swimming pools, and a tidy little place at the beach like Marion Davies had, and a little lolling between pictures at Palm Springs, plus a few shakes of the dice at Vegas or Sun Valley, and a brace of maids and a cook for Gen and picnics with the Brothers Warner on Sundays. The Warners would bring the hot dogs, of course.

The only difference between the dream and what actually happened is that Jack Warner must have forgot to tell his people that Gleason was coming. When he arrived at Burbank, fat and sassy as always, no one seemed to have heard of him, or, if they had, they assumed that he was Jimmy Gleason's lazy kid.

He did several pictures, though. Before he started rehearsing, Gleason tried to explain to the producers, as modestly as possible, that what he really was, what he had established himself as, was a comedian. For this information, he received several polite nods.

One picture was called *Navy Blues*. It starred Jack Haley and Jack Oakey, but not Jackie Gleason. The part was small and ineffectual. Jackie said that he sometimes felt like a real sailor who wakes up on a street corner and is surprised to find that they're shooting a picture around him. Then there was a picture called *All through the Night*. In this, Gleason was cast as a gangster. A third gem was entitled *Springtime in the Rockies*. In this one, Jackie was cast as Betty Grable's manager.

He begged them to cast him as a comedian, and he took a job at Slapsie Maxie's Restaurant to show Hollywood how funny he could be. But the best the Warner Brothers brains could do was to look Gleason over seriously and then suggest that if he could lose a hundred pounds they would see what they could do. Dieting and suicide are synonymous to Jackie Gleason, but he went through the torture of pushing plates away and, when he had dropped one hundred pounds, the producers looked at him again and decided that he was indeed a good-looking young man. "The only trouble is," they said, "now he's not funny."

Jackie was co-starred in a motion picture called *Tramp, Tramp, Tramp* (the other star was Jack Durant), but no one remembers seeing it. He was sick of Hollywood when he went over to Twentieth Century-Fox and was cast as a bass fiddle player in Glenn Miller's band. This was a picture called *Orchestra Wives*.

Glenn Miller was resistant to laughter. The reason for this was that he had a tender spot in his side, and when laughter was involuntary (he had good control) a nerve in his side ached acutely. He laughed every time he saw Gleason come on the set. In time he asked director Archie Mayo if he could be excused while Gleason was rehearsing so that he could spare himself pain.

The stagehands and the assistants on the set also roared at Jackie's japes. He seemed to be funny to two men who stood on the side lines watching: George Durgom, who had once chewed chiclets at a Gleason performance, and Leo Talent, head of Glenn Miller's music-publishing company. Mr. Talent, a young man of good looks and enormous respect for musicians, had never been known to laugh on purpose, but he laughed on the set of *Orchestra Wives,* and so did the song plugger who had once scouted Connie Haines.

Between scenes Gleason renewed acquaintance with Durgom and was introduced to Leo Talent. They were not the kind of men that Jackie would drink with after working hours, but they were the kind he could admire for professional reasons. Jackie is to musicians what a buff is to firemen, what an *aficionado* is to a toreador, what a bobby soxer is to Sinatra.

He could always compose torch songs in his mind. He could hear them, but he couldn't hum them properly and he couldn't set them to music. When he first began to work in the Club Miami, he acquired the habit of sitting at the piano in the dawn hours when the place was empty except for the scrub lady, and with one fat finger he would punch keys and try to transmute what he heard in his mind onto the keyboard. He always loved Dixieland bands; he worshiped old-time jazz; he could sit for hours and listen to a moody man hit sad chords on a piano. If he liked a recording, he would play it over and over, for an hour or more, and sit and listen to it, eyes focused on a table top, or on a wall. His frank worship of men who could squeeze the high ones from a trumpet, or trickle the triplets on a clarinet, or rap a boogie beat with a wire whiskbroom on drums was as pathetic as an urchin's stare through a candy-store window at Christmastime.

Jackie got along well with Durgom and Talent. Both loved jazz and both were frustrated musicians. Once Talent had played first violin on the Boston night boat, a lonesome calling. Bullets Durgom had got his name in the days when he attended Bloomfield High School, when he was so short and so speedy as he zipped up and down the corridors that the nickname had been applied, and had stuck. He had brothers nicknamed Buckshot,

Beebee and Touchdown. He was a second-generation Syrian who could prove that he loved music earlier than Gleason: at the age of seven Bullets carried water to the piano player in a silent-movie house at Mount Pleasant, Pennsylvania.

Gleason was a bust in Hollywood. He had gone to the Coast to make himself known nationally—perhaps internationally—as a true artist among comedians, and he had been defeated because no one had the time to study his talents and fit those talents to a motion-picture script. The producers had shoved him into any fat-man spot available and had ordered him to utter lines which were alien to him.

He recognized the defeat after the second picture. After that it was a matter of keeping a job and working at it. Before he got to Hollywood a letter from Jack White of the Club 18 had been dispatched to a motion-picture writer, Maurie Suess.

"When this kid arrives," White wrote, "keep him away from the Hollywood s—— ——s. He's a big, irresponsible kid. Don't let him get mixed up with these characters, please." Suess wondered what he could do to "protect" a grown man who was known to have a will of his own. Still, he met Jackie, welcomed him to Hollywood, and, to set the friendship off on familiar terrain, announced that he too had been born and raised in Brooklyn. ("I never even saw grass until the day they buried my uncle"; "The only way I would tell it was spring was when the radiators stopped knocking in the poolroom.")

These two got along. Suess recognized almost at once that this young man had an extraordinary talent and, with it, no fear. The writer, a fat, bald cigar smoker who chattered in nervous bursts like Jack E. Leonard, was shocked by the lack of fear. "This kid," he wrote back to Jack White, "has a notion that all he has to do is to go out to Burbank and knock everybody dead with jokes and he's in. It doesn't work that way."

As the disappointments increased by day, the fun became more riotous at night. Gleason hung out with the New York crowd— those expatriates who believed that Hollywood was a good place to make quick money, but that the only things which could be called permanent in the theatrical business were built around Shubert Alley, Billy LaHiff's Tavern and the Lambs Club. Among

his evening-hour friends were Sid Silvers and Rags Raglund.
When they got drunk, or tired, they registered in local hotels as
the Messrs. Eberhard, Faber and Ticonderoga.

At the bars he picked up new friends and new tabs. He was
paid on Thursday afternoons and he was broke by Saturday,
often on Friday morning. On Mondays he frequently telephoned
Suess and said, "Pally, I've got to go to work."

"Doesn't everybody?" Suess said.

"You don't understand, Maurie. I got no money to get to work."

"You're kidding. You got your check from Warner's. What happened?"

"Oh, you know. A little ball."

Maurie Suess met him on these mornings and handed him a
quarter.

"What's this?" Jackie asked.

"Look, you fat lump. That's a quarter. A dime for the bus to
Burbank, a nickel for a cup of coffee, and a dime to get back.
When you get in, call me and I'll take you to dinner."

Gleason held the twenty-five cents in a motionless hand and
looked at Suess with large, sad eyes. "Okay," he murmured.
"Okay."

Gleason's average evening was spent in a gin mill, sometimes
in several of them. The moment he walked in, Jackie beamed
with opulence and a relaxed and warm feeling toward the world.
He started by ordering a bottle of Canadian Club. In a few minutes he acquired new friends. The party left the bar for a table.
The bottle was tipped by sure hands and Gleason ordered another, plus a tray of sandwiches.

All hands talked motion pictures and personalities, and told
the slightly soiled Hollywood anecdotes. If the night was pay
night, Jackie remained at the one place until closing time and
turned his $250 check over to the waiter. If he owed more than
the check could cover, he signed a separate tab for it. Should the
night be other than pay night, and his credit in a challengeable
state, Gleason moved briskly from place to place signing "small"
tabs in each—spreading the risk, as it were.

One of his best friends at this time was Martha Raye. They
made the stops together and could create their own laughter as

they went. Still, Jackie was a little upset to find that Martha was better at finding new friends than he. On occasion, fifteen or twenty men and women got into the entourage and followed the two from one oasis to another.

"Martha," he said one night, "I don't like to mention the subject of money with a dame, but your friends are ruining me."

"How, Jack?" said the lady with the broadest smile.

"I'm paying tabs for fifteen or twenty people every night."

"Oh," she said. "Is that all? I'll pay the tabs."

"That isn't what I want."

"Look, kid. I'm making more than you. Let me carry it a while."

The first night they tried the new system, they picked up seventeen dear friends and everyone turned out to be thirsty. When the place was ready to close, Miss Raye called for the check. She studied the figures and signed with a flourish. The headwaiter took the check and beckoned to Gleason.

"Miss Raye is a good customer here," he said to Jackie. "However, she is one of those generous persons who spends beyond her means. Now will you please countersign this check as a guarantee that she will pay?"

At the time there was a madhouse in Hollywood called Slapsie Maxie's. It was probably the only place in America where, if the script called for squirting Seltzer on someone, the management chilled it first. It was on Beverly Boulevard and it seated 250 masochists and had two stages, one over the other. The owners advertised "No waiting." This did not apply to customers, but rather to actors. On the lower stage a dance number would conclude, and at once the curtains on the upstairs stage would part and a comic sketch would begin.

Most of the patrons were actors, singers, dancers and producers and writers. There was a touch of the Club 18 in the place, and a slight aura of the Miami Club too because, although the actors had scripts and the management paid top writers like Harry Crane as much as $1,000 for a short script, the actors were always in a mood to throw it away. Patrons such as Gene Kelly, Peter Lawford, Martha Raye and many others used to play bit walk-on parts for no fee. Much of the material used was spicy, and some of the kinder patrons referred to it as "clean burlesque." The waiters and the customers were almost always a part of the show, and the show was never the same two nights running.

The restaurant was named after the one-time middleweight champion of the world, Maxie Rosenbloom, who, in his fighting days, preferred to slap his opponents dizzy rather than stiffen them with a single punch. Although the restaurant bore his name, Rosenbloom did not run the business. This was done by a short, soft-spoken man, Sammy Lewis. He was highly regarded in the trade and was opposed to excessive drinking, eating and love-making. Lewis had a single weakness: he thought he could cure maniacs.

Rosenbloom starred in the restaurant and it was a novelty to the patrons to see an ex-pug with a busted nose stand on the stage and trade cracks with comedians. Sample:

MAXIE: I'm an actor.

COMEDIAN: You're a bum.

MAXIE: I'm a cinema actor.

COMEDIAN: You're a cinema bum.

COMEDIAN: God, you're ugly!

MAXIE: You're drunk.

COMEDIAN: You're still ugly.

MAXIE: You're still drunk.

COMEDIAN: I'll be sober in the morning.

This was pathetic material, even when it was new, but the patrons seemed pleased that a man they regarded as being punchy could utter any lines at all. Rosenbloom was not punchy; in fact, he had more cerebral buttons than many of the patrons. He was a shrewd businessman with a short temper.

Sammy Lewis hired Gleason for $150 a week. In time the price would go up to $325, but $150 was good starting money because it was in addition to the $250 Warner's was paying him. His employers at the studio could not understand how a man could stand in front of cameras and hot lights all day and then go out and clown before a live audience all night. They would like to have found a clause in the contract forbidding him to work at night, but, in its absence, they watched to see whether he would show up each morning at eight in Burbank.

Gleason did.

Ironically, he was a smash hit at Slapsie Maxie's, and the producers and executives who scorned his work by day paid to see him work at night. They came backstage to pump his hand and to tell him that he was an artist. Some agreed with Fanny Brice that Gleason's work was comparable to Charlie Chaplin's best. It was common for big-name producers to watch the show and walk out wiping their eyes and saying, "That's the funniest man I've ever seen."

They broke his heart because, while he rated their boozy hugs and congratulations at midnight, they ignored him in the morning. He went home to the Garden of Allah lonely and tired. No one knocked on the door and offered him a new contract. No one tried hard to borrow him from Warner Brothers. And, from day to day, he watched screenings of comedians with less talent than he had, and he wished that there was some way that he could circumvent Hollywood and bring his work before the millions of moviegoers for their approval. There wasn't any way.

On stage and off, Maxie and Jackie were not the closest of friends. Rosenbloom, not quite sure of himself as an actor, resented the ad libs which seemed to gush from Gleason and which threw Maxie off the script. When this happened, the fighter often threatened publicly to walk off the stage, but the thing which aroused all of Maxie's resentment occurred whenever Jackie, on stage, said, "You poor soul. I feel sorry for you." The comedian said it once when Rosenbloom was doing an impersonation of Noel Coward. Maxie stopped working and chased Jackie off stage and up the aisle.

On another occasion Rosenbloom was supposed to draw a laugh on his own ugliness by saying to Gleason, "I had four hundred and fifty fights. What's your excuse?" Gleason snapped, "Betting on you!" and the fighter walked off stage yelling, "I'm not gonna work with that guy any more. You can't depend on him."

What friction there was between Gleason and Sammy Lewis was a matter of Jackie's drinking. The comedian might have made it a little less acute by doing his drinking elsewhere, but once he learned that Sammy was opposed to it Gleason pointed it up sharply. Each evening when he reported for work he walked into the Lewis office and roared, "Sambo, who's the funniest man in the world, Sambo?" And Lewis would whisper, "Jackie Gleason."

Jackie then demanded a glass of whisky. Lewis said no. "Okay," said Jackie. "If I don't get it, I don't go on." Lewis understood the threat and knew that the young man was not bluffing. So he got a water goblet, filled it with whisky and, without a word, passed it to Jackie. This happened many times and, after Jackie drank it, he would hurry up front and on stage. In a moment Slapsie Maxie's was engulfed with laughter and Gleason would shout from the stage, "You see, Sambo?"

Lewis tried to curb the drinking by having Gleason live with him. "Me," said Lewis to his new star, "I drink maybe four ounces of liquor a year. The only way I can get into trouble is if I drink it all on one night." He brought Gleason to his home and pointed to a liquor cabinet, a dark, polished highboy. "No matter what happens," Sammy said, "you and I can get along if you keep away from that liquor cabinet. If you touch it, Jackie, I'm warning you that that is something I will not forgive."

Some nights, after Slapsie Maxie's closed, Lewis stayed to take a closer look at the books. Gleason went directly home to the Lewis place, and by the time Sammy got home Jackie and whatever friend accompanied him were fairly mellow. Sammy would run directly to the liquor cabinet and inspect it. It had not been touched, and the lock had not been tampered with. This posed a unique problem because Sammy knew that Jackie was always broke, and there was no other liquor in the house.

Years later Gleason explained it to Lewis. "Sambo," he said, "you're such a simple soul. When I wanted a drink, all I did was take a screw driver and remove the entire back of your liquor cabinet. That was all."

One night Gleason got falling-down drunk at a friend's house and he was taken home by Joe Bigelow, a writer. · Bigelow propped the actor against the doorjamb with one hand, unlocked the door with the other, and dropped Gleason inside. Bigelow took a cab and went directly to his own house. When he inserted a key in the door, it was opened and Jackie Gleason was standing inside. This so unnerved the writer that he shook for days.

Later Gleason explained this by saying that he was not as intoxicated as he had pretended to be. When he was dumped inside the door, he ran around to the back of the house, through an alley, and hailed a cab. He promised the driver a bonus if he could get to the Bigelow house quickly. Joe had already given Jackie a key to the place, so it was simple to let himself in and wait for Bigelow to show up.

At Slapsie Maxie's, Jackie was a comedian and also a master of ceremonies. Among the acts he introduced were Ben Blue, Sid Tomak, Joe Frisco and Julie Oetjens. He also did imitations and a wild trumpet solo. One night he went on stage with no rehearsals and said that he had just come from seeing a new motion picture called *Johnny Eager,* and if the audience would sit still for a moment, he would like to show them what it was like. Gleason then did a burlesque of the entire movie, playing all the principal parts himself. It was one of the funniest things ever seen on the Coast and the audience loved it, but it left Lewis cold and angry because Gleason required almost two hours to do it and this killed one of Lewis' short shows.

Comics have favorite comics. To Jackie Gleason, one of the funniest men he has ever seen is Ben Lessy, a local Hollywood comedian. Jackie cannot look at the man without snorting and almost wrecking himself laughing. It isn't necessary, most of the time, for Lessy to say anything. Jackie has only to glance at him and he is "dead." This might not be worth discussion except that, by a million to one chance, the funniest man in the world, as far as Ben Lessy is concerned, is Jackie Gleason. In Lessy's case, he doesn't even have to see Gleason; all he has to do is to hear the name and he guffaws from memory.

Both worked at Slapsie Maxie's, but they could not work together. Sammy Lewis tried to team them once and gave up. He paid a good sum of money to have a sketch written in which they would burlesque a song-writing team. They were introduced as "Your favorite song-writing team. Hogers and Rammerstein." They dressed separately and came on stage from opposite sides.

On the first night, they came on in stiff-brim straw hats, striped blazers and flannels. At mid-stage, they turned to look at each other. That was enough. Both pointed mutely and started to laugh. They leaned on each other—while the audience wondered what was so funny—and then they fell down and laughed and rolled. Lewis had to ring the curtain down and he was angry. He ordered them to try the sketch again and again, but it never worked out. Neither dared to look at the other. Not a line of dialogue was ever uttered.

Hollywood was not a total loss to Jackie. He made a lot of new friends, and a lot of so-called important people had an opportunity to watch him at work. Besides Lewis and Bigelow and Harry Crane and Ben Lessy and Maurie Suess and Bullets Durgom and Leo Talent, he had made friends with a host of others, including Rags Raglund, Sid Silvers and Jack Philbin.

The last one—Philbin—had a beautiful front. He was tall and dark and lean, a clotheshorse who gave an aura of having been everywhere and seen and tried everything, a man who might have been suckered into a lot of confidence games and was now prepared to invent a few.

Philbin came from Swampscott, Massachusetts, the son of the owner of the Province Inn, a newspaperman's hang-out. His mother was a wit who loved the theater and who drove more music and less tavern into her son's heart. He had grown up to be a carnival bum, a song plugger, worked for Paramount Pictures song company, married Marion Hutton, organized a show for Ina Ray Hutton and her band, and had a predilection for bossing any operation on which he worked.

Among the keys to strange homes in Gleason's possession was one from Jack Philbin. One afternoon Jackie took a girl from Warner's up to the house on Woodrow Wilson Drive. Philbin wasn't home, so Jackie used the key and walked in. They waited and helped themselves to a decanter which stared at them from a highboy.

When it began to get dark, the girl said that she wanted to go home. Jackie was agreeable, and he phoned for a cab. The dispatcher wanted to know where Gleason was, and Jackie couldn't remember the street. He looked all over the house for a trace of an address, or some letterheads, but there was no clue. The girl got panicky, and Jackie phoned Durgom at his office because he remembered that Bullets knew Philbin and therefore might know where Philbin lived.

The girl at the switchboard said that Mr. Durgom was in New York at the Park Sheraton Hotel. Gleason phoned long distance and got Bullets on the wire.

"This is Jackie. Where does Philbin live?"

"Woodrow Wilson Drive. Why?"

"I'm stuck there with a girl and I don't know where I am."

"Hah?"

(*Click.*)

Another of the new friends Gleason made was Davey Shelley, a short man with brown wavy hair, who was an excellent raconteur. Shelley, the stepson of producer and song writer Buddy De-Sylva, moved in the better circles of Hollywood and had a degree of taste. He had met Jackie at the Club 18, and the two merged their individual escapades.

In a moment of prosperity Jackie once tried to give a couple of his suits to Davey Shelley and Davey turned them down.

"What's the matter?" Jackie said, hurt.

"I won't wear them," Davey said without rancor, "because you're the only slob I know uses cloth buttons."

"What the hell's the matter with cloth buttons?"

"Everybody in Hollywood knows you always lay your arm on the table so that people can count the four cloth buttons on the sleeve. Nothing doing."

As the swallows return, with regularity, to Capistrano, so do the Broadwayites return to Times Square. The period of time is not the same, because, in the case of the swallows, they have read the publicity about their annual migration and they know that they had better get back on time. The Broadwayite is different. He comes back from Hollywood when he is quote fed up close quote. This can happen in a month, a year, five years. If he is under contract to a studio, and highly successful, he does not go back to New York when he is fed up, but is sure to make the pilgrimage when he is "fed up to here."

Gleason was "fed up to here," had worked out his last option, had said good-by to Sammy Lewis with a promise to return to Slapsie Maxie's for a later date, and had stepped aboard a plane bound for New York. He was going back to see Genevieve and the little girls. He didn't want to see any more palm trees; he was sick of sun-kissed oranges and directors and Santa Monica and patriotic speeches and three-toned foreign sports cars and suède shoes and smoked glasses.

He had made a mistake. Gleason had left Broadway too soon and, bull-like, he had lowered his head and charged west to bust the gates of Hollywood. All he had busted was his head. Now he was hurrying home to Gen for first aid.

Jackie has always been gifted with a brilliant imagination. When he imagines a plane falling in flames, he rides it all the way to the ground. So, when he got into the Hollywood-to-New York plane, he jammed his 270 pounds into a seat and, quickly and contritely, said a few prayers for safe deliverance. He had a feeling that all planes were meant to fly serenely except this one.

And, just this once, he was right. The ship took off low and straight and thundering out of Burbank Airport on a cool, sunny morning and lifted slowly toward the purple and white Sierra Madres and then made the long slow turn eastward. Far below were the neat scars of the highways and the pimpled villages. The plane droned on and on, lifting slightly in the thermal currents and dropping slightly. Jackie did not relax.

The pretty stewardess came aft with magazines and the morning newspapers from Los Angeles. Gleason closed his eyes and pretended to sleep. A clever observer would have said that he was not sleeping because fingers do not drum on the arm rests at a time like that. The stewardess got a pillow for him. Jackie kept thinking of all the sane actors he knew who took the sleek trains to New York. He stared, heavy-lidded, at the thin silver wing which held everything aloft—the people, the engines, the mail, the luggage, the high-octane gasoline.

The plane droned on and the brown mountains below slipped slowly under the wing and slid back and back until they were lost in haze. The engines thrummed, the fingers drummed.

The stewardess was up in the pilot's compartment. When she came back, she paused at each seat and said something to the

passengers to the left, and those to the right. When she got to
Jackie, she said, "Fasten your safety belt, please."

The fingers stopped. "Why?"

"We're making an emergency landing."

"Emergency lan—why? What happened?"

"I don't know, sir. Would you fasten your belt, please?"

Jackie swallowed. Well, he thought, here it is. Found dead on
a prairie somewhere.

He fastened his belt tight and looked around. No one was
panicky. The passengers seemed bewildered; some pretended to
be amused. He looked out the window. The plane had come
down a long way. He saw streets and houses and cars and a few
large legible signs. These things moved under the wing swiftly,
blurrily. By pressing his cheek against the window, Gleason
could see a patch of woods straight ahead. He mumbled to himself, "God did not give people wings to fly because he did not
want them to fly." Flying was for the birds, in every way. The
ground kept coming up closer. Jackie took a breath and held it.

The big plane came down easily, swinging first on a wide
tilting arc to the left, then over to the right. The engines seemed
to be barely turning over, and one was backfiring. The trees came
up closer and closer and they fled behind the plane faster and
faster and then there was a pause, a sort of holding of breath,
then a bump, then cushioned air, then another bump, a bump,
then rubbled rolling, then the plane stopped.

Jackie concluded a prayer he'd started what seemed a long
time ago. Then, as casually as a motorist in a strange town, he
said, "Where are we?" Someone said, "Phoenix." Gleason said,
"Phoenix," and smiled. The plane taxied a little bit and then, after
a wait, everybody got out. The people stood around talking and
speculating. A maintenance truck came up and backed up to
the plane.

"What's that for?" Jackie said to a man in uniform.

"The truck is going to take your baggage to a bigger field in
Phoenix. There's a plane waiting."

Gleason tapped his chest. "Not for me it isn't, pal," he said. "I'll
take it from here." The man looked dumb-struck. "Get my bags
off this nickel rocket," Jackie said, "and I'll find a train."

He took a taxi into Phoenix and discovered that he did not have enough cash to buy a railroad ticket. The air line was willing to refund some money on his ticket, but not at once. They would mail it to him in New York. So he did something that few men would do. Jackie went from store to store, in Phoenix, trying to cash a check. He told them that he was an actor, that he was solvent, and he repeated again and again the story of how the cruddy plane had come down in this cruddy place and he would not go back to the plane even if it meant walking home. The shopkeepers could hardly be more attentive and less sympathetic.

Gleason began to believe that all of Phoenix was on relief when he met a hardware merchant who said, "I got the money, and I can cash that check, son, but I got to have some positive identification."

Jackie looked out through the front door and there was a motion-picture house across the street. From where he stood he could see that the picture playing was *Navy Blues*. "I'm in that one," he said.

"You are?" the hardwareman said. "Well, now."

He turned the store over to a clerk. "You starring in that picture, Mr. Gleason?"

"Well," said Jackie modestly, "not exactly starring, but I'm in it from start to finish."

"Then you have no problem," the man said. "All we have to do is go across the street, look at the pictures out front, and see you. Then we come back and cash your check."

Gleason had an uneasy feeling. He walked across the street with the man, and they studied the stills out front, and they studied the stills in the lobby. No Gleason. Jackie said that that was very funny indeed. However, if the man would accompany him inside—Gleason would buy the tickets of admission, of course—he would see for himself that Jackie was a big part of *Navy Blues*. The hardwareman was agreeable. When they got inside, the picture had been on almost an hour, and so they sat silently, waiting for a glimpse of the comedian. There were all kinds of action, but Jackie wasn't even in a background shot. The picture ended, and the newsreel started.

"Wait," Jackie said. "I'm in the opening of the picture."

The hardwareman was agreeable. He composed himself and waited. After the newsreel there was a mystery picture, and they sat through that. The hardwareman thought that it was pretty good. He confessed that he had no idea who had really committed the murder until the last minute, where the murderer held the cop at bay with a gun and confessed the whole thing without realizing that all the other cops were closing in on him. The hardwareman liked mysteries.

Next was the coming attractions, and they sat through that. Then came *Navy Blues* again and Gleason ran down the cast of characters until he saw his name. He jogged the hardwareman and said, "See?" pointing, but the cast of characters was now in slow dissolve and there was nothing to see. So he sat and watched the whole first part of the movie and, when he finally saw himself, fat in whites, standing on a corner with Jack Haley, he almost punched the hardwareman and whispered, "See? See? There I am. See?"

The hardwareman said that there was no doubt about it—that was the same man who was sitting alongside him all right, and he would be glad to cash the check and help an actor out of trouble. However, as long as he had seen this much of the picture, would Mr. Gleason mind sitting a few minutes more until it came to the part where they had walked in? Gleason swallowed, and sat.

It was dark when he walked into a railroad station and said, "How long for the next train to New York?"

One of Jackie Gleason's unrecognized assets is an intangible called front. He has it at all times. No matter how badly matters are going, and even when he is aware that they are going poorly, he wears the big smile of confidence, jets of optimism spray everyone within hearing, and his sparkling eyes, his disdain of doubters, and his take-charge attitude make him a supercharged salesman of success.

It didn't work on Mrs. Gleason. It might have been negotiable currency anywhere else, but to Gen it was as patently counterfeit as Jackie's picture on a four-dollar bill. She knew him better than he did and, what is always tragic in a wife, she understood his weaknesses better than she did his strengths.

So, if his ego needed bandaging when he got home, the job was turned down by his wife. She was angry, and rightfully so, because he had stayed away from home for so long, because he had sent very little money, because she had pumped pals for news—bad news—and had heard it.

There were accusations. And denials. There were rising voices. And threats. The separations were lasting longer. The periods of contrition and forgiveness were shorter. It was easy for Genevieve to play the wronged wife because her personal reputation was of the best and Jackie's wasn't. It is a good thing, at times, to play this role provided that you are not still in love with the man and aching for him to come back.

Gleason left home. He lived for a while at the Hotel Edison, and for another while he stayed at the Hotel Astor. He hung out in Toots Shor's restaurant and he lived big. Gleason always lived big whether he was working or not. His credit was good, even though he was known as a man with the chronic "shorts." Mr. Shor was fond of him and permitted him to sign restaurant checks for unlimited amounts. Mr. Robert Christenberry, managing director of the Hotel Astor, permitted Jackie to sign for everything including his laundry, but balked once at his "coming downstairs and borrowing cash from our cashier."

Willie Webber was busy all over town yelping that "Jackie is back" and looking for work. Some clubs said that they had no spot for Gleason's type of talent. Others said that he drank too much, and they couldn't afford to take a chance.

Still, he got a job in a Broadway play called *Along Fifth Avenue*. It broke no records, but Jackie drew $600 a week—his highest salary—while it lasted. It was not a notable play, but in it was a sketch about the French Foreign Legion which seemed to leave the Broadwaywise crowd helpless in laughter. It opened with three weary members of the Legion coming on stage leaning on each other as they crossed the burning sands. Behind them came Gleason, dressed in an impeccable Legion uniform (side curtains and all), with all the insolence of a latter-day Reggie

Van Gleason. He was heavy with medals and at his side was a beautiful blonde, in shorts, carrying his golf bag.

Of those who saw it, Milton Douglas, a singer and booker of hotel floor shows, said that he would never forget it. He had never seen Jackie Gleason before, but Douglas left the theater believing that this was the funniest man he had ever seen. On another night a short, dapper man named Myron Kirk, an advertising executive who booked big stars for radio, left the theater with the same feeling. Gleason did not know either of them.

The show closed, and the comic was out of work again. Webber got him a short booking in Lou Walter's *Artists and Models.* This paid him $400 a week, but not for long. There was another period of unemployment and a job as master of ceremonies at Loew's State. This one netted him $750 a week, about 18,700 per cent more than he got for the same work at the Halsey eight years before. He was getting top billing on the marquees and he began to live and act more and more like his childish imaginings of the Big Star.

Emotionally, Jackie Gleason was a youngster and his passionate likes and dislikes, his enthusiasms as well as his apathies, were those of an adolescent boy of sensual appreciation. He wanted what he wanted when he wanted it. This is not to imply that Jackie was demanding; he wasn't. His impatience was gleeful rather than glowering. If he ordered a pizza pie, or a new car, he sat shaking with excitement until it arrived. When the writer began to write his biography, Gleason waited three days, then stuck his head in the doorway to my office, clenched his fists like a baby in a high chair who sees ice cream coming, and whispered, "I can't wait to read it!"

He has a quantity of strong, seemingly small characteristics, yet when fitted together like colored pieces of mosaic, it is these "small" things that form the personality known to millions: he tips too much; gives away too much money; undergoes periods of deep remorse; has sudden exultations and passions; is fiercely loyal to "the gang"; is richly endowed with sentiment, and rarely makes an enemy. In Jackie's case, the emotional pendulum swings in a wider arc than in most humans. He can be happier than most of us, and sadder. His main characteristics, the two items

which are with him all of the time, are: (1) a passion for constant
approval; (2) a desire to "go first class."

Everyone has some of each. Few people have them in the
Gleason proportions and, coupled with his adolescence, they
have helped rather than hurt him. They have given him the aura
of the regular guy, the sport, the man most of us would trust, the
sympathetic samaritan.

These qualities were taking firmer and firmer shape during
the post-Hollywood time. His own leanings, coupled with a sense
of what the public wanted, combined to make today's Jackie
Gleason. The calendar had not leaned on him yet. He could still
phone Julie Dennehy and her new husband, Jim Marshall, and
yell, "Let's go bouncing!" and then, because Jackie had not yet
learned to drive, he would charter a limousine and chauffeur and
drive over to the old Brooklyn neighborhood, pick up the Mar-
shalls,· and start off at Pop Proce's place. The stops, after that,
were many, and they would bounce as long as there was any
resilience left. When the bounce was gone, Gleason would drive
back to his hotel, sometimes remembering briefly the nausea, and
the laughter (both actual) of the evening. Home again, he would
give the chauffeur a big tip and say, "Tell the boss to send the
bill."

When he worked, he did little bouncing. He might drink after
hours, but he was never known to be drunk on stage or with
work pending. Sometimes his hang-overs would seem to draw
his individual nerves as tight as E strings, and on many a cold
morning Jackie mopped the spangles of sweat from his forehead.

One Sunday morning he was ordering his skittering fingers to
button up his shirt when Jimmy Ryan came in.

"I'm dying," said Jackie.

"I've seen more carefree days," Ryan said.

"Well, keep your coat on. You're coming to Mass with me."

They went to Mass and Gleason prayed for a job. He needed
work badly. On the way home Ryan said that a sensible man
did not have to put up with a hang-over if he had a little nutmeg
around the house. Gleason, whose mind is always open to new
inventions, said that he had not heard of nutmeg as "the thing,"
but he was willing to try it.

Jimmy Ryan said that he would stop at his place and get the nutmeg. Jackie got home and, in his delight at learning the antidote to the hang-over, phoned everyone who had been at the party the night before and invited them over to try Ryan's panacea. It is a commentary on human intelligence to say that everybody came.

When Ryan arrived, he displayed a small bag. "Nutmeg," he said.

"Nutmeg," Jackie said, pointing.

"Now," said Jimmy, "I will need a little milk to go with the nutmeg."

"In the kitchen," said Jackie. "Help yourself, pal."

"It won't hurt," said Ryan, "if we throw in a little brandy too."

Within an hour everybody felt better. Some were looking up the word nutmeg to find its magical properties. The party ran out of brandy and Jackie ordered more. By midafternoon, the jokes were flying and the management had phoned twice to request less noise.

The supply of nutmeg got low, and Ryan suggested that all hands had better cut the use of the nutmeg and the milk a little bit. This was done without objection. By evening someone said, "The hell with the nutmeg. That stuff could kill a guy."

No one left for three days.

Now and then Willie Webber sold his comics. When he found them and agreed to manage their affairs, they were always small and hopeful. They filled the waiting room of his office on Broadway every morning. It was Willie's job to find work for them, to build up their earning power and their prestige. He did this to the best of his ability.

When they became "too big" for him to handle, he took them to Music Corporation of America and, for 5 per cent of future earnings for a few years, sold them to the big agency. One day Willie called four comedians to his office (including Gleason) and told them that they had outgrown him, that they were big enough to expect national representation. He was about to sell them, not down the river, but up.

Three of the actors agreed to be sold at once. Only Jackie

refused. "You're good enough for me," he growled, and walked out. To make certain that Willie Webber understood what he meant, Jackie borrowed $150 and bought a solid-gold money clip, inscribed, "To the World's Best Manager—Jackie."

One of his many short engagements of this period was at the Bally Club in Philadelphia. After the last show one night Jackie washed up, donned a fresh shirt and tie, and hurried out the back alley to go next door to the Rathskeller, where his friend Jackie Winston was playing. At the end of the dark alley he turned left to go down a flight of steps into the Rathskeller and fell to the bottom. It required no doctor to tell Gleason that his left arm was broken, but Winston and others got one out of bed who examined the arm, set it, put it in splints and told the patient to return in the morning.

The patient did no such thing. He returned to his suite at the Sylvania Hotel and at 3:30 A.M. phoned many of his Philadelphia friends. "You guys like to celebrate something odd," he said to each one. "So come on over right away. I just broke my arm." On that memorable morning—November 10, 1943—a score of Philadelphians got out of bed to dress and bend an elbow to a broken arm. The cost of liquor and food reached such proportions that the management told Mr. Gleason that it would like to see some money before he checked out.

This was a matter of acute embarrassment for Jackie because he was so low on funds that he was signing the tips for ice water. He awakened in the afternoon with an arm like a washboard and two things were apparent to him: no one would book him with a broken arm, and he would be wearing this splint for six weeks at least.

Gleason called Jack White at the Club 18 in New York. He used his sweetest, old-pal tone and he said, "I'll tell you, Jack. I just finished a bit here in Philly and I've got to go to Michigan in five weeks so I figured I might as well be working in the meantime. You got anything?"

White thought about it and said, "Well, yes, Jack. I can use you right now. It's funny that you should call me because I was talking about you only last night. I was saying that that fall you do is one of the funniest bits I've ever seen. Sure. Come on in. Can you make it tonight?"

"Certainly," Gleason said. "I'll be there. By the way, Jack, can you advance me five hundred? I'll tell you frankly, Jack. I was taken in a crap game last night and—"

"You bum!" White snarled. "I walked right into this, didn't I? Okay. I'll wire the dough."

Gleason gulped. He was afraid to mention the broken arm. The money arrived and he paid the hotel bill, the few bar bills around town, a couple of personal loans here and there, and he took the train to New York. At the Club 18, Gleason walked in wearing a tan Worumbo coat with empty sleeve and cape effect. The left arm, hanging on the chest, looked bigger than a cricket bat. When anything struck Jack White funny, he always covered his eyes with his hand. He shrieked, pounded the bar with his fist, and said, "Jackie, that's one of the funniest bits I've ever seen."

The young comedian had to admit that this was not funny, that he had a broken arm. White sobered abruptly. How could a comedian draw laughs with a busted wing? Jackie said that it could be done, that he had a dozen jokes lined up about broken arms, and that the fracture could be turned into a very amusing thing. Jack White was still worried, but he was willing to give it a try.

"Go back and make up," he said. The kid was into him for $500. He had to take a chance.

Joe Frisco was in the dressing room. He sat facing a cracked mirror and he hit himself twice with an old powder puff. He was made up. Jackie came in and introduced himself. Joe Frisco, as a stuttering comedian, had been in this business since before Gleason was born.

The older man asked what happened to the arm, and Jackie must have made a funny story out of it because Frisco, who is not much of a laugher, began to laugh and he slapped the dressing-table top and said, "This calls for a bottle." They sent Jackson for some Scotch, and the two men sat and began to tell stories about the Coast and about the people they both knew and about the theater.

They told stories and drank. And drank, and told stories. The

call came for them to go on stage and they walked out, stood in
front of the band facing the audience, burst into laughter, and
sat down. There was no show. They went back to the dressing
room, noting only that Jack White didn't seem to understand the
humor of the situation, and sent for another fifth of Scotch. They
told some more stories and, wiping their eyes, waited for the
call for the second show.

It didn't come, and they didn't notice. They sat in the little
dressing room for hours, and after an interminable time Frisco
said to Gleason, "Better take a look out and find out what's going
on." Gleason went out in the little hall and looked. He came back
and said, "The tables are all piled up on top of each other. Guess
everybody's gone home."

They put on their jackets and started out. The way out was
through the little hall to the bandstand, down among the tables,
past the bar, and out the front door. They got as far as the bar when
they saw Jack White, alone in the club, standing at the cash
register. The single yellow light shaded part of his face. They
understood at once that, rather than go back for them, he had
waited out front alone, knowing that there was no other exit.

"Just a minute," White said. Both men paused, executed a
fancy turn, and leaned elbows on the bar. White started working
on Joe Frisco first, reminding him of all the times he had pulled
the sharks off Joe's back, how he had staked him to money, how
he had got jobs for him when no one wanted him. Then he called
Frisco some of the vilest names ever devised by men with short
vocabularies. Not a word of rebuttal was uttered by Frisco or
Gleason. Jack White kept shouting until he ran out of names.

"And as for that fat bum with you," he said, "he's just no damned
good at all. He conned me with a broken arm. This much I can
tell you, I am going to sit in this club from now until six A.M.
and I am phoning every club owner between here and Texas—
I'm not kidding about this thing—and when I get through with
you guys, neither of you will ever get a job anywhere. As far as
I'm concerned, you're both in the gutter."

There was a little silence. "Got anything to say?" he roared.

Jackie shook his head silently. Frisco gulped twice and murmured, "H-h-have you g-g-got a bottle of c-c-cold beer handy?"

White's cold rage collapsed. "What's the use?" he said, and brought beer and glasses out for three.

This was the first and only time Jackie had ever been drunk on the job.

There is a large circular bar in the front part of Toots Shor's restaurant, and at any hour of day or night during this period, customers could find Jackie Gleason holding up the western side of it. This was not solely for drinking purposes, although there was always a glass in front of Jackie. To the comedian, this bar meant "Time to relax." He used it as a rendezvous for old friends, a place for roughhouse kidding with Shor, a backdrop for business contacts, a setting for brushing up on news about the theater, the world of sports and, last and least, news of the world. The same set of tired faces could be seen around this bar at any noon hour, and the same half dozen would still be there at 4:00 P.M.

At times Jackie owed considerable money to Shor. He signed all bar and restaurant checks "jackie gleason"—just like that—and the bill reached $800 when Jackie was still out of work. In the late afternoon; while Gleason was worrying about the debt and Shor wasn't, Jackie got an offer to hurry over to a big Brooklyn theater and act as master of ceremonies for one show for $200. At midnight he was back in Shor's place and Toots beamed as Gleason came in, walked by, and pressed a hundred dollars into the palm of Joseph Harrison, the headwaiter. When Jackie came back to the bar, Toots said, "I don't really give a hoot, but will you please tell me why you gave that century to him?"

"Sure, pal," said Jackie, stuffing the other hundred into his pocket. "I haven't tipped him in a long time."

When the bill began to creep above $800, Jackie told Shor that he wouldn't sign any more checks.

"Who's asking you for money, you creep!" said Shor with manly affection. "If you're tired of signing your own name, sign mine."

"Okay," said Jackie, and immediately invited some friends in for dinner. When it was over, he studied the check and marked down a ten-dollar tip for the headwaiter and five dollars for the waiter. "I'd have made it more, my boy," he said to the waiter, "but you know how cheap Toots is."

Once, when the two friends had an argument, Gleason broke
it into laughter when he roared, "One more word out of you,
Toots, and I"ll break my pencil!" On another occasion he wanted
to take a girl out to dinner on New Year's Eve. He needed a
little pocket money, even though he was going to sign the check,
so he took the girl's watch and hocked it for tip money. On still
another afternoon—a Sunday afternoon to be exact—Paul Douglas invited Gleason out for some friendly drinking and, at the
first stop (Shor's) Jackie sauntered up to the bar and said, "A
triple gin with a beer chaser, please."

Douglas was ashamed. "This is the first stop, you big slob.
Take it easy."

"Okay," Jackie murmured. "Skip the beer."

Another member of the Shor set was Lee Meyers, a dark,
wavy-haired press agent who says little but is sure that everything is going to happen for the worst. His voice is perpetually
hoarse from shouting tired horses home. Sometimes he does publicity for the elegant corporations who want their press notices
filtered, and sometimes he does work for clients who would rather
have things kept out of the papers than put in.

Meyers and Gleason got along. They became such fast friends
that sometimes Jackie shared Lee's apartment. There were three
Gleason virtues which excited Lee Meyers' admiration. One was
sincerity; a second was Gleason's ability to go on a "deep-thinking
binge"; the third was that, in a group of freewheeling sports,
Gleason always managed to get his money on the bar first.

In 1943 the United States Armed Forces began to call some of
the fathers of America for war duty, and Gleason showed up
beaming, with chest out and stomach in. The Army doctors gave
him a thorough examination. The findings were: left arm broken,
healed crooked; area between thumb and forefinger nerveless
and numb; polynoidal cyst on end of coccyx; inductee a hundred
pounds overweight.

The verdict: "Go home."

Toward the end of that year Willie Webber managed to find
work for his "boy." Gleason went back to the Club 18, with past

sins forgiven, at $600 a week. Afterward, he got a solid break in a
hit show—*Follow the Girls*. This was the raucous comedy in
which the star, Gertrude Niesen, sang the plaintive and risqué
hit "I Wanna Get Married."

Jackie's comedy was rich and loud and the cast was surprised
to note that he did not rehearse carefully. On the contrary, he
barely riffled through the script, yet not only knew his part well,
but seemed to know everyone else's lines too. In show business it
is not unusual to find an actor, or actress, who is a "fast study,"
but it is phenomenal to find one who can stand in a corner with
a lengthy script, flip the pages slowly, and then announce, "Okay.
I know the part. Let's go." Gleason could do this every time he
was cast in a part, and his memory was such that, years later, if
he was given a cue line, he could recall almost an entire script
word for word. At the same time, if he was asked the date of his
marriage, he could not remember.

His confidence in himself often caused a little trouble. For example, in *Follow the Girls*, he was so smart-alecky that he often
departed from the script to ad lib lines aimed at someone in the
audience. This irritated Miss Niesen, who is small and pretty,
like a baby tiger is small and pretty. She was too fine an actress
to show irritation on stage, but in the wings her father used to
whisper to Willie Webber, "Tell your boy to stick to the script.
Now mind what I say."

But after a few weeks Miss Niesen became accustomed to
Gleason's antics and she dissolved in laughter; Jackie, who thrives
on anyone's laughter, thereupon directed all his asides to the
star, and peace followed.

In time even the best plays close, and when *Follow the Girls*
faded from the Broadway scene, Willie Webber began the same
monotonous round of places likely to need a funnyman. In most
cases he conducted such negotiations alone, but this time, through
a lapse in managerial acumen, he took Gleason with him to see
Sam Rausch at the Roxy Theatre. In those days the Roxy featured a first-run motion picture, plus a stage presentation with a
"name" star.

Rausch welcomed the two men to his office and sat down at his
desk to listen to Willie's sales talk in Gleason's behalf. He didn't

need it, really. Rausch had seen Jackie in *Follow the Girls* and he had seen him at the Club 18, and he was already sold on Gleason's starring in a stage show at his Roxy. Still, it is always refreshing to listen to a Webber sales talk because it is done in basic English, with gestures and heart. Jackie sat listening, and it was obvious that he needed the job and was nervous about his chances.

"Willie," said Rausch, "what do you want for Gleason?" There was a loud silence, in which Jackie could hear a ringing in his ears. "I will give you a four-week engagement," Rausch said.

"Well," said Willie, as though this was something he would do only for Rausch, "I would accept three thousand dollars a week."

Rausch leaned back to look at the ceiling and pursed his lips. Gleason jumped to his feet and, looking at Willie accusingly, shouted, "I'm not worth three thousand!"

Webber gasped for air, stricken with shock and pain. Rausch's eyes came off the ceiling and he laughed so hard that he bent forward with his elbows on his knees.

"Okay, okay," he said. "You get three thousand."

When Jackie went on for the first show at the Roxy, he cracked jokes, did funny bits of business with his hands and eyes, kidded the audience, did a prat fall, introduced an act, and was off in six minutes. Rausch complained that he wasn't getting much for $3,000 a week.

"Don't worry," Willie Webber said. "He's very nervous right now. After the first show he'll start spreading it a bit." The second show lasted six minutes. The third lasted eight. The fourth was clocked at six minutes. At last Rausch complained to Gleason. The actor listened, and then shook his head sadly.

"Mr. Rausch," he said, "this act is so rich that the audience can't stand more than six minutes of it."

A few weeks later Jackie was working for $150 on the "Edelbrau Hour" over radio station WOR. He had an enormous talent for comedy and a supreme confidence in himself as a performer, but, economically, Gleason was a dunce.

He earned $3,000 one week, $150 the next, and nothing on the third. Somehow, in spite of the disparity between these weeks, he managed to remain permanently penniless. He had no insurance;

he did not own a stick of furniture or a car; and, quite often, since
he was paying weekly for the clothes he wore, he didn't really
own the shirt on his back.

Jackie met Lee Meyers on Sixth Avenue one afternoon and
found a point of mutual commiseration: Jackie was out of work
and broke, and Lee was down to one press-agentry account. This
was the Chamber Music Society of Lower Basin Street, a har-
monic hoyden of the air waves. The program specialized in the
musically unusual: philharmonic harpists rapping out "Mississippi
Mud" and Dixieland clarinetists having a go at "Anitra's Dance."

The program needed an artist for the next week's program and
Meyers recalled that his pal Gleason had talked about playing a
trumpet. It occurred to the press agent that a comedian doing a
trumpet solo would be in key with the Society of Lower Basin
Street.

"If I can talk the producer into announcing you as a trumpet
player," said Meyers, feeling his way, "it would be a hell of a
switch. Do you think you could go out and learn a song for next
week?"

"Pal," said Jackie, in the manner of a man who knows that one
of us is worrying needlessly, "pal, you know me. I'll do it and I'll
be great."

"What kind of money would you want?"

"Fifteen hundred," said Gleason.

"Jackie, the show is sustaining. You can't get fifteen."

"What can you get for me?"

"Scale."

"What's that?"

"About eighty bucks."

"Oh, no. Not me, pal. Not me." There was a moment of awkward silence between friends. "Can you get seven-fifty?"

"No."

"See what you can get."

"Do my best, Jackie."

Lee Meyers talked it over with the producer of the show, and
he thought that a comic blowing a trumpet solo was a great idea.
So great, in fact, that he was prepared to shoot every loose dollar

in the budget on it—$350. Gleason heard it and said that he
would do it for his friend, and the lousy $350.

The show was rehearsed in a Blue Network playhouse in the
East Forties. To cut expenses, it was rehearsed only on show day
and it was rehearsed all day long. Lee called for Jackie and took
him to the playhouse. There, a group of musicians whom Meyers
referred to as Dr. Henry Hotlips Levine and His Barefooted
Philharmonic was waiting for the star of the week, Jackie Gleason,
to pick up a trumpet and show his wares.

"Listen," said Jackie to Dr. Levine, "I don't want to play the
thing right now. Just run through it and time it for me. I'll play
it at the dress."

At the dress rehearsal, Gleason held the trumpet bravely,
pressed it to the left side of his mouth, and blew mightily. What
came out was sorrow, not music. He smiled a little and said,
"I'll get it in a minute." He didn't. The producer began to moan.

"We announced this guy in last week's program. Now what?"

Jackie asked the professor to stand behind him and to press the
proper valves down while the comedian supplied the blast. Hotlips did it and out came the right notes, but they were frightened
notes.

"Don't worry," Jackie said. "I'll give you six minutes tonight.
I'll play it right."

When the show went on the air that night, the producer glistened with moisture. Jackie was introduced as a great comedian
whose passion was the trumpet, and, to the accompaniment of the
Barefoot Philharmonic, he blew three mighty blasts on the instru-
ment, then took it away from his mouth and said, "And now,
ladies and gentlemen, I want to tell you something about my girl
friend, Laura, the one who ran off with the trumpet player." The
orchestra played a bar or two more, then died in mid-note. The
producer was in anguish. The technicians stopped working to
listen.

Jackie told a forlorn story of poor Laura and the insidious
trumpet player with the cracked lip. He told it for six minutes. It
wasn't Basin Street Music, but it was so funny that the gales of
laughter from the men in the orchestra almost drowned the

punch lines. Jackie blew one last note of wild defiance into the
microphone and left.

Within fifteen minutes the network switchboards were
swamped with phone calls. Most of the listeners said that this
one was the funniest program they had ever heard. The producer
began to feel happy about his trying experience. In a day or two
there were so many pats on the back from network officials that
Lower Basin Street switched tactics and went out to find comedians who were part-time musicians. They tried Zero Mostel and
a few others, and one evening they auditioned a Danish concert
pianist named Victor Borge. He became a permanent feature on
the program.

In theatrical circles there is a game called "the challenge." To
play it, all the contestant needs is a tremendous capacity for
liquor. The only other requirement is that he be rash enough to
challenge another person to a drinking bout. The arenas for these
struggles are to be found in many hotels and apartments in New
York, Chicago and Hollywood. There are other places, but if a
brandy battle of consequence is being staged, it is usually fought
out in one of these cities.

Unlike boxing bouts, which can be won on points, the challenge
can be won only by a knockout. One of the contestants must fall
unconscious, fall asleep, or run to the bathroom in hysterical
haste. The winner needs only to be alive and vertical, or almost
vertical. It is not necessary for him (or her) to be able to speak
intelligibly or even to be able to speak at all. If the eyes are
open, and the contestant is able to move, either by the use of
feet or hands, or both, he is declared the winner.

Gleason, so far as the record shows, only challenged twice. He
won the first, and there is a slight suspicion that he threw the
second match; in any case, he lost it and was never known to
challenge anybody again.

He was staying at the Hotel Astor, in the early part of 1944,
when he enunciated the first challenge. Down the hall from the
Gleason room was a suite occupied by Jay C. Flippen, a tall,
bushy-haired man who was also a comedian and a night-club
master of ceremonies. This suite was called the Chez Jay and it

became a Saturday-night hang-out for theatrical figures. Most of
the people who showed up at these parties had a lot of fame, and
little money. Each, however, had a little credit somewhere, so
there was not much of a problem regarding *who* would get the
ham and the bread tonight and *who* would go for the brandy and
ice.

At the time, a horse player who worked at the Copa to keep
his bookie solvent was paying serious attention to a beautiful
and well-known singer. They had been talking marriage and, as
soon as there was a lull between meets (after Hialeah and before Churchill Downs, for example), they would be married. The
girl, with all her fragile beauty, had a reputation at the Chez Jay
for not caring too much whether anyone served a drink to her or
not, because when she drank nothing happened. This was dis-
concerting to some of the other bottle battlers, because when they
drank something happened every time.

A few evenings before this particular event the horse player
phoned Jay C. Flippen (as he usually did in such situations) and
said, "Jay, I'm going out of town for a while and I want you to
watch over my girl. Take good care of her."

It is part of the adolescent code of Broadway that, when a pal
phones with a request of this type, every member of the group
will defend the girl to the death. So Flippen was prepared to
baby-sit until the bridegroom-to-be got back to town.

On the Saturday night under discussion, the girl made a careless remark to Gleason about drinking. None of the belligerents
remember the exact wording, but it had something to do with
what disgusting bums men could be under the influence of alcohol, while ladies, in the same circumstances, remained ladies and
yet drank their men under the table.

Gleason made the challenge at once. The rest of the party was
hushed, and when the girl accepted and, as the challengee, chose
brandy, there was a general hubbub and the spectators moved
chairs up to form a circle and watch. Under the rules, spectators
can drink as much or as little as they please during a bout, but
their drinks are not counted, as is the case with contestants.

Jackie (no fool he) asked if it would be all right to stage the
bout sitting or lying on the rug because then, in case unconscious-

ness overcame either contestant, there would be less risk of injury in falling. The girl thought about it and agreed. She sat on the rug, pulled her skirt tight around her, and stared at the hulk who was just settling on the rug opposite her.

The chairs were drawn up in a circle, and the brandy was produced. There are two ways in which a match of this type can be scored: by counting the individual drinks, or by counting it by bottles. Neophytes usually do it by drinks. An umpire pours one for each contestant, and when both glasses are empty he pours another round. In such a match, some years ago, Mark Hellinger and Toots Shor were in the middle stages of the battle when the umpire, Jimmy Cannon, had to be carried out.

A fifth of brandy was placed on the rug before the girl, and another before Jackie Gleason. There was no umpire. They were to drink slowly and steadily, with much conversation and storytelling, and when both bottles were empty two more were to be brought in. A match of this kind sometimes endures for five or six hours, although the average time for show-offs, braggarts and alcoholics is something under two hours.

At 1:00 A.M. both were moving steadily, and the stories told by the talented spectators induced hysterical laughter. Jackie showed a fine mist on his forehead and his breathing could be heard two corridors removed from the scene. Facing him, the girl was bright, chipper and ladylike. She consumed her brandy straight and scorned chasers because sodas tend to fill the stomach.

Around 2:00 A.M. some of the noncontestants were unconscious on the bed and Mr. Flippen was yawning. Dave Shelley (he who can't stand cloth buttons) was standing at a front window conversing with Lee Meyers, who was aching for a morning *Mirror* with the complete racing results. At 2:30 A.M. three more noncontestants were on the floor, outside the circle, snoring. Gleason was now drinking from a prone position, and conversation slowed down as two more bottles of brandy were brought in.

The odds on the match had shifted heavily in favor of the girl, who was still birdlike and bright. Here and there a five-dollar bill was shown and matched, and the records of the two contestants were recited as though they were gamecocks in a pit. At 3:10 A.M. the break came. The girl's complexion changed, in a trice, from pink to green. Without a word, she turned on all fours and crept toward the bathroom.

Gleason, feeling unconsciousness coming but anxious to have a symbol of victory, reached for her slipper and yanked it off as she left the room.

Then he tried to get to his feet, made it, lurched out into the hall, got halfway to his room, and fell. In the morning a German waiter, carrying a breakfast tray, paused over the sleeping Jackie and, thinking that the actor must have sustained a heart attack in the hall, yelled, "Mister Gleezon! *Was ist los?*"

Jackie opened one eye and saw that his right hand was clutching a slipper. He smiled and went back to sleep.

On the other occasion in which Jackie played the challenge, the game was a matter of necessity. He wouldn't have played it, in truth, if he hadn't been ashamed of owing Shor so much money. It was a summer day, and Jackie was standing out in front of his friend's restaurant. He was broke, and he would have liked to have been inside laughing and drinking, but he felt that he had sponged on Toots enough, and he wasn't going to sign any more checks until he had paid off a little cash.

Some friends paused on their way in to say hello, and Gleason said, in each case, that he was waiting for someone, that he would see them later. Lee Meyers came along, skidded to a stop, and asked what the trouble was. Jackie told him. Meyers thought about it.

"Why don't you do what the rest of us do?" he said. "When we're broke, we don't sign anything. We just walk in, walk right up to Toots, call him a fat bum, and challenge him. Naturally, Toots thinks he's the best drinker in the world, so he gets mad and sits down and orders two bottles of brandy. Who cares who wins? You drink on the cuff all afternoon."

There was a certain amount of logic in this approach, so Jackie rubbed his hands together and, wheeling with Meyers, went through the revolving door and walked up to Shor and said, "Whoever told you that you could drink, you fat bum?" Shor almost ruined the sequence by bursting into laughter and yelling, "Look who's calling who fat!" But in a moment the challenge had been accepted and the two battlers were sitting waiting for two bottles of brandy.

At the table was a third man, a noncombatant. He was Jimmy Cannon, the best writer among the *Daily News* alumni, and a sports columnist. He was short and dark and angry-looking. He had a head that looked as though it had been screwed onto his shoulders and someone had forced one turn too many. He was convalescing from a stomach operation and, as he sat at the table with Shor at his side and Gleason facing him, he cut his single lamb chop cellophane thin and he took tiny bits of the creamed spinach his doctor had ordered him to eat.

The bottles arrived and the drinking started. Lee Meyers came over to offer advice to both contestants. Cannon, who has not been caught smiling since the advent of the lively ball, was in no mood to watch idiots swill booze. Still, they sat at his table and called each other names and drank. Gleason drank swiftly and lost swiftly. With no warning, he became nauseated and damaged Cannon's table.

Jackie excused himself and got up. Jimmy Cannon said nothing. Quietly, fiercely, he sawed at the lamb chop. A waiter changed the tablecloth and Shor said he always knew that Gleason couldn't drink, and, if he wanted another beating, let him come back to the table like a man. That's exactly what Jackie did. He came back to the table, looked sorrowfully at Cannon, and apologized. Cannon didn't answer. He was on the creamed spinach again. Jackie poured a drink, brought it to his lips, and the odor induced more nausea. The tablecloth was ruined.

The comedian got up, staggered as far as the archway which separates the bar from the restaurant, did a half spin, and fell on his back. Two waiters hurried over to help him. At that point Cannon spoke for the first time.

"Let the bum lay there!" he snarled.

The waiters permitted Mr. Gleason to lie in the archway. For some minutes customers were escorted around the body to their tables. Jackie never again challenged anyone.

Sometimes, when he was lonely, he phoned Genevieve. Her attitude, however, was cautious and suspicious and his gropings toward remembered companionship left him with empty hands. He couldn't stand to be alone, and so Jackie would go to Jimmy Ryan's club on Fifty-second Street, or phone Julie and Jimmy Proce and Paddy Noto and go "bouncing," or call one of many girls he knew and try to arrange a date.

If he was seen in public with the girl, he was condemned because everyone knew that he was married. Some, bravely drunk, would demand to know why Jackie didn't spend more time with his lovely wife and two lovely children. At this he sometimes shrugged. At other times he murmured, "It's a long story, pal," paid his check and walked out.

Sometimes, if it was still early, he took the girl to his suite and mixed a drink. If she was on the formal and slightly hostile side, Gleason had a device that seldom failed. Under the bed was an old broken-down record player. It had a loose connection, and while Gleason stirred the ice into the drinks he wandered toward the head of the bed and, with his foot, gave the record player a little kick. This was sufficient to start a record entitled "How High the Moon" and was followed by "Love, Your Magic Spell Is Everywhere," which, in turn, was followed by "I'm in the Mood for Love" and "I Only Have Eyes for You."

What with the drink and the music, and Jackie's portrayal of the lonesome boy, a girl could hardly do anything except relax.

The world of radio made a belated feint at Jackie Gleason in August 1944. He had been a guest on several programs, and he had, for a short time, been on the "Edelbrau Hour." But now Willie Webber booked Jackie to star on the "Old Gold Radio Show" at $1,000 a week. It was a pretty good show. Two of the supporting acts were singers Perry Como and Andy Russell. Gleason lasted ten weeks and the $10,000 lasted eleven.

Frequently, Jackie borrowed money before he earned it, and Willie Webber, who always showed up the morning after a broadcast for Gleason's check, puzzled and pouted over payments of $200 and $150. When Jackie was a guest star on the "Kate Smith Show," Webber paid a spy to watch him and to prevent him from drawing any money in advance. The spy reported back, at showtime, that the comedian had not borrowed any money and had talked to no one except a network executive who had shaken hands with Gleason and left.

In the morning Webber collected Jackie's pay—sixty-four cents. He had the check framed for his office wall, knowing that Jackie would pay him his commission sooner or later. It would take time, but all bills would be paid.

When Gleason was solvent again he decided to move. He was at the Edison Hotel (he would be back there again) and a great number of the guests on the upper floors were going out of their minds listening to Dixieland bands at three and four and five in the morning. The complaints piled up on the manager's desk daily, but, he was an admirer of Jackie's, and he hated to throw him out. Instead, he waited until Gleason was away for a week or two, and during that relief the manager had the suite sound-proofed.

When Jackie returned, he staged a big band party in his quarters and had twenty or thirty friends over for a "ball." Before dawn he phoned the manager.

"Any complaints from next door?" he growled.

"No," the manager said.

"Then," Gleason snapped, "they must be listening."

Around this time he rented a big apartment on East Thirty-sixth Street. It had twenty-foot-high beamed ceilings and a wrought-iron balcony and a lot of period furniture that looked as though it had come out of Rudolph Valentino's Falcon's Lair. He was in it but a short time when he phoned Webber.

"Pal, I got to have a pool table."

"What for?"

"To shoot pool on, my friend."

"Now, Jackie, I don't know."

"Go out and get me a pool table. It doesn't have to be new, just as long as the cushions are good and the cloth isn't ripped. It shouldn't come to more than a hundred or a hundred and fifty. You can take it out of my end."

"When do you have to have it, Jackie."

"Right now."

To the kid from Halsey Street, this was a distinguishing mark of success. He shot pool at all hours of the day and the night in his own home. Then, as suddenly as the table came, it disappeared. All it had proved to him was that he still had the sure touch with a cue.

The war ended and among the homecomers was Sergeant Tony Amico. He phoned Jackie, said he had been discharged and, in a timid way, wanted to know whether Gleason wanted to redeem his old pledge. Jackie could hardly have been more joyous. He demanded that Tony take a cab and come over right away—and "bring your things."

Tony had been married since the old Club Miami days, and the marriage hadn't quite worked out. So he was separated, as Jackie was separated. The sergeant reminded Gleason that he had once said that "someday, maybe," when Jackie had made a big hit and a lot of money, he would employ his old pal as a valet, or dresser, or man Friday. Had the time arrived?

"In a way, yes, Tone," said Jackie. "In another way, no. I can make ten or fifteen times what I made back in Newark, but it isn't steady dough. Sometimes I make a lot. Sometimes there isn't a dime coming in."

"I understand."

"I'll tell you what. You got a job?"

"Nothing."

"Okay. Suppose you move in with me. Hell, we might as well be broke together. And I'll tell you what I'll do. You act as my valet, or butler, or whatever you want to call it, and I will pay you seventy-five bucks a week when I'm working, plus board and keep, and nothing when I'm broke. Does that sound any good to you, Tone?"

Tony Amico beamed. "Best offer I've had all week," he said. "Sure, that's great."

"It's a deal?" Jackie asked, with hand outstretched.

"It's a deal," said Tony. They shook hands on it.

Tony had a fine, perceptive mind, and he understood this deal better than Jackie. Gleason always needed someone to talk to in the lonely hours, but it had to be someone he could trust. It had to be someone who was better at listening than at speaking. This person would also have to be someone who could reciprocate the affection that Jackie feels for a real friend. In addition to all this, it would have to be someone who was willing to act the part of a manservant, with all the duties that would entail.

Amico of the pearly teeth and deep dimples was one of the few men who could carry out an assignment like this without losing the friendship, the employer-employee relationship, or his own self-respect. Tony took the job and loved it. Gleason, for the first time in years, felt at home at home. Now, if he could get some work . . .

Jackie might have had a good job the following week if he had not smelled decay in a new play. It was called *The Duchess Misbehaves,* and in it Jackie was to play the part of the painter, Goya, who painted the nude duchess. He read the script and didn't like it. The comedy, he felt, needed strengthening and some of the situations sounded weak. It was a musical, and before the rehearsals he asked the producer for permission to call in a writer friend, Joe Bigelow, to doctor the script. Permission was granted, and the two men worked far into the night on East Thirty-sixth Street and there isn't any doubt that, if they had been permitted to go on doctoring, they would have devised a brand-new play in which the sole resemblance to the original would have been the name Goya.

Jackie phoned the producer one day and asked for permission to put in two more songs. The producer said no. In that case, Jackie said, I quit. In that case, the producer said, you'll do nothing of the kind. Your contract is for the run of the play. Read it again.

Gleason reread the contract. It was for the run of the play all right and there was no way out. Under Equity rules, Gleason had to appear in it and had to stay with it.

In the morning he made three phone calls. One was to the producer; one was to the brothers Shubert; one was to his own doctor. The message to all three was the same: during the night something had happened to his knee and the pain was terrible and interminable. Would they all come right over, please, and see what they could do? They would, and did.

The producer brought his own doctor. The Shuberts had one

too. And, with Jackie's physician, it was a good medical gathering. Gleason was propped up in bed. Three pillows were under the knee. Several yards of bandage were around the knee, and this was held on with one-inch adhesive. Over all was about six ounces of Mercurochrome.

The Shubert doctor tried to touch the knee lightly and Jackie roared in pain. Tony came running from another room and looked accusingly at the doctor. The producer's doctor was not intimidated and he tapped the knee with one finger. The comedian screamed and punched one hand into the palm of the other. The three doctors went into a huddle and their diagnosis was that Jackie had a focus of infection in the knee resulting from a throat disorder. There was no way that anyone could prophesy how long it would take for him to recover and there was no point in holding him to a contract which he wasn't physically able to fulfill.

The Duchess Misbehaves opened, and it closed. And yet, the specter of the great painter, Goya, achieved a revenge upon Gleason when, shortly afterward, a girl friend of Jackie's named her wire-haired dog De Goya. Soon she brought him over to Jackie's apartment. De Goya was a well-behaved dog with slight delusions of grandeur. He did not like to lie on the floor; De Goya preferred chairs and couches. He had long, untrimmed toenails.

The furniture had tight, shiny, figured satin covers. When the lady and De Goya left, Gleason and Amico sat on the floor until long after dawn snipping thousands of loose threads. Afterward, they waited in silent tension as the landlady critically inspected the premises. Then they vacated the apartment and went back to the Edison Hotel.

The Duchess Misbehaves closed ignominiously. So did the apartment on East Thirty-sixth Street.

If Jackie Gleason had assessed his career at this time (it is very doubtful that he did), he would have had to concede that he had reached his peak as a night-club comic and was not destined to go any farther. He was now known in the trade as a smart, earthy comic with no known fears. He was worth between $500 and $1,000 a week to any club which could afford him. His engagements were chronicled in the theatrical trade journals and his buffoonery filled space for the Broadway columnists. He was in good odor with most of the club owners, but he lacked a touch of greatness. Perhaps he lacked a hallmark of character, a specialized style—something which made comedians like Bert Lahr and Lou Holtz and Bert Wheeler and Milton Berle worth $5,000 or more a week.

Another thing which mitigated against Gleason was that he was something of a slob in the trade. He didn't stand on the niceties of ethical dignity. If your comedian was ill, you could call Gleason at noon and he would report for work at 8:00 P.M. the same day. If a performer was hurt, and Gleason was his friend, Jackie would take his place for nothing. Further, he had no economic bracket, as witness the fact that on one evening he would run across to Brooklyn to act in a show for $200, while, in almost the next breath, his manager was demanding $3,000 a week at the Roxy Theatre. The word also got around that he was "on the sauce"— a heavy drinker—though this was unjust because, with the exception of the Club 18 session with Joe Frisco, Gleason had never failed to appear for a scheduled performance in full possession of his faculties.

At this stage—late 1945 and 1946—it looked as though Jackie Gleason, after ten years of the hurly-burly and heartaches of learning a trade, would not achieve his goal of being "bigger than Berle." The closest he would come to this would hinge on a phone call from Nicky Blair to Willie Webber.

"Willie," said Blair, "I want to see you. Come right over."

Nicky Blair is a club owner of standing, and the history of this dark and murmurous man goes back to the 1920s, when Greenwich Village was an important stop on the night-club circuit and Larry Fay and Helen Morgan were big names in the business. At the moment he owned a part of a night club called the Carnival, a gay little place on the ground floor of the Capitol Hotel. In this venture, Toots Shor was a fairly silent partner.

"You know," said Blair, when Webber sat in his office, "some friends and I are running the Carnival. We had Milton Berle booked to go in, but he has come down with laryngitis and one hell of a cold. He won't be able to start, Willie, and we were thinking of using your boy Gleason."

Willie thinks fast and accurately. His shiny skull pounded with the possibilities: (1) Gleason envied Berle and would whoop at the chance to do a better job than Berle; (2) no comedian in possession of his senses would want to walk into a place where the patrons thought that they were paying to see Milton Berle— but, where Berle was concerned, Jackie Gleason was not in possession of his senses; (3) Berle must have been promised a lot of money for the appearance.

"How much?" Webber said.

"Three thousand."

"I think it will work out."

"Good, Willie."

That night Jackie's pride was in flower. He showed up at Shor's saying that he had been asked to step into the Carnival for a week while Berle was ill. He would not take a dime less than Berle had been promised, he said, and, if Berle was sick for a week and working on a guarantee, then Milton should pay Jackie the $3,000, not Nicky Blair. It was soothing to the ego to know that, if Berle wasn't available, they would pick Gleason. But that wasn't sufficient for Jackie. He wanted to be funnier than Berle and he wanted everybody to know that he was funnier.

The management of the Carnival played the situation for the extra dollars, by neglecting to announce that Milton Berle was ill. On opening night the club was full of people who liked Berle and who were paying to see Berle. In fact, the management waited until the single spotlight was on the stage microphone, and Jackie was in the wings waiting to go on, before they announced, in an off-stage voice, that Milton Berle had been taken ill and, in his place, the services of that well-known comic, Jackie Gleason, had been secured. The boo from the crowd could be heard in the street.

Jackie grinned through it, held his hands up for silence, and said, "Folks, flattery will get you nowhere." He went into the fastest line of jokes he had ever used and, in ninety seconds, he had the patrons laughing. In three minutes, the laughs were cutting in on the next joke, and by the time he walked off the applause was so thunderous that some of the customers stood to display the final accolade. Blair ran to Gleason and threw his arms around him. Nicky always admired courage.

He finished his week well, but Berle did not pay him; Blair did. Secondly, Jackie heard that Berle was promised more than the $3,000 given to a substitute. Third, as a matter of professional courtesy, Jackie expected a thank-you note from Milton Berle and did not get it. He would not forget these things.

A few weeks later Webber asked Jackie to accompany him to the opening of La Conga. A Webber client named Lenny Kent was opening, and he needed a few name stars to drop in and wish him luck. Jackie said that he would be glad to go. They sat at a ringside table.

Berle was also present. He was introduced first, and he came on stage with pad and pencil, pretending to copy the jokes of others. He looked around and drew a laugh when he said, "Out in front I see two of my favorite comedians—Jackie Gleason." When the laugh died, Gleason roared, "I wish you were *one* of mine!"

The next meeting of these two occurred at the Copacabana. The ringside tables were laced with celebrities. Milton Berle was at the microphone calling actors to the floor. His device was to get a celebrity to the microphone, say something funny and, before the other could reply, grab his arm and yank him away from the microphone so that whatever was said in rebuttal was lost in the vacuum.

Berle called Gleason to the floor and Jackie strode, beaming and bowing, into the trap. When he was at Berle's side, Milton tried to say something into the microphone, but Jackie snatched it away. Berle then tried to grab Gleason's sleeve, and yelled "ouch!" The sleeve was full of straight pins. Jackie smiled at the crowd and said, "I helped you out at the Carnival, pal. But I couldn't do it tonight for five thousand." He walked off.

Every actor's ambition, at one time or another, was to play the Palace Theatre at Times Square. In the old days this was the glittering temple to the two-a-day art—the mecca of all vaudevillians. It was as far from the Halsey Theatre as the office of the mayor of Wet Moccasin, Oklahoma, is from the White House.

And yet, when the Palace got around to summoning Gleason, it was not the Palace Theatre in New York—it was situated in Columbus, Ohio. There, what was left of vaudeville was being shouldered off stage by motion pictures.

Jackie got top billing. His name was in lights over the top of the marquee. Others on the bill were Marva Louis, Guy Kibbee, Tommy Reynolds and His Orchestra, Eve Condos, and a motion picture called *Betrayal from the East*, with Lee Tracy.

He turned down another booking because his name wasn't set in big enough type. The Loew's office had booked him as an Extra Added Attraction at the Capitol Theatre. The main attraction was to be Jimmy Dorsey and His Orchestra. Gleason said he'd appear provided that the newspaper ads carried his name, at the bottom, as big as Dorsey's was at the top.

On the day of the opening Jackie barged into Webber's office, past the young comics warming the bench and into the sanctum.

"Look," he said, flashing a newspaper advertisement. "One third billing." (His name was set in type one third the size of Dorsey's.)

"So?" said Webber.

"So," bellowed Jackie, "I'm not going to show up."

"Now wait a minute," Willie said.

"Now you wait a minute," Jackie said. "I get a lot of kicking around and I don't like it. You're my manager. You call those people and tell them that they violated the agreement. As a result, I won't be there."

"It's on the marquee," said Willie softly.

"I wouldn't care if it was in Roman candles. I'm not going."

He didn't. The only concession he made was to phone Jimmy Dorsey and say, "I got nothing against you, pal. But . . ."

A man must have a fierce kind of pride to drop a big date at the Capitol Theatre when he has no money. Gleason has that kind of pride—or vanity, or ego. The profession is full of actors like him, but few have it to the degree that it has obsessed Gleason. He wants every last measure due him, not a bit more, not a whit less. He will do fifteen minutes of jokes for $10,000, and he will do an hour of the same at some communion breakfast for nothing—but don't chisel him on the billing in either case.

Instead of the Capitol, Jackie was booked into the Chanticleer in Baltimore. When he arrived, he was in one of his "deep-thinking binges" and wasn't very funny. The only thing he liked about the club that first night was a line of chorus girls who knew how to dance. They had life and sparkle and, by inquiring around the Chanticleer, Gleason learned that a girl named June Taylor had assembled the girls, worked out the choreography, and trained the group.

Jackie met her. She was a little blonde, a girl with ageless eyes who smiled only when there was something at which to smile. She introduced her husband, Sol Lerner, a New York lawyer, and the three sat at a table and discussed show business. Miss Taylor said that she too had danced at one time, but after a serious illness had quit to train others. She now had six fine girls, including her younger sister Marilyn, and, with any luck, the show would keep moving, right into New York.

Gleason was impressed. This woman did not talk "big"; she talked sense. She seemed to know music, too, and whenever she wanted to stress a musical point, her foot began to tap the floor, her palm hit the table, and she whispered the notes of the song at the tempo she thought was right for it.

"Does the audience change here with each show?" Jackie asked.

"No." Sol Lerner shook his head. "They come into town and they stay."

"That's great. I got material for one show."

"You're a big fellow," said June, "and I notice that you're light on your feet. How about doing a number with my girls?"

"Sure. But I need a fast tempo. Something that really moves."

"That's no problem. I know a number called 'Steppin Out with My Baby' and it comes up fast like this." The foot and palm and lips began to move and Jackie cocked his head and listened. "I'll stage the girls around you," Miss Taylor said.

"It's gotta be fast," he said. "Let me show you." And Jackie hummed "Just One of Those Things" in racy, bouncy style. June Taylor nodded with the tempo.

"It can be done."

A few nights later Gleason opened with an array of pretty girls around him. It was fast and bright and it set the key to the whole show. It conditioned the customers, and although it wasn't a new idea by any means it was new to Gleason, and he found that it started the show in high gear.

Jackie seldom forgot anything he learned.

In the early part of 1947 the talk everywhere was of television, and the people were out buying ten-inch sets or the giant twelve-and-a-half-inch size. Small metal trees bloomed on the roof tops of the nation. The bartenders were among the first to learn to spin dials and flip switches. In wavering pictures and quavering voice, the whole world began to come into each home on an opaque glass screen.

Gleason could not afford to buy a set. As always, he needed work. Webber was phoning all over the East, and as the late spring arrived Jackie was still sitting in Toots Shor's; still waiting for the word; still meditating and spinning a coin on the bar and watching it settle. The best that Willie could get was a week end at Ross Fenton Farms in June, and, as Jackie said in exasperation, "What's that? A taste of work. I need more than that. Much more."

At the bar, Jay Jackson, an announcer, sat at his side and said, "How are things?"

"Lousy," said Gleason.

"Need some dough?"

Jackie brightened. "I could stand a little eating money."

"I haven't got much, Jack. I can spare twenty, though."

"Twenty!" Gleason snorted. "I need two thousand!"

In his room he paced the floor, tired of borrowing, tired of signing tabs, sick of kicking himself for always spending more than he made, worried about a score of bills closing in silently from all sides. He had no place to go. Everybody in the world had someplace, someone, something.

Jackie remembered that there was a headwaiter in town who admired him almost to the point of idolatry. Maybe—just maybe —he could phone the headwaiter and work him for fifty dollars for a week or two.

"This is Jackie," he said sweetly, unctuously. "Gleason. Remember me? Good. Look, pal, I'm in a little jam. I need fifty clams in a hurry. What? The Hotel Edison. You will? Say, that's swell of you, pal. Thanks."

He could hardly wait. Fifteen interminable minutes passed before there was a rap on the door. When he opened it, with a low bow, there stood a waiter with a tray. On the tray were fifty cherrystones.

The next noontime he was at Shor's again and he was telling the story of the fifty clams to Davey Shelley and Lee Meyers, and they looked glum and unenthused. Jackie, who often provides his own morale lift, clapped Shelley on the back and said, "Pal, I'm going to take you and Lee someplace."

"Where?"

"First, we got to do it the right way." He looked in his pocket and he had two dollars and two nickels. "Yes," he said, "that will do it."

"What are you talking about?" Meyers asked.

"You guys are with me. We brush this joint off, and you're both with me. First, a phone call."

He disappeared into a booth, left the door open, and talked for a minute. Then he came back.

"It will be here in a minute," he said brightly. "Bartender, give us a small refill before we go."

"What will be here?" asked Davey.

"When we go, we go first class, don't we? A Cadillac is coming."

"Nuts," said Shelley in disgust. "Where are we going to go in a Cadillac?"

"You're with me, pal."

In ten minutes a uniformed chauffeur came through the revolving door and looked around. He tipped his cap. "Mr. Gleason," he said, "the car is outside."

Jackie made a fluttering motion with his hands. "And away we go."

The three finished their drinks and piled into the back of the big black limousine. Gleason gave the chauffeur an address. Three men, with a total of perhaps seven dollars among them, rode noiselessly and elegantly through the streets of New York,

across town, over to Eleventh Avenue, and up the West Side. The
chauffeur stopped at Sixty-eighth Street, pulling up beside a play-
ground. He looked back at Gleason. Two men in the back looked
at Gleason. Jackie got out and held the door for the other
two.

In front of the glittering bumper of the car was an aged Italian
with handlebar mustaches. Before him was a little red-and-white
cart with a little red-and-white umbrella over the top. The sign
said, "Hot Dogs." The Italian looked up happily and said, "Hey,
Mister Jack! How you do!"

Gleason, with dignity, said, "I want you to meet my friends,
Mr. Shelley and Mr. Meyers."

Davey, who was afraid that he was in some sort of an emotional haze, nodded to the man and whispered, "What are we
doing here?"

Jackie ignored him. He spoke to the merchant. "I'll have one of
those—" he pointed. "Put some of that delicious stuff on top,
please." The Italian lifted a bluish frankfurter and slapped it in
a white roll. He drew a mustard stick back and forth across it.
Then he took a can of ground hot Italian pepper and shook it on
the frankfurter. Carefully, and with dignity, he shook the water
out of a forkful of grayish sauerkraut and placed it on the rest
of the stuff.

"Now, my good man," said Jackie, "what do we have for a
beverage?"

"Always the same, Mister Jack," the merchant said. "Orange,
grape . . ."

"I will have the usual," he said, and turned to his friends.
"Forgive me for jumping in ahead of my guests," he said, "but I
go crazy over this man's frankfurters and I can't wait."

"Nothing for me, thanks," said Meyers.

Shelley shook his head sadly. "I know I'll hate myself for this,
Jackie, but I'm going to skip this treat."

Shelley counted. Gleason ate eleven of the hot dogs, paid the
man, complimented him on his delicious wares, and promised to
be back. Then, with Lee and Davey looking uneasily at each
other across Gleason's chest, they drove back to Shor's restaurant
in the rented Cadillac. When they got out, he thanked the driver,

tipped him with what money he had left, and said: "Tell them to send the bill, please."

Two weeks later, in desperation, Jackie accepted the week-end job at Ross Fenton Farms. This is a big summer club just behind Asbury Park, New Jersey, on the edge of Deal Lake. They wanted a comedian who could do impersonations, so on Thursday night Jackie went down to an Asbury Park hotel with Jay C. Flippen and Shelley.

They sat in the room and ordered a few drinks. Jackie was worried about his impersonations because he hadn't practiced them in a long time. He stood, turned his back on his mystified friends, and then turned to face them, using the flat, querulous voice of Cary Grant.

"Now look here, Judy," Gleason said.

"Who is it supposed to be?" Shelley asked, interrupting.

"Who is it supposed to be?" Gleason roared. "Who is it supposed to be? It's Cary Grant, that's who it's supposed to be!"

Shelley shrugged. He looked at Flippen. "Does it sound like Cary Grant to you?" Flippen said nothing, just shook his head dolefully.

Gleason turned his back and then swung around and did another impersonation. It was pretty sad. He tried a third one. He turned his coat collar up, stuck his upper teeth out over his lower lip, twitched a couple of times, and said, "Okay, Louie. Drop the gun."

Shelley began to snap his fingers excitedly. "I know that one," he said hopefully. "At least I think I do—Bogart?"

Gleason put his finger tips on his hips and nodded sarcastically.

On opening night Shelley and Flip sat at ringside as Jackie came on stage, beautifully attired, and went into a little speech about how happy he was to be back in good old Asbury Park, of how nice it was to see so many old friends out front, and of how sorry he was that he was going to be present only for the week end. He said that he would like to open his little act with a few impersonations.

Jackie turned his back, swung around, and started to say, "Now look here, Judy." He didn't get through the whole sentence because, through the haze, he could see Davey Shelley shaking his head no. For a moment Jackie compressed his lips and maintained his composure. Then he roared with laughter and the people out front looked at one another to find out what was funny.

"Seriously, ladies and gentlemen," he said, wiping his eyes, "my first impersonation will be of that well-known movie star, Cary Grant."

He turned his back, swung around slowly, and, to his horror, there was Davey still shaking his head dolefully. This broke Gleason up. He became hysterical. He leaned on the piano and shook. The curtain came down. The manager fired him. When he was asked why, the manager said simply, "The man has no act."

Jackie was never so poor that he couldn't afford a little charity. When he had no money, he donated time, the only commodity he had. There was a man on Broadway named Gay Brown (author's note: a fictitious name) who ran a small sound-tape business. Someone told Jackie that Brown had a bad heart and no money. Gleason had a talk with the man and found that his major work was trying to get backstage at theaters to interview name stars. He carried a tape recorder, did a short topical interview, and then tried to sell the tape to a local radio station for whatever small sum the traffic would bear.

Sometimes Brown was admitted backstage. More often he was turned away as a nuisance. Gleason studied the pale face and said, "Let me do some of this stuff. I know a lot of stars. I'll put a few laughs into the talk."

Gleason lugged the tape recorder around and fashioned the interviews. The radio stations bought these tapes because, for a small amount of money and no effort, they acquired the services of a well-known comedian and a news-worthy celebrity.

One warm afternoon Lee Meyers and Jackie were walking on Fifth Avenue when Brown waved hello and stopped to talk. The little radio man said that things were going better for him and, as he was talking, he toppled into the gutter. Jackie crouched beside him and held Brown's head on his knee.

"Quick!" he said to Meyers. "Get some brandy. This is a heart attack for sure."

Lee ran down Fifty-second Street and turned into the first

172 THE GOLDEN HAM

open saloon. "Hurry!" he said to the bartender. "Jackie Gleason's out there with Gay Brown. Heart attack. Come on, brandy!"

The bartender ran for a bottle. "Who," he said as he poured, "had the attack?"

"Brown, of course. What's that got to do with it?"

"For Gleason," the bartender said, "brandy. For the other guy, who's paying for it?"

Another of Gleason's private hobbies was picking talent. Few understood better than he how difficult it is to get "the one big break." Few worked as indefatigably to discover talent and to give it an encouraging shove.

And yet there was a weakness in his selection of talent. Unconsciously, Gleason confused class with talent, or perhaps it was that the little people who needed help had to have class first before he could recognize their talent.

Class is a difficult quality to define. In a word, it is the quality of the nonwhiner; one who accepts the buffeting of life without complaint; one who will give freely of his possessions to his friends even when there isn't much to give; a person whose loyalty to others who have class is unqualified and without limit; one who lives large and carelessly even when he's penniless.

Gleason, who seldom boasts, once defined class this way: "I was in New York and I had a little dough and I wanted to gamble. I called a joint in Las Vegas and I said to the guy, 'This is Jackie Gleason. Will you please put a hundred on the red for me?' and the man said, 'Just a minute, Mr. Gleason. Hold the phone.' I waited, and in a minute he was back. 'Sorry, Mr. Gleason,' he said. 'You lost.' 'Thanks, pal,' I said. 'I wired the hundred to you a half hour ago.' That's class."

Sometimes Jackie discovered people who had already been discovered. A case in point is a tall redhead whom Gleason called "Little Abner," but whose legal name is John Pierre Lescoulie. Years before Lescoulie thought of leaning against the bar in Shor's, he was a radio hit on the West Coast and had amassed a fortune and spent it. He was also a serious student of Shakespeare and this did not seem to fit with the big toothy smile, the flaming hair, and the shy, All-American-boy attitude which marked Lescoulie as the type who would look more at home as a disciple of Benny Goodman.

Little Abner arrived at Shor's place at 11:00 P.M. every night. He had a job as a lonesome disk jockey on radio station WOR, and his program opened at 2:00 A.M. and closed at 5:00 A.M. He was in the restaurant to try to get some celebrities to appear as guests and to swap small talk between the spinning of the records.

Toots noticed him first at the bar a few times, said hello, got talking, and found that this big quiet kid had class. This qualified him for membership in the Shor Set and an introduction to charter member Jackie Gleason. Lescoulie and Gleason became pals almost at once. Jackie appeared on Jack's program many times. Often they made a night of it, carrying packages of beer and sandwiches to the studio. On the air, they chatted, swapped Broadway gossip, told jokes and background stories of songs and, in general, had a "ball." In the final hour of the broadcast, after 4:00 A.M., Lescoulie played only the best jazz records and at this time there was no conversation. Gleason listened reverentially.

"You got class, Little Abner," Jackie said one evening. "Someday you and I are going to be working together."

Lescoulie, who was working, believed the man who wasn't.

One of the facets of everyday living in which Gleason had little faith was life insurance. No matter how it was discussed, the quotient was death and this was something that always seemed remote. Now and then he would buy a policy under prodding, and, in time, lack of premium payments would cause it to lapse, or borrowings against the face value would reduce it to the status of a low-interest loan. Once in a while someone else would insure Jackie. Willie Webber took out a policy for $50,000 in the early 1940s, paid premiums on it for a long while, and almost collected the money in 1947.

Gleason had had a pain in his side for days. He did not see a doctor until the pain became unrelenting and could be relieved only if he drew his knees up. The examining doctor sent him to the Hospital for Joint Diseases, where it was established that Gleason had a ruptured appendix.

Frankie Hyers, the Club 18 comic, phoned Willie Webber in the morning with the doleful news.

"Better hurry up to the hospital, Willie. Jackie is in bad shape. They sent for the priest."

Webber taxied uptown with his son Stewart and found Hyers downstairs in a waiting room. The faces were grim.

"Let's go up," Willie said.

"No," Frankie said. "They're going to call down."

Willie waited five minutes. "I can't stand it," he said, and got into an elevator. In the room, a curtain was around the bed. A doctor was busy with a hypodermic. A nurse, cool and starched, turned the bedclothes down. The patient, flushed and moist, gulped barrels of air. A priest packed the instruments of eternity and nodded as he left the room.

The nurse looked at Willie. "He can't see you now," she said.

"Is he all right?"

"As well as can be expected."

"What's the doc giving him?"

"Penicillin."

"What's that?"

"A new drug. You'll have to leave now."

They left. The word hit Broadway. Bad news has zip. It leaped across the roads, curled around the skyscrapers and licked its way along telephone wires. Gleason was dying. Gleason was dead. Gleason had died screaming for a priest. Gleason had a priest. Jackie had been a good guy. Why is it the good ones always go early?

Nobody thought to tell Gen the news that day. Nobody.

Two days later Webber and Stewart tiptoed into the hospital room to whisper hello to The Greatest. They were stunned when Gleason, sitting high on the bed, sang out, "Well, Baldy. You thought you'd collect that fifty G's, eh? For your information, my friend, I'll outlive you."

Webber was so relieved that when Jackie was discharged the agent took Gleason to his own tailor and loaned the comedian

$800 for eight new suits. A week after that the tailor phoned Webber.

"We like Gleason," he said. "Nice boy. Do us a favor and take your business somewhere else, Willie."

"Don't be fresh to me. What happened?"

"Last week the suits fit fine. He was back today. Now he's too fat for them. We can't afford him."

When Gleason is healthy, he is very, very healthy. His body is full of verve and the tanks are topped off with high-octane energy. Fat or thin, he walks fast, talks fast, thinks fast. He almost burns the oxygen through which he strides. Phones are flipped to ear, pencils execute dervish dances on paper, telegraph wires sing with messages, people enter a room with him, listen, nod and leave, and Jackie never seems to tire.

He was healthy now, but he could not get a real job. He could get a few weeks at Billy Rose's Diamond Horseshoe, or he could get a few weeks on radio, but nothing lasted. Willie Webber waited until Jackie was working before he dropped the fat one.

First, Willie explained it to Mrs. Webber. "Take this radio show he's working on," he said. "I have to leave the house at the beach at nine A.M. Right? I drive in and pick Jackie up at ten. I drive him to wherever they're rehearsing. Right? While he rehearses, I sit. When they call time for lunch, I go with him to Toots's. We eat. Then we go back to rehearsal. I sit all afternoon. Comes six, maybe, rehearsal is over and we go back to Shor's. We eat. Then we go to the studio and wait for showtime. He does a show and now he wants to relax. Where can he relax except Shor's? I'm not much at drinking so I stand around at the bar laughing. Sometimes my stomach hurts. At some hour of the morning, I go get my car and drive out to the beach.

"This is a living? I love this boy and he must love me or he would have gone over to a big agency long ago. But I figure if I let him go now I can add a few years onto my life."

That day, when Webber met Jackie, the manager made a little speech. "Look, Jack," he said. "I don't think that I can do anything more for you. You need *all* of somebody's time. I tried to do it, Jackie, but I'm not getting any younger. I'd like to spend more time at the office."

Gleason studied his friend's tired, pinched face and then he said what he always says when a decision hurts him. "If that's the way you want it, pal . . ."

Within a few days Tony Amico quit. He too had a deep affection for Gleason, but he was possessed of a despairing feeling that neither he nor Jackie was getting anywhere in life.

"A guy I knew in the Army," said Tony, "has a little restaurant in Dallas. He wants to give me a partnership, but I don't know what to do."

Gleason looked up from his toast.

"Take it," he said.

"I don't want to hurt you, Jackie."

"Take it. Things are slow up here."

"I figured that you and me . . ."

"Don't worry. We'll be together again." Gleason held out his hand. "If the thing doesn't go, you can always come back."

It didn't go. Tony liked Dallas, but Dallas did not even notice his presence, and, rather than admit failure to his friend Jackie, Tony re-enlisted in the army and served a hitch in Korea.

This, perhaps, was the real low point in the career of Jackie Gleason. On the personal side, he had lost his wife, his manager, his valet. On the professional side, he was a funnyman whom no producer took seriously; an artistic bum who could be substituted when a better man was sick; a comedian of no particular character; a theatrical personality who was *almost* a star. This was bad, because Gleason was too big for the small clubs and not big enough for the $5,000-a-week places.

It added up to unemployment.

Jackie Gleason will often brood alone, but never in public. The bluff exterior, the hearty greeting, the quick quip are all a part of the man who has "class." He will not whine and, if he manages to borrow ten dollars, he will be the first to toss the ten on the bar for the next round of drinks. But this was a very bad time, and it seemed to go on unendurably.

He wired Sammy Lewis in Hollywood and Sammy replied that Jackie had a job, for as long as he wanted to work, at Slapsie

Maxie's. The salary would be $325 a week. It sounded good.

It wasn't, really. He had to send $150 to Genevieve, and he needed $100 to live in an apartment on South Sycamore, and, after Social Security and taxes had been deducted, he had very little bar money. He needed booze money at home too, because Gleason liked lots of people around, and among the people he like to see regularly were Paul Douglas, Sammy Lewis, Davey Shelley, Jay C. Flippen, Frankie Hyers and his writer friend, Joe Bigelow. Some of them brought "broads," but, since Jackie could never remember the names, all girls became Mildred and all boys became Tom.

Still, for many weeks Jackie behaved with, for him, discretion. He drank little, he worked hard, he went on a diet, and he dropped to 178 pounds. He looked so young, so handsome, so angelic, that Davey Shelley was touched. Davey's stepfather, the composer-producer Buddy DeSylva, was planning a lawn party on his estate. This was to be anything but a brawl. Only ladies and gentlemen were to be invited and one would no more reach toward the butler's tray of Martinis more than once than one would be caught diving into the swimming pool in one's underwear.

"This once," said Shelley, "I think it is safe to invite you."

"Pal," said Jackie earnestly, "you know me."

"That," said Davey, "is the inner voice which keeps ringing the warning bell. All I can tell you is that everybody who is anybody in Hollywood will be there. This is a real opportunity for you. You stay sober and I'll move you right in with these people."

"You know how I handle these situations," said Gleason.

"Okay. But I want you to build up to it. Oliver Hardy is going to be there and this is a guy you always loved. Every move you make you're doing Oliver Hardy, and if it isn't Hardy, it's Lloyd Hamilton. Let all these people take the floor, Jack. You hang back. You be the nice quiet guy and they'll all go crazy about you."

"Pal," said Jackie. "We have nothing to worry about. Not a thing in the world."

Two days later Shelley watched Gleason being fitted by a tailor with a new suit for the party. Jackie was standing on a small platform and the tailor was measuring the shoulders and the sleeve length. It was an Oxford gray cheviot model, thirty-nine dollars anywhere.

"I want to look right for the party," Jackie said gravely.

The tailor was snipping cloth from the bottoms of the trousers to make cloth buttons for the cuffs.

"That material will come off on chairs and rugs," Shelley said.

"This?" said Jackie. "Never. This is real French cheviot. This runs to a lot of dough, but I told the tailor I'll advertise his joint, so he's letting me have it for thirty-nine bucks."

Two days before the big party Gleason arrived at the DeSylva mansion in the afternoon. He was about as far from being intoxicated as he was from being sober. Some friends of Mr. and Mrs. DeSylva's were sitting around the big swimming pool. The conversation was subdued. The French windows from the drawing room were open and soft music could be heard. Gleason gave all hands a big hello and a deep bow. He looked around, serenely ready for anything.

"Davey," he said, "you know I'm the world's greatest swimmer. I was a lifeguard once and—"

"You going to start telling me lifeguard?" Shelley snapped. "You were never near water in your life unless you fell in that Brooklyn canal."

Jackie smiled pityingly at one and all. "The world's greatest swimmer," he said softly. He held a hand out toward the water. "Would you join me in the pool? We'll do a couple of laps."

"Nothing doing," said Shelley. "The man just put the chlorine in."

"Don't worry," said Jackie. "I won't swim in that particular spot."

He went inside, put on some swim trunks and came out thumping his chest. The air was cool, and most of the guests took their tall drinks and moved inside. Davey stayed to watch because he had a big stake in what this man might do—a happy home, for instance.

Jackie plunged in gracefully, swam down to the shallow end of the pool, turned like a professional, swam back to the deep end with long, slow strokes, swam back again, turned, floated on his back, spit a stream of water, flapped his arms against his sides and barked like a seal. In ten minutes he was out. He looked a bit blue, and Shelley went inside and turned on the hot water in the shower. Jackie ducked in, soaped himself briskly, hummed an aria, got out and dressed.

"Well, pal," he said to Davey. "Let's have a little nip."

Shelley was worried. He had seen all of these signs before, and they were not signs of happiness. He fixed two drinks and felt nervous and he knew exactly why he was nervous. Then he noticed that Gleason's eyes were getting red. They became redder and redder and they bugged out more and more until they resembled two hard-boiled eggs in a bowl of chili sauce.

"There's something wrong with my eyes," Jackie said. "I can't see."

"It's probably the chlorine, Jackie." Davey jumped up and ran into the drawing room. One of the guests was a doctor. He called Gleason out and put him on a couch and examined both eyes. Then he phoned a drugstore and asked that a lotion be sent up at once.

"You lie down and stay that way," the doctor said.

"It's just as easy to drink lying down as it is standing up," Jackie said. "So, if you people don't mind, I'll have a drink."

It is *not* as easy to drink lying down as it is standing up, but Jackie did it anyway. When you are supine, and you cannot see the fluid level in the glass, it is not even good for furniture. He also asked for a cigarette and, as he couldn't see an ash tray, the debris went on the floor.

"Well," Mrs. DeSylva whispered at one point, "there goes my rug." When she saw the couch going too, she said to her son, "You brought this bum out here—why can't he drink like other people?"

"Now I can't see at all," Gleason murmured.

"Maybe," said the doctor, who was now tuned in on both ends of the dialogue, "you'd better put him in the breakfast room. Put out the lights and draw the blinds. That might help."

Gleason was assisted to the breakfast room, but he is not a man who can sit alone in darkness very long. Drinks helped to while the hours away, and Davey brought them. In the evening, more guests arrived and Cass Daley cooked spaghetti, but she cooked so much that everyone had to get on the phone and call more guests so that the spaghetti would not be wasted. The doctor put some drops in Gleason's eyes, and Davey said he was blind in a way other than visually, and matters became mixed up when somebody phoned Irving and Jill Weiss and Jill got on the phone and said, "Well, I'm cooking spaghetti too so I'll bring it with me, and I've got some hot sausage too."

By the time the ladies got to warming the stuff that had already been cooked and cooking the stuff that had only been warmed, they too were in a brave state of mind and someone dropped four ounces of cayenne pepper into the spaghetti to give it body and authority. This had the effect of making the spaghetti so powerful that the cooks dumped in other ingredients calculated to kill the cayenne pepper.

Gleason roared, "How about me? You got me in the dark and I'm hungry."

This excited the pity of the cooks, so they tried a family-sized platter of spaghetti and hot sausage on him first. He wanted wine with it because, as he pointed out, any old slob knows that spaghetti is nothing without wine. So wine was brought and he finished a bottle of that.

Afterward, he felt considerable pain and he clutched his eyes and announced that he was going to sue everybody. "And find out the pool man's name," he bellowed. "I'm going to sue him too."

Shelley has "class," but he decided to stop defending his friend for the moment. He asked Sid Silvers to take Jackie home. Silvers is a small man with a tremendous singing voice. The car he had parked outside was probably the first Whippet ever made. It gleamed in the darkness.

Jackie was led to the car and Sid got in and started the motor.

"Sid," Gleason mumbled, "I'm afraid I'm going to be sick."

"Okay, okay," said Silvers, "but not in this car you ain't."

Jackie, who could now see a little bit, got out of the car with elephantine dignity and walked over to a pair of potted evergreens which framed the entrance to the DeSylva estate. In a few minutes Jackie was roaring like a wounded whale and the guests lined up at the French windows to watch. From a distance, both trees now looked Christmassy. Gleason emitted a cry of anguish and Davey ran out to find out the trouble.

Jackie was standing staring at the two trees. "Didn't I have a piece of sausage?" he asked.

Shelley nodded.

"Then," said Gleason, "where the hell is it?"

Shelley is a hard loser. The following day he was in the Gleason apartment reconstructing the mistakes of yesterday and talking about the big party to come.

"Don't worry," Jackie said. "There will be none of that at the party."

"I'm kind of worried," Shelley said. "You know anything about a salad fork?"

"Do I know anything about a salad fork?" Jackie moaned. "Of course I know something about a salad fork."

"Well, we can't have any of that business like yesterday. I got Sammy Lewis coming too and I better nod to you guys when you're supposed to take this or that."

"You're my friend! Would I make a bum out of you?"

"Be careful, even with the butler, Jack. He and his wife worked for the Duke of Windsor. So, please, Jack . . ."

"Look. I'll go like anybody else. I'll wear the new suit and I will do exactly what everybody else does."

"That's the boy," said Davey. "Go like anybody else but yourself. And don't start this business of 'I'll have a double for openers.' Just say, 'I'll have a little Scotch and a lot of water in a tall glass.'"

"Okay. Stop worrying."

"Jackie," said Shelley plaintively, "this time I'd like to see you last. You know something? I've never known you after one o'clock in the morning."

"Stop worrying, will you?"

On the afternoon of the party Jackie found himself flanked. Shelley had him by one arm; Sammy Lewis, the other. On the way out they whispered last-minute instructions on lawn-party behavior.

"The best thing," Sammy Lewis said in a soft aside, "is not to

say anything. Then you can't get into trouble. I'll point out these
people and tell you who they are—"

"You'll tell me!" Jackie bellowed. "You slob. You run a saloon
and you don't know these people any more than I do. Don't tell
me how to act!"

The cherubic trio came onto the lawn in a loud argument.
Lewis, who averages four drinks of Scotch per year, drank all
four at once and, while Davey and Shelley strolled from group
to group saying hello to the ladies with the big hats and the
parasols, began to stagger and shout.

"Get a load of *him!*" Jackie snorted. "Briefing *me!*"

Jackie's behavior was good. It had to be. Shelley seldom released his arm. Sammy Lewis took the other arm, even though
Gleason should have been holding Sammy's arm. Davey, who
was wearing his most courtly manners, introduced his friends to
Mr. and Mrs. Allan Ladd, and Lewis, now bobbing lightly in
the breeze, said, "You're Sue Carol, aren't you? I didn't recognize
you. You got so fat."

Gleason pried both men from his arms and muttered, "Here
I go to the bar. I got to have a couple of belts fast."

He had a few fast drinks, and Shelley, watching all the nice
people under the big green tent, felt a chilling shudder go
through his frame, so he had a few, and afterward he noted that
whenever Jackie was thin he no longer sounded funny—he
sounded surly. Gleason was making witty remarks left and right,
but the guests gave him a faintly amused smile and turned away.

In the chill of the evening, the party moved indoors and Jackie
saw Sammy Lewis almost pass out in a chair, and it made him so
jumpy that he felt he ought to have a few more just to face the
truth.

In the drawing room, Johnny Mercer, at the insistence of the
guests, stood and sang a new song which he had written with
Bobbie Dolan. Irving Berlin played a few favorites on the piano.
The hostess said that everybody had to do something. Phil
Silvers got up and told some stories that were so funny that
Jackie said, "I'm going back to the bar. I can't stand that bum."

"Why not?" said Shelley, becoming a little loud himself. "He's
a nice fellow."

"I don't mean as a fellow," said Gleason, shouting. "I just can't stand a guy who gets laughs. If I don't hear his jokes, I can't re-peat them."

When Jackie returned to the living room, there was no availa-ble sitting space so, in the new woolly suit, he lowered his body onto the off-white chenille rug. By now he was in the aloof mood, looking around at the girls, flicking ashes on the rug, and exud-ing silent wisdom and mystery.

Leo McCarey, director of *Going My Way*, saw the ashes fall-ing and asked David Butler to "grab that fellow's cigarette before it goes into the rug."

Gleason heard it and said, "I can handle the cigarette. It so happens that I heard about you and Gene Fowler and those guys. Now don't start to tell me, pal."

Johnny Mercer arose hurriedly and began to sing another song. Jackie yelled over the music. "Good writer, but a lousy singer." He arose haughtily and, on one side, he looked as though he was wearing a snow suit. As he passed Mitzi Green, who was listening to the song, he whispered, "No sense drinking cham-pagne out of a glass, honey," and picked up a bottle of cham-pagne and poured it over her head.

One guest said, "This man must be out of his mind!" Mrs. De-Sylva began a litanous chant with "Oh, my God! Oh, my God!" Jackie walked over to a couple standing on the perimeter of the room—Jack Donahue and his wife, Arlene Dahl—and he said, "Like to meet the girl, Jack." Mr. Donahue introduced the come-dian to his beautiful wife, who was wearing a full-length white gown.

"How do you do." Gleason said, bowing from the waist. "Would you mind lifting your dress?"

Donahue said softly, "Shut up, will you!" Mrs. Donahue seemed puzzled.

"Just a little bit, please," said Gleason, waving upward with both hands. "Just to the ankles."

By now the singing had stopped and everybody was interested. Mrs. Donahue, figuring that resistance would get her into a deeper dilemma, raised the front of the skirt a tiny bit.

Jackie slapped his thigh. "Just as I thought," he said. "All these beautiful broads got big feet."

The party seemed to be peopled with wax images for a mo-

ment. Davey Shelley broke the silence by asking, "Anyone care
to join me in getting drunk?"

Hollywood can tire a man of cosmopolitan interests more
quickly than any other city in America. From the air, Los Angeles
looks like a huge silent butler laden with crumbs of bungalows.
In character it is neither western nor southern; it aspires to be
New York, but it comes closer to Pittsburgh with palm trees.

And yet it is a good city, a huge hick with straw in its teeth
sprawling between the San Gabriels and the sea. It is 10,000 nice
little neighborhoods separated by billboards announcing the
wares of morticians and by painted signs on rocks announcing
the second coming of Our Lord. It is bigger, topographically,
than New York and yet it uses 3,000 policemen to New York's
20,000. Almost all of it is in bed by eleven and up by seven
drinking smogged orange juice and dressing, not for motion
pictures, but for the Douglas plant or Lockheed.

Gleason thought that at Slapsie Maxie's a producer might see
him and give him a second chance at motion pictures. This didn't
happen. In the autumn of 1948 Jackie surrendered and took a
train back to New York. Hollywood had beaten him again. This
time it had been no contest.

If there is work in New York, the fall is a good time for it
because that is when the new shows are being cast and tried out,
that is when the night-club owners dust off the cash register, that
is when agents are booking talent. Jackie came to New York
radiating charm and friendliness. No one met him at the train.
No one asked for his services.

He took a couple of rooms at the Edison Hotel and told Irwin
Kramer, the manager, that he didn't know what he was going
to do. He knew that he had talent; he knew that he could make
people laugh; he knew that he was unafraid of work—but night-
club owners, producers and agents merely looked at him, howled,
held their aching sides, and walked away.

With no job and no money, Jackie still threw wild parties at
the Edison and signed his tabulated checks at Shor's. He had
lived at the Edison, in the same suite, some time before, and
Gleason had become accustomed to the horrendous complaints of

neighbors who did not appreciate two choruses of "Melancholy Baby" by a five-man band at four in the morning.

One of the oldest band jokes came out of this kind of situation. Max Kaminsky and his brassy five were tootling loudly and well one dawn when a man in a bathrobe knocked at the door and said, "Do you know there's a lady sleeping next door?"

"No," said Max sweetly, "but if you'll hum the first four bars we'll fake the rest."

In New York the newspapers were full of advertisements for television sets and aerials were being mounted on roofs all around the metropolitan area, but it did not occur to Gleason that this new field of entertainment might mean employment for him. He had watched television at the homes of friends and he had seen some of it in saloons, but it was feeble stuff, a combination of chopped dramas and antiquated motion pictures. Even when it was entertaining, the picture was too small and it often disappeared in a maze of diagonal stripes, or else the actors spoke but no sound came out.

No one—least of all Gleason—could imagine that the picture tube would ever be able to compete with live entertainment or with full-size motion pictures. Even the few who took it seriously admitted that a performer who worked a year to draw up an acceptable routine was dead after one shot on television because, in that one appearance, he had been seen by almost everybody in the area.

One of the men who took it seriously was Milton Douglas, the one-time singer who had seen Gleason do a Foreign Legion sketch in *Along Fifth Avenue*. Douglas jimmied himself into television early and did not laugh at it. He worked hard to understand it, to bend it to the yoke of showmanship. Douglas was in television when a director had to do everything around the set except paint it. In the back of his mind, Milton Douglas felt sure that vaudeville, dead and buried on the stage, could be revived in front of cameras in the guise of a variety show with a funnyman as master of ceremonies.

There were others like Douglas, but they weren't great in number. Some had failed in other lines of show business and turned to television for a final fling on the wheel of fortune. A

few tried it and gave it up because they felt it would never be a
commercial success. The cost of putting a can of baking powder,
or a cake, or a bottle of beer before an audience cost too much
per home.

Jackie was more concerned with the services of a manager. He
needed one to find work for him, to worry about his finances, to
argue for a bigger salary, to order his whole life. He was telling
this to Kramer of the Edison, and Kramer said that he knew
such a man and would talk to him. Gleason asked who the
manager was and Kramer said, "Let me talk to him first."

Kramer saw his man—Bullets Durgom. Time had changed
Mr. Durgom. He was now a personal manager. Whereas once
he had been chasing bands and singers, now they were chasing
him. Whereas once upon a time Gleason had offered him a job,
at Frank Donato's Colonial Inn, as a stooge, now the stars were
offering him a part of their income to take care of their careers.
He still chewed gum, and his baby face still looked doleful even
under the most ecstatic conditions, but now, to his select clients,
he was a brother, a friend, a cashier, a wife, a doctor, a banker,
a bleeding heart, a confessor, a dupe, a dope.

That's a theatrical manager. A good one.

Durgom listened to Kramer's plea for one J. Gleason. The jaw
muscles stopped chewing for a moment and recognition came
into the sorrowful Armenian eyes.

"Yes," he said, "I've seen Gleason a couple of times. Big fat
guy. He worked at Slapsie Maxie's and he was at Fox for a
while. He's a big talent, Irwin, except that he uses blue material.
He never got off the ground with the public. Maybe he's a little
too sharp for them, a little bit too hep."

This did not sound like reassuring talk to Irwin Kramer, and so
he spilled on. Bullets listened a while and said, "You know
something? I saw Gleason at Fox doing a thing with Glenn
Miller, and Jackie Gleason is the only person who ever made
Glenn laugh." There was a smidgin of reverence in the tone. "He
almost killed Glenn Miller. When Miller laughed, it hurt his
stomach. He couldn't laugh and he didn't want to laugh." He
shook his head. "It almost killed Glenn. I'm telling you."

"Well, do you think that—"

"And Archie Mayo. Mayo is the director. Gleason broke *him* up right on the set. This Gleason is a very funny man."

Durgom and Kramer ended the conversation in Jackie's suite. It was December 1948, and they came to an agreement almost at once. Bullets was to get 10 per cent (and later, 20 per cent) of whatever Gleason earned and he started his work by announcing that he was not going to book Jackie for any jobs. "That's an agent's function," he said. "I'm going to enhance your value, build your career, make you valuable. Let the agents work for you."

He got up to leave.

"Well," said Jackie. "It sounds like a start. When do I see you again?"

"I'll be around," Durgom said. "I operate out of an office on the Strip in Los Angeles."

Gleason looked hurt. "That isn't going to help me here. I'm a New York guy."

"Don't worry about it," said Durgom. "You're going to be all right."

A few days later Bullets stopped in at the Edison and Jackie said hopefully, "How about it? You got any news for me?"

Durgom shook his head negatively. "Nobody knows you," he said.

A week later he was back and Jackie asked him the same question. Bullets shook his head no. "Everybody knows you drink," he said.

. Jackie clenched his fists in exasperation. "How is it," he roared, "that nobody knows me but everybody knows I drink?"

A short job came along. It wasn't much. Back to Baltimore in a night club. Jackie took it and he went to Maryland and worked hard and tried to keep his weight down. He was moody and spent much of his time alone.

One day he ran into a priest named Father Howard. Gleason's beautifully selective memory placed the priest and the original situation at once. Years before, when he had been working at Leon & Eddie's, he had seen a Roman collar at a back table and, between shows, had stopped to chat. They had talked of philosophy, and life, and the rigors of marriage, and had parted with a cordial handshake.

Now they met on the same note and, over coffee, they bridged the gap of the years, and Father Howard was saddened to learn that Jackie was no longer living with Genevieve.

"I'm surprised at you," the Father said. "Marriage is a sacrament."

"I know. I know," Jackie said.

"It can't be treated lightly."

"I didn't treat it lightly. I'm not going to argue who's right and who's wrong, Father. All I want to know is how many fights can a guy stand? Or a woman, for that matter?"

"Were you a good husband to her, Jackie?"

"Oh, that. I suppose I went out a lot with the fellows, and maybe I drank too much, but that's all part of the game I'm in."

"Did you ever stop to think that maybe all of her so-called hollering was for your own good?"

"Maybe it was, Father. But I'm sorry. I don't want to be reformed. A man can do a lot worse than come home drunk."

"It's still a sacrament."

"Sure it is, but I've been asked to get out. Invited to leave."

"Offhand, I'd say that you both have pride. That's one of the seven deadly sins. Do you go to Mass, Jackie?"

"Lately, Father, yes. I'm not going to lie to you. I've missed plenty of times."

"Confession and communion?"

"Sometimes. Not too often."

The priest sighed. "Well, you're staggering, my boy, but you seem to be staggering in the right direction. You know what I think? I think that the drinking, in itself, is not the important thing right now. And I think that the nagging is equally unimportant. What is important is that two people, in good faith, asked the blessing of God on their union and He gave it. Therefore, they owe it to Him to stick by the contract and to give the love of two parents to their children."

"Father, it won't work. It just won't work."

"Nothing works unless you will it to work."

"Honest, if I went back with Gen it would only start all over again. I know what I'm talking about."

The priest talked on, softly, agreeably, sympathetically. Gleason argued firmly, less firmly, murmuringly. At last, against every warning in his mind, he did as he was told: he phoned Gen in New York and said that he had been talking to Father Howard and that Father Howard thought that they should start all over again. He had a lump in his throat. Gen cried and said that she could take a train to Baltimore and that her mother would watch the children for her—if he wanted her to take the train.

Yes, he said, he would like that. Mrs. Gleason went to Baltimore.

Always Jackie Gleason has tried to measure up to his own idea of what a good boy should do. Often he has failed, but he has never given up trying. Genevieve never had this problem. She was a good girl all the way—without effort and without sacrifice.

They were happy for a time. When they returned to New York, the Gleasons appeared before Father "Moose" McCormick at St. Gregory's Church in Brooklyn and repeated their marital vows. It felt legitimately good to Jackie to be back in marital harness and be with his children. If there was any recompense, this was it.

Inside, he felt hopeless and licked. He was bucking an impossible combination. He was sure now, after ten years, that he was not a good enough man for Gen, and she was not the lovely, laughing, sophisticated girl he should have married. Under the sacrament of matrimony, he felt that he was pulling toward the materialistic pleasures of the world, while she was pulling toward the rewards of eternity.

They had little to talk about.

A year later she chided him about reading books on metaphysics and the occult sciences. He was risking mortal sin in reading that stuff, she said. He disagreed. Since when is it a crime to try to learn something, he wanted to know. There were lots of things, she said, that a good Catholic did not want to know.

This topic led to more arguments. Each was tenacious. There was no room for compromise. It's a sin. It is not a sin. Yes it is. No it isn't. Don't tell me. Don't try to tell me, either. Ask a priest. Ask one yourself. I'm only trying to tell you. Don't bother. . . .

In California, Gen asked Jackie to go on a retreat. There, she was sure, he could speak to the priests and ask them if it wasn't a sin to read books which pretended to discuss the hereafter. Jackie felt no mounting urge to go on a Catholic retreat, but, still trying to live up to his own standards of the good boy, he went.

A retreat, to a Catholic, is a time and a place for meditation and spiritual inventory. Some require a week; some are done on a week end. The Catholic man should make one once a year, at least. Usually he goes to a monastery or to a retreat house administered by priests of a given order, and there he sleeps in a barely furnished cell, gets up early for daily Mass, listens to lectures designed to help him calculate the worth of his own spiritual life, recites the rosary and other prayers aloud with other retreatants, is given time to sit in his room and meditate, takes walks around the grounds, says the Stations of the Cross, eats well and in silence while someone reads aloud, goes to bed early, and gets home on the following Sunday evening with a reasonable idea of whether, as a practicing Catholic, he is climbing or skidding.

Gleason went to the Jesuit Fathers Monastery for a week-end retreat to find out if he was spiritually bankrupt. He checked in with the other men, and the priests greeted one and all heartily and assigned cells for prayer and meditation. If Father Maher, the master of retreat, had known what was coming, it is quite possible that he might have gone on a retreat of his own.

Jackie had questions to ask. These turned out to be numerous, incessant and almost interminable. Wearily, Father Maher selected Gleason to do the spiritual reading at mealtimes. If Father had a notion that a few hours of oral reading would tire the Gleason tongue or mind, he underestimated his man.

A young priest was assigned to sit beside Jackie during the readings. All retreatants are enjoined to silence as the reader sits behind a lectern in a large bare room, around the perimeter of which are tables and benches. As the others eat, he reads from a book, and even the reader is supposed to maintain silence except for the written words before him.

In theory, this works well and is an excellent form of discipline. In practice, however, Jackie found that there were words, in

French or Latin, which he could not pronounce and did not understand. Every time he reached one of those words, he paused,
jammed his index finger against the word, turned to the priest,
and said, "How do you pronounce this one?"

"You are supposed to remain silent except for the reading."

"I know," Jackie said a little bit louder, "but how am I going
to read if I don't know how to pronounce the word?"

"Skip it then."

"I'll do nothing of the kind! You tell me how to say it or I can't
go on."

As an act of humiliation to be offered up, the priest told him.
Jackie beamed at one and all and went on until he hit the next
big multisyllabled rock. The same scene ensued. Some of the
retreatants laughed, and this too is against the rules. Jackie's big
baritone Brooklyn voice made this one of the liveliest retreats
known to the Jesuits.

Of the several conversations with Father Maher, one established the pattern. Gleason started off by wanting to know the
attitude of the Church toward psychoanalysis and psychic mani-
festations. With patience, Father explained that the Catholic
Church is not opposed per se to any medically approved form
of psychiatry; some psychiatrists, in fact, had claimed that confession as an emotional experience—as opposed to the spiritual
values—is a form of psychiatric therapy and that the Church has
been practicing it for 2,000 years. The Church is opposed to deep
analysis, Father said, because it has seen evidence that deep
analysis often changes the personality of the patient and gives
him a new set of values which are not always consistent with
what he had been taught. For example, if a woman patient has
been guilty of adultery and part of her trouble stems from feel-
ings of guilt, the Church cannot agree with an analyst who tells
the woman that she committed no wrong, that she was merely
expressing a new-found freedom. In the eyes of the Church, such
a person is guilty of mortal sin if she committed the act with
premeditation and a knowledge that the act was sin.

So far as psychic phenomena are concerned, the Church does
not subscribe to them because it has seen no evidence to support
such extrasensory contentions. And yet the Church does not ac-

tively oppose anyone's searching for the truth, provided that the searcher does not become unbalanced along the way. In the early centuries, Father Maher pointed out, the Church taught that there were evil spirits that tried to influence the lives of good people. No one had actually seen the evil spirits, and yet, hundreds of years ago, pious, God-fearing people had been known to change, in a trice, to monsters of evil.

"Then it's not wrong to read about it, Father?"

"No, no," the priest said. "I cannot put it that squarely. Everything depends upon how much of this stuff you can handle without becoming unbalanced about it. I know people—good friends of mine—whom I would warn away from both these subjects because they are easily led, easily channelized, in their thinking. They fall for every new fad, every line of propaganda, that comes down the pike. No, my son, only the spiritually strong and those who have mental muscles can afford to dip into this stuff."

"Well, is it a sin if I read about it? My wife says it is."

The priest thought about it a moment. "How long have you been reading this stuff?"

"Five years. Maybe seven."

"Then I would say that it is not a sin. You are here, aren't you? After five years of exposure to this stuff, you are at a retreat for Catholic men. If Freudian analysis or psychic phenomena had any influence over you, Jack, you would not be here. Now, let me ask you a question: Do you think that you can continue to 'handle' this stuff without hurting your original faith?"

"Of course I can."

"Then I think that Mrs. Gleason is wrong. You see, Jack, it's like asking me if a policeman can be trusted to spy on a gambling ring without succumbing to a bribe. You would first have to show me the policeman."

Jackie returned to Genevieve in triumph, but he did not move her to change her opinion, which was that there are some things which are not good for a Catholic to know. He continued to read; she continued to worry about it.

Now and then they went out for an evening. Sometimes it was refreshing, more often it wasn't. The schism between these two could be bridged and hidden at home, but not in public. In a party at a night club, it was plain that Genevieve was not to be numbered among the Jackie Gleason fans. He told jokes, and sometimes the entire party howled with laughter—all except Mrs. Gleason. They would wipe the tears from their eyes and ask why she wasn't laughing. Gen would shrug and murmur: "I've heard these jokes before."

On his side, Jackie did not make a strong effort to bring the union to the state of happiness it enjoyed ten years before. He acted like a man serving out a sentence with no hope of parole. He took Genevieve out when he ran out of excuses for not taking her out. At other times, if he could duck out and join the gang at Shor's, he would remain out until dawn and then come home surprised and outraged that his wife should feel angry. The truth is that he no longer felt relaxed in Gen's presence; she knew him, she understood him, and she did not forgive him. Hers was the voice of righteousness pointing an indicting finger at him— and he couldn't take it.

Ironically, he felt closest to Gen when he was hurt. When he was out of a job, or sick, or the world had bruised him, it was Genevieve and only Genevieve who could soothe him and make him feel equal to getting up on his feet and fighting once more for the recognition he deserved. When life was good to Jackie, Gen seemed to fade from his thinking.

The domestic arguments and accusations continued. Sometimes he threatened to leave. Sometimes she suggested that he leave. More and more, the massive ego in him which prompted him to want to become a star was being kicked and bruised at home. The deeper the hurt, the more he became convinced that he had been cast as a sinner, Gen as a saint, and the girls, Geraldine and Linda, as innocent angels.

The question was "How long?"

Durgom had been doing a little innocent spying on his new client and he felt optimistic. He had heard that Gleason was attending Mass regularly—sometimes every morning for a week —and this pleased Bullets because some of the Broadway agents had represented Jackie as an unreliable character. Secondly, he learned that Jackie was again living with Mrs. Gleason and the children and, to a chronic worrier like Durgom, this too was a good sign. The only great mistake the new manager made was when he said, "Jackie, I think that you're a little bit too thin to be funny. You need a little more beef for laughs." Gleason can put on sixty pounds with less encouragement than that, as Bullets discovered too late.

The one drawback to a good relationship between manager and client, in this case, was that Jackie Gleason needed constant, unremitting attention. No one can manage Jackie's affairs and go off to California for a week or, for that matter, to a near-by lake for an hour. He is afflicted with problems he wants to discuss. The business of being funny, to Gleason, is a very serious business and it requires daily conferences as one of its components.

Bullets went off to California to straighten out some motion-picture business and Gleason felt the loss at once. Then too, Durgom had other clients. The Wesson Brothers were in the Riviera at $2,500 a week, and he managed Andy Russell, Connie Haines and a band or two.

"It won't work, pal," said Jackie, shaking his head. "It just won't work. I know me."

"It works with everybody else," said Bullets. "What makes you so different."

"I need a guy here morning, noon and night. Somewhere near by I need someone I can turn to at any hour for advice." He shook his head. "It's gotta be that way."

Durgom did something unusual. As a client, Gleason was not earning anything at the moment, but Bullets went out and found ex-song plugger Jack Philbin and made a deal with him.

"Jack," he said, "here's the situation. I've signed Gleason, and someone has to watch this guy while I'm on the Coast. And I mean watch him. I'm willing to make a deal with you that you be the guy who represents me whenever I'm in California."

"How much?" said Jack Philbin.

"Even up—I'll split the commissions with you."

Philbin thought about it. At the moment, he would be getting

50 per cent of nothing. Still, it could turn out to be a good thing
because he was aware that Gleason was a man of talent. Philbin
said yes.

Jack Philbin is a tall, slender man of ruddy complexion and
graying hair. He has all of the amiable attributes of a retired
confidence man, plus the tired, jaded smile of the Broadwayite
who has had it. For a while he had plugged songs for Paramount
Pictures, and for another he had been a vice-president of General Artists Corporation. As a song plugger for Glenn Miller,
Philbin had become acquainted with Bullets. He could do a little
of everything—judge a song, bang out a little ragtime on a piano,
assess a band or an act, shoot a little golf, frame a witty retort or
play gin rummy well enough to lose only to the right people.

Now these three started on a long, long roll of the theatrical
dice.

Almost at once the first television job materialized. It turned
out to be the wrong comedian in the wrong part, but it was a
job. William Bendix had been starring in "The Life of Reilly" on
radio with success. Now Pabst Blue Ribbon, the sponsor, wanted
to try it on television and, quite naturally, it expected Bendix to
assume the role.

However, Bendix was also a motion-picture star and, to his
anguish, it was pointed out to him that his contract forbade any
television work at all. In the impasse, a substitute was needed
and one Irving Brecker suggested Jackie Gleason.

Durgom thought that it would be a good deal. So did Philbin.
Gleason didn't think it made any sense at all. All of his life he
had been the wise-guy comedian, the smart-aleck know-it-all.
Conversely, Bendix, as Reilly, played a lovable dope who was
always making the wrong moves with the best intentions.

"Take it," said Durgom. "It's a start."

And it was. The series was made on film and Jackie played
Reilly in twenty-six of them. When it was over, Pabst Blue Ribbon dropped "The Life of Reilly" and began to sponsor boxing
matches.

Philbin and Durgom asked General Artists Corporation to get
some fresh work for Gleason and they booked him for a personal

appearance at the Strand Theatre, in New York. Jackie now felt
good. The new team was clicking, and the more work they sent
his way, the better he liked it.

He showed up at General Artists to sign the personal-appearance contract, and when he arrived he turned to the office boy,
a black-haired youngster with big eyes named Jerry Katz, and
said, "Kid, get us a couple of sandwiches. And some coffee. A
piece of pie too." Katz, who was impressed by the magnitude of
the stars, phoned downstairs for the lunch. When it arrived,
Gleason turned to Jerry Katz and said, "Pay the man. And give
him a half a buck tip." Katz did it.

When Gleason left, Jerry followed him to the door, waiting to
be paid, but the great man had a headful of business details and
never thought of the lunch. Afterward, Jerry said to his boss,
"That little item cost me about three days' lunch. I only make
twenty-five dollars a week."

The boss shrugged. "You should know these guys," he said.

"Well, what should I do?"

"You're stuck, kid."

Jackie didn't do much better than Katz. After this brief flurry,
things died again, and, despairing, he went back to California
and Slapsie Maxie's, with the feeling that he had tried, and failed,
at television as well as motion pictures. He had a hopeless feeling that he was going to go through life always miscast. The
motion-picture people had cast him as a gangster, an instrumen-
talist and a sailor. The television people had cast him as a lovable oaf on "The Life of Reilly." In private life he had been cast
as a sinner beyond redemption—a wise guy, a drinker, a spendthrift, a girl chaser, a crude comic.

What was he, really? He was a lonely talent looking for a
medium. He was a man with enormous quantities of love to give,
a man who was gasping to get some of it back. Part of his unique
talent as a funnyman lay in his struggle for affection—the people
will not laugh at you unless they like you.

He knew that. But he also knew that there was some sort of
mist between him and the people. He reached for them, but they
couldn't see him. Always when his big chance came to appear
before multitudes of them, he was somebody else; he was not

Jackie Gleason. Someone handed him a sheaf of pages and said, "Say this," and he said it, but the words were alien and the laughter was distorted and he took the money and went back to his hotel and sent some to his wife and some to the landlord and saved some for a party and wondered if this wasn't the end of the road.

Maybe this was the way it would be always. A fast buck, a few weeks out of work, another fast buck, some loafing, a quick deal, some pacing around a hotel room, a few weeks in a night club, and back to the long-playing mental recording at dawn.

Once, in an interview with Donald Kirkley of the Baltimore *Sun*, Jackie Gleason summed up his entire philosophy in two words:

"I try."

It follows that, as television grew up in New York, Gleason was in California. This happened in 1950, and this adulthood was something that the world of entertainment sensed, rather than measured. Almost overnight, millions of families had television sets and were spending more hours before the opaque screen than they did at cards, in conversation and at church combined. Friends who dropped in for a chat hung up their own hats and coats in an iridescent gloom and saw warning fingers held to lips. The neighborhood motion-picture houses were more than half empty, taverns hung out signs reading "Television Inside," and a new generation became acquainted with such movie stars as Rod LaRoque, May McEvoy, Buster Keaton and Wallace Reid. Television was selling sets of dishes, potato peelers, cigarettes, beer, razor blades, aspirin, vitamins, real estate, rugs, personal loans, refrigerators and canned orange juice. It had something for the whole family—kiddie shows, old movies, late news, mysteries, romance, fights, baseball, cooking lessons, reducing exercises, crooners and a man called the Continental.

The screen was bigger, running to seventeen and twenty-one inches on the average, and actors were learning to wear yellow shirts because they photographed white. Pancake make-up was plastered on the plain face of President Harry Truman, and mul-

titudes were surprised when the new medium took them directly
to the scene of a huge Chicago fire while the buildings were
still burning.

In New York there were two big networks—Columbia Broadcasting System and the National Broadcasting System—and one
smaller one, DuMont. All three were trying to connect their lines
to the Pacific Coast by means of something called a coaxial cable.
The goal was to bring in Times Square and Hollywood and Vine
in successive shots—live.

A small part of the race for 150,000,000 pairs of American eyes
was Milton Douglas, the somewhat prissy ex-singer who wanted
to be a part of the television world. Others were in this race for
the new dollar—motion-picture directors, producers, fading stars,
advertising agencies, the big theatrical agencies, such as Music
Corporation of America and William Morris. Even the office
boy, Jerry Katz, was now selling talent to the all-consuming
eye.

Douglas had sold himself as a television producer to the
Whelan Drug Company. He wanted to stage a one-hour variety
show and the cost was—for that time—high, at $7,500. He
wanted this show to be called "Cavalcade of Stars," and he
wanted it to be on the air fifty-two weeks a year. The bill would
be a whopping $390,000. The feeling was that no product could
sell enough extra merchandise to make up a deficit that size, but
Douglas argued that if the show was staged on the smaller Du-
Mont network and was shown in such big cities as New York,
Pittsburgh and Chicago, the bill could be split among the hundreds of Whelan drugstores and would benefit each one of them.

"Cavalcade of Stars" was on a year in 1950 and it was shown
once a week between 10:00 P.M. and 11. It was a good show,
funny in spots, but it wasn't great. It needed a personality around
whom the show might revolve. Douglas had tried Jack Carter,
and Carter told some very funny stories. But when Carter introduced the jugglers, or the dancers, he did not seem to be a part
of them. The program tried Jerry Lester, an irrepressible comedian who laughed with the audience as the show progressed.

What Douglas wanted was a funnyman who would act as
master of ceremonies and, at the same time, act in sketches; a

man who would run the show, and yet be an important part of it. He needed an actor-comedian who also had the characteristics of a proprietor and father.

In May of 1950 Douglas contacted the William Morris Agency and asked for the services of Peter Donald. The agency was pleasantly surprised, because it had been selling Donald as a wit and raconteur. Everybody was happy except Peter Donald. He was troubled. On a phone call to Douglas he said, "Why do you want me? You need a high-powered star. I'm a low-voltage guy."

"That's exactly it," said Douglas. "We want a slower-paced M.C."

Donald had an engagement in Syracuse, and he went off thinking about the new big job. The more he thought about it, the less he thought about it. After a lot of soul-searching, Peter Donald wired the William Morris Agency that he would not star in "Cavalcade of Stars." The agency phoned and asked him to please change his mind. No, he said, he had given the matter lots of thought and he knew that it would be a great thing for him to get the job, but he was not the man for it.

"This calls for someone like—like Jackie Gleason, for example. You know, big and fast. A lot of personality. He'd be terrific in this thing."

William Morris broke the news to Douglas and suggested several other names, but not Gleason's. He was not their client. Jackie was now working for Music Corporation of America.

Still, Milton Douglas kept thinking of Gleason. Inquiries got him nowhere. Jackie was not in town. Someone remembered that he was in California—at Slapsie Maxie's. That was too far away for Douglas. He had no time to go to the Coast to look at a comic who, possibly, might not be the man he needed.

He was talking to the sponsor's lawyer one afternoon, a man named Arthur Desser, and learned that Desser had some business in Hollywood.

"Do a favor for me," said Douglas. "There's a comedian out there, a man named Jackie Gleason, and they tell me he's at Slapsie Maxie's. Will you stop by and take a look at him?"

Desser said that he would. He had, in fact, seen Gleason before.

"This guy could be the answer to our problem on 'Cavalcade,'"
said Douglas. "But I'm not sure. Tell you what you do, Art. If
he's funny, offer him seven-fifty a week for two weeks."

"Suppose he won't go for it?"

"If he looks good, use your own discretion."

In California, Desser spent an evening at Maxie's and took a
good look at Gleason. The lawyer laughed so hard that he decided that he had better come back again and take a second look
on the premise that nobody in the world could be that funny.
He took a second look, then he interviewed Gleason. They
talked about "Cavalcade of Stars," and Jackie said that he had
seen it in New York.

The lawyer offered $750 a week for a two-week engagement.
Gleason, when broke, is difficult. His answer was "Nothing
doing!" Desser asked what guarantees Gleason wanted.

"Four weeks at least. Why should I go all the way to New
York for two weeks? I already have a steady job."

He got four. Jackie wasn't very happy about it. The whole
deal was merely a quick way of making money. In four weeks
he would have $3,000. Ten per cent of it would go to his agents,
and twenty more to Bullets and Philbin, and some would go
to Genevieve, and what was left would pay a few debts and help
to make him even with the world. He didn't see the engagement
as a chance for a career. He had tried television, on film, and
it had not worked out for him. There was no reason to think
that "Cavalcade of Stars" would be different.

At the railroad station, the whole gang from Slapsie Maxie's
kissed Jackie, hugged him, wished him Godspeed, and he stood
on the bottom step of the Super Chief as it started to sneak out
of the terminal and cupped his hands and yelled, "See you in
four weeks!"

Mrs. Gleason and the girls remained in California for the
fairly obvious reason that it would be witless to move them to
New York for four weeks and then move them back. Geraldine
was growing up to be sweet and serious and ladylike, like her
mother. Linda was moon-faced and black-haired, a gay wit who
looked exactly like her father.

Linda was invited to visit the movie set of the *Cisco Kid* and, while there, posed for pictures with Leo Carrillo and other stars. Someone helped her into cowboy boots and chaps and a ten-gallon hat and put her on a horse. That picture appeared on the front page of *Variety*.

A friend asked to see it and Linda pulled it out from under a chair cushion.

"Why do you hide it?" the friend asked.

"I don't want my father to see it when he gets home," she said. "You see, he never made the front page of *Variety*."

The first publicity release from the DuMont Network has a certain unique value of its own:

"*June 30, 1950, New York*—Arriving from California aboard the Super Chief * Friday morning, Jackie Gleason promptly set to work on plans for his debut on 'Cavalcade of Stars' Saturday, July 8 (9 to 10 P.M. EDST) over WABD and the DuMont Television Network. Jackie is taking over the comic-emcee duties for the star-studded variety show which were formerly conducted by Jerry Lester and Jack Carter.

"Born in Brooklyn thirty-four years ago, the attractive, dark-haired comedian is one of the few who can 'be funny' just because it comes naturally. Having recently completed *Desert Hawk*, a Universal Picture to be released soon, Jackie is enthusiastic about his new DuMont Network program. He feels the 'Cavalcade' format will give him more opportunity to do the kind of comedy he enjoys and is best suited for—ad lib, situation skits, and generally zany fun.

"Among the guests to greet Jackie on his debut, July 8, will be Rosemarie, the petite, now-grown-up child singing star, and Evelyn Farney with her Morrison Dancers.

"The 'Cavalcade of Stars' program is presented each week by Drug Store Television Productions Inc. Milton Douglas produces, Frank Bunetta directing and Sammy Spear in charge of music."

The publicity writer forgot to mention that the show also had two writers: Arne Rosen and Coleman Jacoby. These were

* The Super Chief does not come into New York.

grim men who had a lot of experience writing theatrical sketches. Two more were going to arrive almost at once: Joe Bigelow and Harry Crane. These two were editorial imps who laughed and cracked jokes as they tried their insane ideas on Gleason.

Jackie had a chat with the writers (he has the same feeling about writers that sailors have about compasses: he needs them but he doesn't trust them) and he had several talks with Milton Douglas. Gleason rented two sketches for the opening show and asked Douglas if the budget would permit some dancers.

Douglas said that "Cavalcade" had had six girls, who had been taken right off the stage of the Palace Theatre, but after two weeks they had run out of dances. That could be fixed, Jackie said, if someone was hired to do a little choreography. He had met a girl once in Baltimore who knew dances and dancers inside out. A girl name of June Taylor. Douglas said that that was funny, because he knew June Taylor in Chicago years ago, and her work had been great.

"Will she work cheap?" Douglas asked.

"Who knows? Ask her."

Douglas met June Taylor, broached the idea of a chorus line, and Miss Taylor said that she had seen the show, was acquainted with the style of variety in it, and could get six fairly healthy girls for $50 apiece. Her own services would come to $85 a week. Douglas did a little thinking, and said all right.

This gave Jackie the fast bouncy opening he wanted. When the music wasn't fast and bouncy, he groaned and sometimes he became angry. But June Taylor pointed out to him that she was buying seventy-five-cent orchestral arrangements, and when the day came that they could afford a real arranger, everything would be fast and bouncy.

On the opening night Jackie went through his two rented sketches and they were funny. The writers chipped in a satire on an Italian movie named *Stromboli*, and Gleason played it to the hilt. Even the writers laughed. He got so much good out of their material that they began to think "good stuff" for him. In one sketch there was a half Dutch door and Gleason was supposed to exit through it. The door became stuck and Douglas, watching from behind the cameras, was certain that the scene would be ruined if someone could not get the door to open. Gleason turned to the cameras, snarled something about stuck doors, and climbed over it. The audience giggled. When he had to make another entrance through it, Jackie decided not to try to open it. He climbed over it as though that was the way a Dutch door was intended to be used. The audience laughed. He went in and out and over that door so many times that people were wheezing from laughing. Even the camera crews were roaring.

When the show was over, Milton Douglas mopped his head and said, "He'll do. He'll make it." Executives of the network who saw the show agreed that this was indeed a very amusing fellow, but they wanted to see him once more before signing him to any long-term contract. If he could be that funny twice in a row, he was the television find of the year.

For the second show, the writers suggested a satire on a whisky advertisement which proclaimed The Man of Distinction. Gleason, as The Man, would be posing for a photograph, but the photographer would keep coming out from under his .black hood and complaining that Gleason was not putting enough feeling in the photo. Jackie would demand that the photographer assume the proper pose, and the cameraman would thereupon sit in the chair and drink the whisky. They would take turns doing this until both became intoxicated, and the scene would close with Gleason under the hood taking the photographer's picture, etc., etc.

"It's a good idea," Jackie said, "but you're going to need one hell of an actor to play that photographer."

"We were thinking of that," Coleman Jacoby said, "and there was a guy we did some work with on CBS, a really terrific little guy named Art Carney."

"Never heard of him," Gleason said.

"Great," said Arnie Rosen. "This boy's got it."

"Can we get him?"

"We can try. He's been doing a butler part for Morey Amsterdam on DuMont."

"See if you can get him."

They got Art Carney, and the second week turned out to be

more riotous than the first. Carney was the prissy perfectionist of a photographer and Gleason played the part of a society playboy named Reggie Van Gleason III. For this he devised his own costume, his own technique. He wore an old-fashioned gentleman's cape, a top hat, and a square mustache. He kept his eyes heavy-lidded and half-closed, exuded the aura of a drunken snob, and burped at one and all.

This time the producer laughed.

Douglas wanted to sign Jackie to a long contract, but was now fearful that the new man knew his own worth and would ask for too much. The producer was lucky, in a way. Gleason furnished the springboard for the deal. He wanted to know if he could borrow $5,000.

The owners of the show—Product Advertising Corporation (the Whelan Drug people)—might have been happy to give him $5,000 but, as long as he asked for it as a loan, they made it a loan. They also got his signature on a contract, which eventually ran from June of 1950 until June of 1952, and which reached $1,500 a week. The sponsors deducted $450 a week on the $5,000 loan; $150 a week went to Durgom as manager; $150 a week belonged to MCA; Genevieve got some; taxes got some; and what was left to Jackie often amounted to $90.

One week, when he had a toothache, Jackie permitted a dentist to shoot penicillin into his jaw and the jaw swelled so much that he could not speak. He missed the show that week and the sponsors would not pay him. They said that his illness was not their fault and that it had caused them to cancel the rental of an elephant. Douglas learned that at the moment Gleason was broke, so he went to the sponsors and asked for some money for the sick man. He came back with $200, which Jackie accepted gratefully.

Milton Douglas had the restraint and abnegation necessary on the part of a producer to keep a star like Jackie Gleason fairly happy. Some producers will not listen to suggestions or changes from an actor. Douglas isn't one of them. He listened and, when he found himself in sympathy, he adopted Jackie's idea. When he wasn't in sympathy, he tried to be firm (and sometimes was), but sometimes he was persuaded to try Glea-

son's way. Douglas had the gentlemanly attitude of a tie salesman at Sulka's, but on the few occasions he locked horns with
Gleason he absorbed a little bit of the Brooklyn technique.

The first rift came about when Jackie announced that he
wasn't going to rehearse. Milton Douglas had a silvery laugh
left over from his operetta days and he enunciated it.

"Of course you're going to rehearse," he said. "No rehearsal,
no show. Everybody rehearses."

"Except me," said Jackie. "It makes me stale."

"But how will you get to know your part?"

"Let me read it once, pal. That's all I need."

"How about the others in the cast?"

"They're pros, aren't they?"

"Jackie," said Douglas plaintively, "all I want is a good performance and a successful show."

"Me too," said Gleason.

On the third week the new star got around to reading the
script of the hour-long show the day before the performance.
To the amazement of Douglas, Bunetta and Joe Cates, assistant
to the producer, Jackie riffled through the pages of dialogue,
threw the script on a table and said, "Okay. I got it."

They had a run-through (a reading by the members of the
cast, usually done sitting in a circle with scripts on knees) and
Jackie turned out to be right. After a casual look, he had memo-
rized the script. Except for missing a single word here and there,
he not only knew his own part, he knew everybody else's too.
This phenomenal memory was constant; he could do it at any
time. So phenomenal, in fact, that it came as almost no surprise
at all to find that his memory regarding his private life was
poor. He had the memory working where he needed it—in his
profession—and nowhere else. Unless, of course, it was something he enjoyed remembering.

Douglas learned to dispense with all except last-minute rehearsals. The next disagreement occurred when Jackie invented
a new character to try out on the show. This one was called Joe
the Bartender, and it was a Brooklyn monologue built around
Poppa Proce, the neighborhood bartender who wore his white
apron up over his chest, and Mr. Dennehy, Julie's father, who

was the ghostly customer in the scene. Gleason, with hair parted
severely in the middle and plastered down the sides, drew an
imaginary beer and talked out of the side of his mouth about
his real boyhood friends—Teddy Gilanza, Jimmy Proce, Bookshelf Robinson, the Dennehys and others. It was an acute portrait of a real Brooklyn bartender and it went over with the
audience, except that, on one particular night, Gleason was on
the air when a tactless carpenter began to repair a light on stage
with hammer and nails.

The sound of the hammering was picked up by the micro-
phones, and Jackie, in mid-routine about Brooklyn and the
Dennehys, could hardly believe his ears. Milton Douglas, behind the cameras, waved frantically to the carpenter to stop, but
the man was busy.

It usually requires less than three seconds for Jackie to comprehend a situation like this and to do something about it. He
stopped talking, inclined his head a little, and smirked. "They're
hammerin' on the pipes again," he growled. "A lot of good it
will do them."

When the show was over, the comedian came off stage seeth-
ing. He went to his dressing room, thrust his arms into a bathrobe, and waited. The writers came in, some friends stopped
by, and finally Milton Douglas walked into the room.

"It's all your fault."

"Jackie—"

"I said it's your fault and nothing you can say is going to
change me. You're the producer. You're running the show."

He was pacing back and forth in the little room, the robe
flapping in the breeze.

"I sympathize, Jackie—"

"That's not enough."

"What the hell do you want me to do?"

"Do your job. It's up to you to see that the stage is clear at
showtime."

"Now, look, Jackie, I don't have to take this—"

Douglas began to thread his way through the crowd toward
the door. Gleason reached over and stopped him.

"You listen to me," he roared. "Nobody leaves this room when I'm insulting them!"

These things were of small consequence; if anything, they showed that Gleason was now taking television seriously. It was no longer a fast buck and back to Slapsie Maxie's. He was surprised and pleased to find, for example, that people now recognized him on the street and he could hear them say, "There's Jackie Gleason." This was new and nice.

He tried to work with the writers, and for a while he had himself billed as the last writer on the list. This is common to big stars who fancy themselves as latent scribblers or as executive producers, but in Gleason's case he invented characters with the help and connivance of writers, and he also added good bits of dialogue and situations.

Still, he could be a chronic pain to the men who labored over the scripts. Many a time he showed up a few hours before "Cavalcade" went on the air waving a yellow copy of the script, shaking his head sorrowfully, and murmuring, "This won't do. This will not do." If the show was not successful, he sought out the writers and said, "I told you." If the show went over big, he slapped the writers on the back and roared, "Well, we fooled 'em again!"

Once he balked at a situation in which he was to play a pompous and sarcastic shoe clerk who was trying to fit a size three shoe on a size seven dowager.

"Pal," said Jackie to Douglas, "this sketch is no good."

"I think this one can be very funny," Douglas said.

"I don't," Jackie snapped.

Douglas looked at the studio clock. "It's post time. What are we going to do?"

"I'm the guy who has to go out there and do it."

Douglas laughed. "I agree. You're the one who has to go out there and do it, but the fact is that this is the sketch and we don't have another one and all I can suggest is that you do your best to make it funny."

Gleason shrugged and walked away. That night he made a minor classic of the shoe scene. He tried harder because he didn't believe that it was funny, and the scene became such a standout that it was repeated several times in later years.

Sometimes, when there wasn't much of a supporting cast, Milton Douglas would put himself on as a singer—his old trade— and Jackie would stand in the wings and make fun of him. When the producer casts himself as an actor, a critique is almost axiomatic. One night Douglas sang a classical number attired in a hempen garment held together with a sash.

Apparently Jackie hadn't expected it, because he came out of his dressing room, took a look on stage and, backstage, did a devastating satire on Douglas singing.

"You know why he gets into those rags?" he asked no one in particular. "Because he looks lousy in a tux, that's why. How can you say a guy looks crumby in a rope?"

One of the writers said that Jackie was ruling the show with an iron head. "Cavalcade" was getting a high rating for a small network—the rating was 25—and the writers felt that their work had something to do with it. Gleason felt that his artistry had something to do with it, and it may be that Douglas felt that his perspicacity in picking a new star and new writers had something to do with it.

Rosen and Jacoby showed up one noontime with a complete script. They thought it was funny, but they knew that they would have to read it aloud in the face of a master of comedy. Jackie sat, unshaven, in a bathrobe, and he nodded briefly to both men.

"Okay, pal," he said to Jacoby. "Start reading."

Jacoby shook the script out and opened his mouth to read. At this moment a white-coated waiter wheeled in an operating table full of Chinese food. Everything was steaming. There were quart containers of chow mein, broiled shrimp, won ton soup, lobster Cantonese and soy sauce.

The steam pervaded the room and Jacoby had to remove his glasses and polish them. Gleason looked at the tableful of food and, without looking up, growled, "All right, Coleman. Come on. Get on with it."

The writer read half a page. "Okay," Jackie said. "Okay. I

got it," and he stood and fell on the food with both arms flailing.

In 1950 and 1951 Jackie's love of food seemed to increase. Coleman and Rosen accompanied him to Hartford to watch him break in a personal-appearance act for the Capitol Theatre in New York. Before showtime he ate a bushel of food, drank everything potable and, in the middle of the act, did a cartwheel, fell down, and couldn't get up.

At four in the morning Jackie began to feel very sick and he phoned for the hotel physician. This innocent showed up in a bathrobe carrying a bag and he examined the patient, gave him an emetic and a hypodermic, and then sat at the bedside listening to the mighty moans. At 5:30 A.M. the crisis had passed and the doctor assured Jackie that he would live.

At 7:00 A.M. Jacoby and Rosen showed up in the room with the spurious ebullience of writers who are nervous wrecks. They noticed the death pallor and solicitously inquired about the health of the star. Gleason told them that he had been a bad boy, had eaten too much and almost killed himself. However, he was now feeling much better, so, in their presence, he phoned room service and asked that breakfast be sent up for one—two double pork chops, a loaf of toast, mashed potatoes, gravy and a cold bottle of beer.

Jackie ate, washed, shaved, dressed and started off for the theater. On the way he was his old happy self, and when he was almost at the theater, he looked at his wrist watch and told the writers that they were all early. Much too early. There was time, he said, to stop at a little Italian restaurant he knew and to kill a few minutes. There they saw him eat lasagna, devour a pizza, and empty a bottle of Chianti.

"This," said Rosen to Jacoby, "is all happening before lunch."

"Before breakfast," said Jacoby.

Gleason did not get sick again that day, and he went on to the Capitol Theatre and smashing success. He earned $8,000 that week end and, with the first big proceeds, bought a mink coat for Gen.

More than a million people now saw Jackie Gleason every

Friday night, and the big networks tried to devise shows which would cut his audience down. One put on a show called "Caval-cade of Sports" (a series of weekly fights), and Jackie lost a large part of his tavern audience at once, but in the homes the wives argued for the Gleason show, while the men fought for the fights and lost. The Proce tavern in Brooklyn was one of the few which solved this impasse by buying two television sets. If you wanted to watch the fights, stay near the front of the bar; Gleason was on the rear set.

Jackie was growing and growing. He was invited to do guest spots on bigger shows, and for this he was often paid $10,000 and $12,500 for a performance. When Frank Sinatra asked him to be a guest on the Sinatra show, Gleason made a stipulation: no fee. Too well he remembered the days when both of them were struggling at Frank Donato's Colonial Inn, and he would take no money from a pal now.

Sinatra had an extra $5,000 in the budget and wanted to give it to Gleason, but Jackie said no. When the show was over, Sinatra was so pleased that he insisted on doing something for his friend. Frankie phoned the Cadillac agency and asked them to contact Gleason and to find out what kind of Cadillac he wanted.

When the contact was made, Jackie dropped his bashfulness. He would like a black Cadillac and he wanted a phone in the back and some special equipment and extras. The bill came to $8,000. Gleason used the car for a short time and then sold it to a sporty undertaker who wasn't particular about how much gaiety had transpired in the back seat.

Of the writers, the one in whom the star reposed particular confidence was Harry Crane. Crane was fat and bald and kept his teeth clenched solely to hang on to his cigar. He could take a slender premise—like the idea of a man falling down a coal chute—and work it up into a twenty-minute sketch, complete with fist fights, love, police and ringing bells. He was hired on a Tuesday and Bullets Durgom said, "Now this is Tuesday, kid. The show goes on Friday night, so you haven't got much time."

"Well, he's got some sketches for this show, hasn't he?"

"Nothing, pal. Nothing."

"Then we'd better get busy. Quick."

"Meet Jackie at his place (he was now in an apartment on East Fifty-second Street), oh, maybe about seven. You two got to get together."

"Sure. How many sketches?"

"Two."

"Good God!"

Harry Crane arrived at Gleason's apartment at seven. He would have to sit with Jackie at least half the night to work out acceptable suggestions. Then he would have to sit and write all the next day, get a few hours sleep, and work over the first rough drafts of the sketches the following night with Jackie. No matter how fast they worked, the sketches would not be ready for a first look until Thursday, the day before the show. This is not quite a relaxed opening for a writer just starting on a show.

Someone opened the apartment door, and such a blast of bedlam hit Crane that he thought he might be in the wrong place. He wasn't. There was a party going on. Fellows and girls were dancing; groups in corners were drinking and telling stories. A record player, turned up full, was pounding "Lili Marlene."

"Where's the meeting going to be?" Crane asked Gleason.

Jackie put on his biggest smile and pounded Harry on the back. "Grab yourself a booze and a broad, pal," he roared. "We're gonna swing here."

"Jack, we have writing to do."

"Stop worrying. It will come out all right."

Crane sat. He was frightened. Still, he kept telling himself that if the party kept moving at this speed, it would have to end in exhaustion shortly. It's still Tuesday, he kept telling himself. Wednesday it ain't.

Some of the people tired and went home early. But new hordes kept coming in. At ten Harry lifted his size forty-four frame out of a chair, held the cigar in his hand, and said, "I'd better go, Jack."

"Tell you what," said Jackie. "Meet me here at ten in the morning. We go."

"Wednesday?"

"Yeah."

"All right." Crane nodded toward the gyrating, pulsing figures in the room. "We could never get áway from this."

In the morning Harry rang the doorbell at ten. Nothing happened. He tried again. Then he pounded on the door. A maid opened it. The apartment looked like Yucca Flats. Glasses lay on their sides on the rug. Spaghetti hung like fringe from a table. A record player spun silently. Three dirty dishes leaned against a wall. A lampshade tilted drunkenly.

"Where's Mr. Gleason."

"Sleeping."

"What's been going on here?"

The maid shrugged. "It's like this every morning."

"It's Wednesday," Crane said to no one. "This man has to face millions of people Friday night."

He walked into the bedroom. The blinds were closed, the draperies drawn. Jackie was sleeping with one arm across his face. Harry Crane shook his shoulders until he got responsive grunts. Gleason looked, rubbed his face, and subsided with eyes closed.

"Look, pal," he said. "I'm dead. Just got in. I'll tell you what to do. Let me sleep or I'll be no good to you. Call me at three, Harry. Let's make it at three. Definitely three."

"But, Jack. This is Wednesday."

"Don't worry, Harry." The voice was fading in sleep. "It's going to be beautiful."

At 3:00 P.M., Durgom answered the phone. "Yes, Harry. . . . You're absolutely right, Harry. . . . Hell, I'm worried too. Tell you what to do. Make it for seven sure. This thing has got to be done. Yes, he's up. He's straightening out now. I'd put him on but he's in the bathroom. . . . No, I'll see that you two are alone. No visitors. Nothing. No phone. . . . Seven sharp, Harry."

At seven o'clock, Crane found that he had a tic in his shoulder. It kept shrugging whether he wanted it or not. He kept doing mental mathematics and he was telling himself that, in exactly 3,060 minutes, this show would be on the air. Millions of people in hundreds of thousands of homes would turn the dial to the correct channel, and a sign would say "Cavalcade of Stars," and then there would be some credits and a dissolve and some fast music and the dancers would come on and then Jackie Gleason would come bounding out, fat and shiny and handsome, and he would say, "Ladies and gentlemen, the script that wasn't written for tonight's show was unwritten by Harry Crane. As we have no script, so we have no show. We will now have a commercial and will sign off until next week, when we will have a new script writer—if not a new star."

The tic was becoming worse. Harry Crane rang the bell to the Gleason apartment and the door was opened at once by a stranger with a slight edge. The place was jumping with music and noise. Harry Crane walked among the guests beaming. "This is ridiculous!" he kept shouting above the music. "This is all crazy. This is Wednesday night." Most of the guests had heard nuttier speeches in their time, so they merely nodded at the smiling man and went on with the party.

"Jackie!" Crane said to the host. "This is fantastic. It's Wednesday night."

Gleason clamped a friendly hand on Harry's shoulder. "Stop worrying," he shouted. "Everything is going to be beautiful. I'll get rid of these people by ten for sure. Then we work."

"But you can't possibly get a show out!"

"Ten o'clock we go."

At ten o'clock the party was going wilder and louder and two girls without shoes were trying to find room to execute a Charleston.

"Jack!" said Crane at ten-thirty. "Listen to me a minute—"

"Know what I'm going to do?" Gleason said. "I'm going to get rid of this gang early—real early. Then I'm going to get a good night's rest and I'll be in shape for you in the morning."

" 'In the morning' happens to be Thursday!"

"We'll rap it out fast. You'll see."

"But Thursday, Jack. This whole thing is insane!"

"Stop worrying."

"Maybe you're right. Yeah. Maybe you're right. I'll stop thinking about it."

"See you in the morning, pal."

"I keep telling myself, I'm in it this deep . . ."

Crane began to think in tics. He decided to fool Jackie. Instead of showing up at ten and finding him dead in bed, he'd arrive promptly at 3:00 P.M., when Gleason would be bright and dressed, and it would be too late to write anything.

At the stroke of three, Harry Crane walked into the apartment, calling, "Jackie! Jackie!" and he found the star dead in bed. By now Crane was laughing because this was better than any script, even though no one would ever believe it. Gleason pulled one eyelid back and asked for a cold bottle of beer. Harry got it and Gleason drank it sitting up in bed glaring at the wall. He opened the second eye and donned an old bathrobe, scowled, smacked his lips, scratched himself and tottered into the bathroom.

Crane fell on the bed laughing. "The show goes on in thirty hours," he was saying, "and nothing has even been written. Nothing!"

Jackie came out of the bathroom slapping a wet towel on the back of his neck. "What's the matter?" he said.

"Show business certainly cuts into your day," said Harry.

"Pal," said Jackie. "That's the idea."

"But Jackie. What about scenery? What about supporting actors?"

"Milton Douglas called last night. He was steamed. He said he had to build sets and hire actors, so I told him to build an interior. I told him you and I would write a sketch to fit the setting. He said what kind of an interior and I said a living room, for God's sake. Now all we got to do is think of an idea to go with it."

Jackie took a shower and Harry rolled a sheet of blank paper into a portable and looked at it longingly. Harry kept jumping at slight noises and thinking of poor ideas.

"There are actors to be hired," he said loudly, "but we don't know what kind of actors. There are sets to be designed and built, but we don't know anything about them except that Douglas is going to build a living room. There are sketches to be written, but we don't know what they're all about because we haven't got any ideas. There are musical cues and background music, but we don't know what or even why."

The phone rang. It was Milton Douglas. Gleason got on, with half his face lathered.

"How can I give you an idea of the opening sketch if we haven't even thought about it? . . . Okay, we're a little late. . . . Sure, sure. . . . But I can't give you an idea, Milt, if we haven't got an idea yet. . . . Give us a little time, pal. . . . Look. I'll be there tomorrow. Just you be there at noon. . . . Hah? Nothing doing. No eight in the morning for me. We start at noon."

Gleason sat at the typewriter and began to peck at it. He typed part of a sketch and then sat and talked it out as Crane took his turn at the machine. As Jackie related it, the scene became funnier and funnier, and, as he told it, he could see the weaknésses in it too and he told Crane how to guard against them. When it was finished, Jackie started at once into a Reggie Van Gleason III sketch which could be played in a living room. After that he made three suggestions about music and cues.

"Don't write the whole thing out, Harry," he said. "Just write 'bit with hat'; 'bit with window'; 'bit with lamp.' I'll know what they mean."

Crane had worked with Broadway and Hollywood stars, but this was the first time he had met one who could devise good sketches, talk them out in detail, anticipate the weaknesses, make it credible, whip up a full-hour television show in ninety minutes and yet act like a man in the throes of an agonizing hang-over.

Harry also noticed that when he had something to contribute, Gleason listened in silence, nodded once or twice, then slapped the palms of his hands together and said, "That's all!" meaning that he understood and approved. Crane was convinced that he had never before met an actor like this one.

At noon on Friday the entire staff of "Cavalcade of Stars" was on the stage of the Adelphi Theatre on West Fifty-fourth Street. The only person missing was the star. The producer was frantic. The director was resigned to the inevitable. Prop men were running around with nothing to do. A cameraman shook his head and said, "How can Frank plan shots for a show nobody knows nothing about? Once he asked Gleason about this little problem and Jackie said, 'You can't go wrong if you just keep the camera on me.'" The assistant to the producer sat on a camera dolly smoking. Actors wandered around the set swapping gossip. Jerry Katz, the one-time office boy, looked sharp and agentish in a new suit.

Jackie arrived at 2:00 P.M. He removed his coat and handed it to someone and asked for a chair. An actor asked if he could have a copy of the script and Jackie said, "I got no time now. I've got to stage this thing." Another actor looked at him hopefully as he stood on the chair to address the cast and staff, and the actor said, "When do I go on?"

"You've been around," Gleason said. "Get on whenever you can."

He turned to the cast. "It's every man for himself. I'm going to read this thing once. Just once. Listen and pick up whatever you can. We haven't got any time."

As he read, he parenthesized and yelled to the prop man, "Get me a top hat. . . . I need a beer barrel. . . . A full bottle of Seltzer."

Crane said, "How can you get a show on?"

"Easy," said Gleason. "No use aggravating yourself seven days a week. I get all the aggravation in one day and put the show on." He could see that Crane did not believe him. "Others work seven days a week and it doesn't come out any better. You'll see."

What frightened Harry Crane the most was that the whole mess made sense. He almost feared that, seven hours from now, a full-length television show would be staged and it would turn out to be rich and funny and right, and then what would happen to all the nice show-business lessons he had learned?

Five minutes before showtime Jackie was in his dressing room talking to Teddy Gilanza, who packed the Adelphi Theatre with old pals from Brooklyn every week. Harry Crane left, muttering to himself, "I'll be stoned!" The show went on and Crane watched it from a saloon and it was rich and beautiful and flawless.

Crane turned to a bar fly standing next to him. "Looking at that fat slob," he said, "you'd think he rehearsed it about four years."

"How do you know?" the bar fly said, half belligerently. "Maybe he did."

One afternoon Joe Bigelow and Harry Crane were trying to write a sketch with the star, and Gleason said that he had an idea for a sketch that would revolve around a married couple—a quiet, shrewd wife and a loudmouthed husband.

"You got a title for it?" asked Bigelow.

"Wait a minute," said Crane. "How about 'The Beast'?"

Jackie got to his feet. "Just a second," he said. "I always wanted to do this thing, and the man isn't a beast. The guy really loves this broad. They fight, sure. But they always end in a clinch."

Bigelow shrugged. "It *could* be a thing."

"I come from a neighborhood full of that stuff. By the time I was fifteen, I knew every insult in the book."

"Then let's try it," said Bigelow.

"But not 'The Beast,'" said Jackie. "That's not the title."

"Why not?"

"It sounds like the husband is doing all the fighting. We need something a little left-handed as a title. You know, this kind of thing can go and go and go."

"How about 'The Lovers'?" said Harry Crane.

"That's a little closer, Harry." Gleason paced the floor. "A little closer, but it could mean that they're not married. We need something that tells everybody at once that they're married."

"'The Couple Next Door.'"

"No. How about 'The Honeymooners'?"

"Aw, no. That sounds like they're lovey-dovey."

"All the better. This dame is very wise and very tired. She knows this guy inside out, see, and he's always got a gripe. Maybe he's a—no, a cop wouldn't do. They got a little flat in Brooklyn. Flatbush Avenue, maybe. Cold-water flat. Third or fourth floor. Hell, I lived in these joints. I know where the sink should be, the icebox—and don't forget the drip pan underneath—the sideboard and the round table. The little gas range. You know? Maybe we got something."

"I got the opening line," Bigelow said. "The guy comes home

tired. He worked all day. He's beat. He walks in, mad at the whole world, and his wife says, 'Don't take your coat off. Go downstairs and get me a loaf of bread,' and the guy gives her a look that would split a grapefruit and he shakes his head sarcastically and says, 'I'm not getting anything. I worked all day. What did you do?' and they're off to the races."

"That's the general idea," Jackie said. "Make it real. Make it the way people really live. If it isn't credible, nobody's going to laugh. The guy at home has got to be able to look at it and say, 'That's the way my old lady sounds.'"

"This can be a thing," said Crane. "A real thing."

"I even know who can play the wife," said Gleason, enthused. "Pert Kelton." He held out both hands for the verdict. "Is anybody more natural than Pert for this bit? Did you guys ever see her in a part where she gets mad at a guy? Holy smoke!"

They talked about it. And talked some more.

"The Honeymooners" turned out to be the most popular sketch on the show. There were others which were given a good trial, and some turned out to have lasting qualities and others did not. There was one called "The Bachelor," a pantomime effort, which struck no responsive chord. The Reggie Van Gleason III character remained one of the best. The same applies to Joe the Bartender, and a whimsically sad character called The Poor Soul. One sketch called "Father and Son" died quickly. Loudmouth Charley Bratten, a raucous know-it-all, lasted for years. So did Fenwick Babbitt, the turning worm.

It was important to Gleason's television career, at this early stage, to invent new characters constantly, to try them out, and to get an accurate index to their popularity. Rudy the Repairman got a long trial and almost made the grade. Another that Jackie always enjoyed doing was Stanley R. Sarg, the television pitchman who sells Mother Fletcher's products between reels of a Mae Busch movie ("For you girls with heavy calves, a cowbell").

At times there were characters within characters. Joe the Bartender used to tell the imaginary Mr. Dennehy about Crazy Googenham, whose sole enjoyment was crashing wakes, and Bookshelf Robinson, who had a big nose and who rolled over in his sleep one night and got his nose caught in his ear, sneezed, and blew his brains out.

The realization that television might be tailor-made for his talents came to Jackie Gleason when, after a few weeks, his show achieved a high rating on a small network. Although he was in competition with the big fights on one network and with fine entertainment on another, one out of every four television sets in the East and Midwest was tuned in on "Cavalcade of Stars" every Friday night. This news, in addition to the new two-year contract, gave him a feeling that a whole new world had suddenly been opened to him—a ·world of verdant blooms and sweet-smelling success; a world, if you please, with no rejection. It was a world largely unmapped, unexplored, but it was uniquely friendly to him. He kept trying to tell himself that it was no longer necessary for a few hundred people to dress and come out of their homes and pay to see him in a night club or a theater; at the flick of a switch, he came to see a million people in their homes, and they sat in their socks and in house dresses and they watched him and laughed and laughed and laughed.

The DuMont clipping service showed reams of copy about him written by radio and television editors, and these columns proclaimed Jackie as a bright new star in Pittsburgh, in Cleveland, in Chicago, in New York, in Boston, in Washington, in Detroit. After so many failures, sudden and violent success can dizzy a man. It didn't do this to Gleason because he had felt all along that he was great; life was a matter of waiting until one was discovered by the people. Now that the discovery had been made, he was not surprised; they were.

He sent for Genevieve and the children and, on many a show night at DuMont, Gen sat in the glass-enclosed director's booth and watched this earthy man of hers cavort and strut and make funny faces and fall down. The children, after the show, often ran up and down the aisles of the empty theater waiting for daddy to get dressed and come home.

Out front were friends from Brooklyn, hogging the best seats in the house and applauding, whistling and stomping whenever

Gleason came on stage. Backstage, Jerry Katz was telling Bullets Durgom that he was now a real full-fledged agent and even represented a pianist—someone named Liberace. Katz, now with Music Corporation of America, was Jackie Gleason's agent too.

Backstage also was Leo Talent, the quiet man of the Glenn Miller group, who now plugged songs and hoped that he could get Gleason to use one or two on his show each week. One was called "Me and My Teddy Bear." Jack Philbin was there too, cool, efficient, sitting astride the biggest parlay of his life. Now and then Julie Dennehy came backstage with her husband, James Marshall, to swap tall stories of the old days when they all went "bouncing."

Sammy Birch, the one-time master of ceremonies who had preceded Gleason at the Halsey and who had given him shelter and had split a fifty-nine-cent dinner with him, dropped by. And Jackie threw both arms around his old friend and asked Sammy how it was going, and Sammy said pretty good sometimes and Jackie said, "As long as I ever have a job, pal, you got one too." He meant it and he never missed a chance to write Sammy into the script. And Sammy worked well in television. He never let Gleason down.

Lee Meyers, the press agent who once put him on the Lower Basin Street program, was hired as public-relations expert for Gleason. George Sossin and his wife came backstage and the three of them sat and laughed and shook their heads over the old Club Miami days. Sinatra, Slapsie Maxie, Toots Shor, Davey Shelley, Willie Webber, Paddy Noto, Jimmy Proce, Al Siegel— they were all there to glisten a little bit over the hard times of the past and to see with their own eyes whether the boy had permitted any of this to go to his head.

He hadn't. He was as big a ham as ever, but no bigger. He loved all the attention and he reveled in it, but he was as loyal to old friends as always, and perhaps more generous.

One afternoon Jackie took Lee Meyers and Davey Shelley to Brooklyn to show them the old neighborhood. Naturally, it had to be done with class, so he chartered a limousine and drove them up and down Saratoga Avenue and Herkimer, Truxton, Somer and Chauncey. He did it with pride.

At one point the limousine was forced to stop because a taxi-cab came to a halt dead ahead. Two men got out. One had a portable radio under his arm. Both men walked into a hockshop.

"That's what I mean about the old neighborhood," Jackie said. "When we hock anything, we take a cab to do it."

At home, matters were no better because success cannot cure a chronic heartache. Jackie stayed out more and more. He could afford more parties and he staged more. He got drunk with the boys, or remained sober with a girl. Women always felt an attraction for him, but now it was intensified because to be seen with him was often good enough to make a Broadway column. The showgirls, the pretty stars, all were eager to be draped on his arm and, from Jackie's standpoint, it was very good. The only thing his new life had lacked, now that he no longer leaned on Gen's sympathy, was feminine flattery. He needed it. He got it.

Mrs. Gleason received the telephoned reports of friends, and thus she knew the worst and she knew it daily. One night he stayed out and went to an after-hours bottle club called The Gold Key. He got home at dawn and, when he awakened in the afternoon, Jackie was penitential.

In the timid tone, he asked Gen if she would like to go out. She thought about it and said yes. They went to a night club with Mr. and Mrs. Arnie Rosen, and Mrs. Gleason was righteously angry. She kept reminding him of past sins, especially the one of last night.

"Take it easy," he begged. "Take it easy, will you? I'll be good from now on."

"All I want to know," she kept saying, over and over, "is what does a man do when he's out until four or five in the morning? I heard that you were at The Gold Key. What's The Gold Key? Why don't you ever take me to The Gold Key? If you can drink with somebody else, why can't you drink with me?"

It wasn't much of a night out.

He worked harder, played harder and ate harder, and it was then that he got his three wardrobes: the one for the times when he weighed 185 pounds, the one for when he weighed 240 pounds, and the one for 280 pounds.

Shortly after the signing of the DuMont contract he was up to

264 in weight, and Toots Shor began to kid him about it. This is strange because Shor is so fat that Jackie once said that watching Toots jog up a staircase was like watching two small boys fight under a blanket.

"I'm fat!" snorted Gleason. "Listen to what's telling me *I'm* fat!"

"I may be fat," said Toots, leaning on his own bar, "but I'm in better condition than you."

Gleason spun a coin on the bar and watched it settle. "You," he said, using a finger to point, "are in better condition than me? My friend, I will bet you ten bucks I can beat you in a race any time, any place."

"For a sawbuck," said Shor, "you're on."

The men around the bar began to listen. Both of the fat ones removed ten-dollar bills from their wallets and Toots said, "I'll race you around the block and the first man back picks up both tens."

"You," said Jackie, "have just made yourself a deal."

Gleason finished his drink, thought a moment, and said, "Tell you what, Toots. I'll race you around this block."

"This one? Fifty-first and Fifty-second?"

"Fifty-first and Fifty-second. We both start together outside that door. You run up to Fifth, around the corner, down Fifty-second, around Sixth, and up to this bar. I run the other way, around Sixth, up Fifty-second to Fifth, and down Fifty-first. Okay?"

"Okay. This is easy dough. It's a shame I have to run for it."

They waddled through the door and the race was on. Toots, laughing, trotted off through the crowds on Fifty-first en route to Fifth; Gleason, grimly, started in the other direction.

As soon as Jackie got out of sight of the restaurant, he hailed a cab. "Pal," he said, easing himself onto the cushions, "just drive me around the block and up to Toots Shor's place." About a hundred feet before he reached the restaurant, Gleason paid the driver, got out, trotted back into the bar without drawing a deep breath, and was pocketing the twenty dollars when Shor arrived.

Toots was partly dead. His skin was purple and his mouth

hung open as he gulped oceans of air. "You crumb," he gasped, "I don't know how you did it, but you won. I'll stand for a round of drinks."

The drinks were served and Gleason warned his pal that Toots ought to take better care of himself, drink less and get to bed early. Shor took it for a while in silence, then his eyes opened wide and he stared at his friend.

"Just a minute, you fat bum!" he growled. "How come you never passed me?"

There was a vague, uneasy feeling around DuMont that, now that they had a top drawing card in Gleason, the bigger networks might lure him away. Few suspicions were as well founded. At the National Broadcasting System, as well as at the Columbia Broadcasting System, the ranking executives had had the word passed to them, and they were now spending Friday nights at home watching Gleason. Jack Van Volkenburg and Hubbell Robinson of CBS made a ritual out of looking at Gleason and then comparing notes. Sadly, they agreed that he was a droll and amusing fellow in front of cameras. How come DuMont had him? No one seemed to know; the talk along Madison Avenue was that someone at DuMont had picked the man out of the blue.

Another man who was watching was Myron Kirk, the advertising executive who had once seen Jackie in *Along Fifth Avenue* and had also seen him at the Club 18. "Mike" Kirk knew that Gleason was funny; he needed no screen to tell him that. And he wasn't worried about Gleason's quick success; Mike had the Buick account and Buick had Milton Berle. This comedian was called "Mr. Television." He had a life contract and no one could topple him from the top of the heap.

The man who had a feeling, neither vague nor uneasy, that Gleason was going to go much higher in the entertainment world was Jackie Gleason. He was as sure of it as he was in the days when, at age fifteen, he had told the kids on Chauncey Street that someday he would be on top—bigger than "Milton Berle and all them guys."

He realized that he had been stalled for a long while. Now he was under way again, and going very fast. Instead of leaning back and helping himself "to a booze and a broad," he began to worry. A big man needs a big team. He was going to need more help than that furnished by Bullets and Philbin and Jerry Katz. He was going to need people on stage and off—efficient people on whom he could depend. Someday soon he was going to need secretaries and producers and directors and musicians and actors and announcers—a lot of people. A lot of good people.

And so, as he met people from day to day, Jackie began to draw together a team in his mind. For example, when "The Honeymooners" went on, Gleason said, "This guy, this what-are-we-calling-him? This Ralph Kramden is going to need a pal. A buddy. A guy who lives upstairs. He's going to have to be funny, and yet he can't be funny like me. I need a good situation comic, an actor. Now, who?"

Someone said that the guy who played the photographer was pretty good. What photographer? Jackie asked. You know, the man said, the one in the "Man of Distinction" bit.

Jackie snapped his fingers. "Carney," he said. "His name is Art Carney. A good man. Let's try him out." Carney was tried out as Ed Norton, and everybody said he was born for the part of the glib, happy-go-lucky dope who lived upstairs. Within a short while Carney developed into one of the finest actors in show business, an actor who could play Norton, could play Reggie's spade-bearded father, could play insipid Clem Finch to Gleason's loudmouthed Charley Bratton, had the versatility of a concert artist who could play Brahms with his back to the piano, sing operatic tenor, and execute a cello solo with his bare feet.

Carney, an insecure, overly modest man earning $200 a week, was and is the antithesis of Gleason. At parties he was a wall-flower. For years he drove an old yellow Pontiac and, even when riches came, he continued to drive the same car. He was a home man who spent much more time over the choice of his children's school than he did over his press clippings. Carney and Gleason seldom found themselves in the same gatherings off stage, and the occasions when Carney remained in town to have fun with the gang were so few that it alarmed his family and his friends.

And yet, one would have to go far back in theatrical history to find a team of comedians—not a comedian and a straight man, but a team of comedians—who complemented each other as these two. Gleason, star of the show, ran against tradition when he insisted that Carney get big billing and more money. When the writers did not give Carney enough laughs, Gleason tossed the script back at them and said, "Write Art in bigger than you have him." When there were bows to be taken before the curtain at show's end, Gleason always screamed, "Carney!" and brought his friend out and led the applause. At rehearsals he taught Art little bits of comedy which Jackie had learned the hard way—in night clubs and in burlesque. On Arthur Carney's side, he said many times that he wanted to keep on playing second to Gleason. "I don't want the responsibility of my own show. This way I make good money and Jackie has to make the decisions and whip the show together."

Gleason was still drawing up a mental team when, at Shor's one night, he was introduced to Lawrence "Jack" Hurdle. This was a big, hearty bald man who, in the long ago, had been Ted Healy's straight man. Later he had directed the "Beulah Show" on radio, had produced the "Ripley Believe-it-or-Not Show," and, in a short time, would be producing "Four-Star Review" and the "Colgate Comedy Hour" from time to time. This was a man who could draw a big show together, cook spaghetti at 1:00 A.M., keep ten thousand jokes and stories in a mental file cabinet, remain out until 4:00 A.M. with the boys, and could be depended upon to laugh it up when others felt blue.

Toots Shor told Gleason that Jack Hurdle also had "class."

One Friday night Jackie needed a girl who could play a serious role. One of the staff recommended Joyce Randolph. She played the part, was told that she did "well," and went home. Months later Gleason decided that Ed Norton needed a wife and, while the writers and technicians were suggesting names, he flapped his arms down and said, "No, get me that girl—that blonde who played the serious part some time ago."

They called Joyce Randolph, and she became Trixie Norton. Miss Randolph's real name was Joyce Sirola. Her people were Finns and they lived in Detroit. Before Gleason discovered her, she had been cast many times as the woman in the mysteries who gets killed.

On Christmas night Gleason walked into a bar blue and alone. He asked for a drink and looked around to see if there was anyone present that he knew. He saw one friend, a man named Eddie Hanley, and Gleason was about to walk over to him when he noticed that Eddie was sitting with a remarkably pretty redhead.

So he sat, brooding over his drink, until Hanley waved to him to come over.

"Honey," said Hanley, "I want to present Jackie Gleason. Jack, say hello to Audrey Meadows."

The trio sat and talked, and Gleason asked the redhead if she was in show business, and she said yes, that she was in a show called *Top Banana*. Gleason knew the star, Phil Silvers, and they talked that up for a while, and then the restless Gleason said, "Let's go." They went to the Biltmore to listen to Freddie Martin's music, and after a while Jackie grinned and said, "And away-y-y we go!" with a funny flick of his elbows, and away they went. This time it was to The Embers to listen to more music, and Jackie, in talking to Audrey Meadows, learned that she was the daughter of a missionary to China, had been raised in China, in fact.

The conversation moved so fast after that that no one noticed the time until Miss Meadows announced that it was 4:00 A.M. and, if the gentlemen would put her in a cab, she would go home and they could go on.

She did. And they did. But Gleason would remember.

Among those who thought that Gleason was a good actor but was *not* destined for greatness were his manager and his assistant manager, the Messrs. Durgom and Philbin. They split 20 per cent of Gleason's earnings, but this was hardly enough to keep them in suède shoes. Added to the lack of faith was Bullets' anger when Jackie signed a seven-year contract with the theatrical agency, MCA.

"The guy walks down the street," Durgom said, "MCA has a piece of it."

When Bullets learned that Music Corporation of America had

lent Jackie $10,000 in return for his signature on the contract, the manager was twice as angry.

"He's a dope," said Bullets. "They should have *given* him that much for signing."

Durgom phoned Philbin from California. "Things aren't going so good, Jack. Close the New York office and come out here."

"What will I do with Gleason?"

"We'll handle him. You and I will go into partnership. We can sell people to pictures."

"You think it will go?"

"How can it miss? We'll go into the Screen Actors Guild."

It should have been a good wedding of talent. Some clients liked Durgom the worrier, who walked around with two telephones in his hand. Some liked the jaded attitude of Jack Philbin, whose tired smile told them I-have-seen-all-and-I-know-all-but-go-on-with-your-story. A good manager and a good doctor have a single thing in common: both have an excellent bedside manner.

They opened a Hollywood office and called it Personalities Limited, which had a lovely exclusive sound, and the partners managed to sign a few people for motion pictures. To keep Jackie Gleason happy, Bullets flew back to New York every time the screams of neglect could be heard on the Sunset Strip.

For some mysterious reason, this wedding of intellect with intellect did not produce substantial profits.

"I just can't make it," Philbin said one afternoon. "I'm not geared to this stuff."

"You're right," said Bullets. "I want to get out of it. You can have the clients that are left. I'll keep Gleason. Honest, Jack, I can't keep running to New York to watch this guy. I even hired an accountant to watch him *and* the books."

The partnership was dissolved, and Jack Philbin, instead of protecting the interests of two female clients, went around and about selling a sort of home water purifier to Los Angelenos.

If Gleason knew that he had been exchanged for two ladies, he gave no sign. He waited quietly until Bullets, in New York, had to make another trip to California.

"Now look, pal," said Jackie. "I got a good thing going for me right here and I need somebody."

"Jackie, don't be unreasonable. What can happen in a week?"

"Plenty. Things are going to go even better for me and I need a man here every day."

"Jackie!"

"Don't Jackie me. Put somebody on the pay roll."

"Who?" said Bullets, who had now uttered the word that Gleason wanted him to say.

"Philbin is a nice guy."

Durgom knew that he had been trapped. He knew that Gleason liked Philbin and had waited patiently for this favorable moment to force the issue. "You'd like to see him get a break, wouldn't you?" Durgom said.

"Certainly."

"All right, Jackie. I'll bring him in. I won't agree to keep him but I'll try him."

Philbin dropped the water purifiers and returned to New York as assistant to George Durgom at $300 a week. No one seemed to divine that Jackie's biggest problem was that he would always need people he could trust to be at his call at all hours. The more people, the better.

When he had Philbin, the new star wanted Durgom. Bullets reminded him that Philbin had been employed so that Bullets could take care of the Hollywood business, and Gleason said, "Nothing doing. I want you here too." In addition, Jackie phoned MCA and said that if Herb Rosenthal, the regular television agent, was too busy to be around him every day that they had better find someone who could. At once the agency detailed Jerry Katz to remain with the star at all times.

In spite of their close association, Katz never had the nerve to mention the $2.80 that Jackie owed him for an old lunch.

"Cavalcade of Stars" starred Jackie Gleason for fifteen months before the big networks decided that they had to have him. The National Broadcasting Company began to ask questions about him at almost the precise time that Hubbell Robinson, vice-president of Columbia Broadcasting System, and Jack Van

Volkenburg, president of CBS, began to take Herb Rosenthal of MCA to lunch.

This was October 1951 and all over the eastern part of the United States youngsters on the street were making funny flapping motions with their arms, rolling their eyes, and yelling, "And awayy-y-y we go!" Other children, pleased with something given to them, would shake their heads elaborately and say, "You're a dan-dan-dandy!" Gleason's mannerisms could be seen in any neighborhood, and adults quoted his best lines and laughed over them, and the combination of Gleason, Pert Kelton, Carney and Joyce Randolph turned out, in the matter of marital vicissitudes, to be so much like millions of other married couples that irritated husbands all over the country held tight fists under the noses of wives and growled, "One of these days, Alice—pow! Right in the kisser!"

To CBS, Gleason was something else. He was a precious property; a sensitive actor who could probably do dramatic parts as well as comedy; a large fiery gem whose many facets had yet to be examined. Some of the executives who had studied his work began to use the word "genius," a dangerous, slippery word. Still, even his detractors admitted that, at the very least, Jackie Gleason had developed the qualities of the true theatrical artist, a person who, by make-believe, could convince an audience that something real was transpiring and could mold and shape the mood of the audience so that, at will, the artist could make it laugh or make it weep.

The Columbia Broadcasting System wanted Gleason and wanted him bad. All they wanted to know from MCA was "How long must we wait for him?" and "How much will it cost us?"

Theatrically, the boy had become a man. Emotionally, the boy remained a boy.

THE PENTHOUSE

"In any case," the writer said, "I think that Gleason is in love. Deeply."

The doctor shrugged. "You know more than I do."

"Oh, no," the writer said, waving his cigarette over the debris of dinner, "don't give me that stuff. You know this man and you know that he is capable of falling in and out of love at great speed. How come this time he has remained constant for three full years or more?"

The doctor shrugged. "I'm not a swami. I don't know. Then again, maybe I do. Yes, maybe I do. He has again met the so-called good girl. You know, men are prone to do the same things over and over. Take a woman who is married to a neurotic who beats her. She complains bitterly, but, if he should die, she picks a second husband who is pretty handy with his fists."

"The trouble with men of medicine is that they try to put everything into a neat slot."

"I'm just giving some offhand guesses." The doctor glanced at his watch. "Let me ask you a question. Will he get a divorce?"

"Is he irrevocably in love with Marilyn?"

"Now, now. You're answering a question with a question."

"Who knows what he'll do. I don't."

"You think it's possible?"

"It's possible."

"Jackie is Catholic. Marilyn is Catholic. Gen is Catholic. You're Catholic. And you think that this is possible."

"It is possible that he may someday be canonized."

"No, no. Wait a minute. I asked a simple question and I want an unequivocal answer."

"You've got it."

"Then it's possible that he might get a divorce?"

"Marriage, Doctor, is a sacrament. It cannot be bent or twisted to suit the whim of a heart. But—wait a minute, now—let me finish. Sometimes the heart of a Catholic becomes more important to him than his soul. It isn't common, but it has happened. How old is Jackie emotionally?"

"Sixteen. Maybe seventeen."

"Now you are beginning to answer your own question. At sixteen or seventeen, life and love are often more important than death and the hereafter."

"He has deep religious convictions."

"Okay. That's the mitigating factor against divorce. So has Marilyn."

"Have you talked to her?"

"A lovely girl. No glamour-puss. Genuine."

The doctor stood and patted his pocket to make sure that he had his glasses.

"It's sort of tragic," he said as he went out the door. He grinned. "You got a happy ending for this book?"

"No," the writer said. "I stink at fiction."

The continuing battle between the big systems of television is not for air space, nor even for time. The battle was, is and will be for the listener. The more listeners, the more sponsors. The more sponsors, the more money. The more money, the bigger the attractions put on the air. What makes this battle interesting is that it is unremitting, and that there is never a permanent winner.

The tide of listeners rises and falls, half hour by half hour. By the millions, people switch their dials from one network to another, or to a small independent station if it has a good show scheduled. This tide—as merciless as a wave crashing on sand—is what keeps television honest. The advertising-agency men, who speak for the sponsors, watch these tides more closely than a village banker watches an alcoholic teller. Today's hit show could be next week's egg, with corners on it.

No frigid, glistening peak in the world is as slippery as the top of the world of television. The moment a show reaches that peak, the competing networks have two options: (1) devising a better, more costly show to take the listeners away from it; or

(2) putting a cheap show on at that time and surrendering. They seldom use the second option.

Each September battle lines are drawn and redrawn, and big stars are moved around the face of the clock to the point where the network executives feel that they will show to best advantage while, at the same time, they have the best chance of robbing the competing networks of listeners.

Thus, when the Columbia Broadcasting System wanted the services of Jackie Gleason, there wasn't a scintilla of sentiment in the deal. They saw Gleason as a new face, a new talent, a new format, something born and bred for television and not borrowed from motion pictures or from the Broadway stage.

Aside from his brilliance as an actor, he would be, in the eyes of millions of people, the average man—frustrated, blubbery, sentimental, scheming and amusing in his portrayal of the very people who were at home watching him. CBS saw this, and CBS also had a notion that they would like to put Gleason on for an hour, opposite NBC's "All-Star Review," a show which clearly had the attention of the majority of listeners. The "All-Star Review," in weekly rotation, featured such top-flight stars as Jimmy Durante, Tallulah Bankhead, Ed Wynn and Martha Raye. If Gleason could not drive them off the air, CBS felt that the least he could do would be to hold them to a stalemate.

There were conferences between CBS and MCA, with the network trying to get Gleason as cheaply as possible, and MCA trying to sell him as expensively as possible. The result of such conferences is almost always a series of compromises between the asking price and the bidding price; between the length of contract desired by the network and that demanded by the star; the same applies to so-called protective clauses, indemnifying clauses, moral turpitude clauses and others. In general, such a contract averages about a page and a half longer than a mutual security pact between nations.

The net effect of all of this was that Jackie Gleason, overnight, was rich and famous. The contract between Gleason and Du-Mont would expire in June, 1952. The new one, with Columbia Broadcasting System, was to begin in September, 1952. In the new one, MCA had represented him handsomely because he would be more than a star in a show; he would produce the show. Jackie Gleason would own it and be the sole responsible agent for delivering it every week on Saturdays at 8:00 P.M. Eastern Standard Time.

This, in the trade, is called a "package." Jackie agreed to devise a one-hour network show, for which he would hire the writers who would write the sketches; retain the orchestra to play the music and then tell them what music to play; do the casting and hiring of other actors; be responsible for the lighting, the director, the producer, the camera work, the properties, the electricians, the stagehands, the carpenters, the dancing girls, the dances, the guest stars, the sets.

Most stars would feel that it is a full-time job trying to be funny for one hour a week. Not so Gleason. He could hardly have been more delighted at the chance to "run the whole show." He had had no experience on the administrative side, but he looked forward to it as though this were just one more step in the climb to success, when, in fact, he was assuming a big business obligation.

Still, if Jackie did not comprehend the enormity of the job, his advisers did. The Gleason lawyer—Robert Schulman, of Washington, a pipe-smoker who has tamed all the tigers in his stomach—advised him to incorporate at once, not so much to ease the tax burden, which was a consideration, but mainly so that the corporation would be responsible for the show.

What came out of this was a corporate structure called jackie gleason enterprises (no capital letters). Two hundred shares of common stock were issued, plus a few shares of preferred, and Gleason owned them all. Officers were needed, and Bullets Durgom became president.

CBS agreed that the weekly budget of the show should be $50,000 for talent and sets. It would cost, in addition, about $70,000 to put the show on the CBS network—air time. The total cost was $120,000 a week. For thirty-nine weeks, it would cost $3,680,000 to see "The Jackie Gleason Show," and this, roughly, would be split up between such sponsors as Schaefer Pen, Schick

Razors, and Nescafé Coffee. Each would have to realize a profit of more than one and a quarter million dollars in extra sales to make the show worth while.

If the show, on any given Saturday, cost less than $50,000 to produce, jackie gleason enterprises, the producer, and CBS would split the surplus. If, let us say, the show came to $45,000, j.g enterprises would get $2,500 and CBS would get $2,500. To prevent Gleason from bringing the show to the cameras too cheap, a clause in the contract said that, in no case, could it cost less than $45,000.

Enterprises hired Jackie for $7,500 a week as star of the show. Thus he stood to earn $292,500 a year, plus whatever profits piled up in enterprises. The least he and his corporation could expect to make would be about $400,000 a year.

If you think that this dizzied our hero, close the book now, because you have learned nothing about Jackie Gleason. He appreciated it, but he felt that he was worth all of this, and that it was slightly overdue. He was sure that he was not any funnier now, in 1952, than he had been in 1942; he understood his art now as well as, but no better than, he had ten years prior. As a producer, he had no experience whatever, but, whereas the average Broadway producer did one musical a year, Jackie was going to do thirty-nine a year, with sketches, and all of them, he hoped, would be worthy of being seen by scores of millions of people.

One of the awkward moments, so far as The Greatest was concerned, occurred just after CBS had secretly closed the deal. Jackie was still starring for DuMont.

"Our deal has seven months to go," Milton Douglas said. "Can you give me an idea of what kind of a new contract you expect?"

Gleason thought about it for a moment. He had been pledged to secrecy by CBS and MCA. He could not say, "I'm signed. I'm going to be one of the biggest entertainers in the world. For the next three years I'm going to be on top, moneywise, prestigewise, showwise. DuMont is too little and too late." He could say none of that.

Instead, he said, "Well, pal," with the happy grin, "I want ten thousand a week and the privilege of doing the show from California if I want to."

Douglas smiled too. "Jack," he said, "I won't say you're not worth it, but it's pretty steep for this group. I'll let you know."

The producer argued for his discovery, but the drug sponsors didn't permit themselves to think about the matter seriously. In substance, they said that the whole show wasn't worth that much to them—much less one actor.

It's a lot of aspirin, at that.

June 1952 was a good time for Gleason to take a long vacation and rest up for the labors ahead. There was a space of three months between the expiration of the DuMont contract and the opening of the CBS show. Gleason never used the word vacation. There were two things which he felt had to be done that summer. One was to draw his team together. The other was to make a personal-appearance tour and earn some loose cash.

When the Columbia Broadcasting System unsnapped the leashes on its publicity chieftains—Jack Goldstein and Dorothy Leffler—the moonlike face of Gleason, in addition to glowing stories, appeared in newspapers from Portland to Portland and from Fargo to Key Largo. At one stage, Jackie even held a mass interview with all of the television columnists—by telephone. Editorially, it was a big splash.

The day the news was published, everybody who knew Jackie knew that he—as the saying went—"had it made." On that day of days Davey Shelley went calling on his old pal. What he expected was a phantasmagoria of broads, booze and thousand-dollar bills. What he saw was Jackie laid out on a bed in his Fifty-second Street apartment undressed, unshaven, uncombed, alone. He was staring at the ceiling.

"What's the matter with you?" Shelley asked.

"Not a thing, pal. Not a thing."

"What's this hermit bit?"

"Just thinking."

"This is a big day, my boy. A large, wonderful day, and look at you. You look like a bum."

"I'll get shaved."

He got up slowly and, from a closet, brought out a trunk and some boxes. Shelley sat and watched. The new boxes were full of custom-made shirts, and this was of special interest because,

quite often, the old ones were given to Lee Meyers, the press
agent, who, in time, passed them on to Davey Shelley. Jackie
opened one box and out of it bulked dozens and dozens of pairs
of socks in blues, grays and browns.

"I met a guy in the sock business," Gleason said gloomily, "and
he hustled me for a gross."

From another box came shoes, and it became apparent to
Shelley that Jackie had laid hold of big fresh bank notes somewhere in anticipation of his new job, because in the box were
twelve pairs of black shoes and twelve pairs of brown ones—
all the same model.

"What's this all about?" Davey said.

"Met a guy makes Sinatra's shoes," said Jackie.

"This is ridiculous!" Shelley said. "You got Sinatra's tailor,
you got his bootmaker, you got his Cadillac; the only thing you
haven't got that belongs to Frankie—"

"Don't worry," said Gleason. "I'll get her too."

He slung the old trunk on the bed. Carefully, almost lovingly,
he packed all his old suits in it, a lot of freshly laundered shirts,
ties, socks, underwear and old but serviceable shoes.

"What's all this?" asked Shelley.

"You interested in horoscopes?"

"Nope. That's a lot of crud."

"For your information, my friend, it's no such thing. Right now
I'm supposed to be playing burlesque in the Adams Theatre in
Newark. Instead of being there, the wheel took a little extra spin
in my case, and I'm signed up with CBS. You know what I'm
doing? I'm thinking that some day I may find myself back at the
Adams, and if that happens, I know I won't have a dime or a
suit of clothes, so I'm sending all this stuff to the Adams right now
and I'm marking it, JACKIE GLEASON, HOLD FOR ARRIVAL."

Shelley said nothing for a moment. He was stunned in the presence of a ham who realized, better than anyone else, that he had
been made big and that he could be made small again just as
easily.

"You got any money?" Shelley asked softly.

"Maybe eighty clams."

"Well, take a tip. You got a good idea here, Jack. But put a five- or a ten-spot in each suit. Then, when you get to Newark someday, you put the clean suit on and you reach in the pocket and you got money to eat with until you get rolling again."

Gleason did it. Before there was any celebration for the new success, the trunk was dispatched to the Adams Theatre and, as it was carried downstairs, Jackie said, "No matter how big I get in this racket, I'll always remember that I got someplace to go."

There is no point, according to the Gleason philosophy, to being a big success unless one is going to travel first class all the way, and among the ways of traveling first class is to have an office and a secretary. The secretary was important. Jackie needed someone who could not only take a letter and type it, but also read his mind between letters and handle his erratic bank account, keep pests away from him, order his appointment sheet so that he could cancel out when he did not feel in the mood to see people, advise him and be completely trustworthy.

Such a person does not live, but that didn't trouble Jackie. He ordered Bullets to look around and find that girl. Durgom was in the office of a friend one day when he saw a girl he had met casually before. She was Lee Reynolds, dark, pretty, an actress, a radio fashion expert, a brain. Durgom talked to her a while, and he listened a while. He had no idea whether Miss Reynolds was a good secretary or a poor one, but he had an idea that her directness, her frankness tinged with sympathy, was exactly what Jackie needed.

"Why don't you come over with me to the Adelphi Theatre," said Bullets, "and see Jackie. He needs a secretary; more than a secretary—an assistant."

Miss Reynolds accompanied the manager. At the Adelphi, she waited an hour and a half to see the man. Then he walked up to her, with his headlights on upper beam, hand outstretched, and said, "I don't know what you can do, but you're hired."

Gleason was a busy executive. He likes to make decisions, and he makes them in a trice. He wanted Art Carney to come over to CBS with him, and Carney's manager, Bill McCaffrey, said that Art couldn't make the switch for less than $750 a week.

"The hell with that!" Gleason roared. "He gets a thousand or nothing." Joyce Randolph, who played Carney's wife, got $300. Jack Hurdle, the bald one who had impressed Jackie as a production executive, was hired as producer of the new show at $750.

Jackie was moving fast, and he had no time for parties, no time for drinking, no time to relax. Next he wanted writers and he wanted good ones. Like Mark Hellinger, Gleason believed that "if you ain't got it in the script, you ain't got it nowhere along the line." He wanted two writers on each script, and it was then that he set up his "team" system. His plan was that Team A would be working on this Saturday's story; Team B would be rapping out next week's show; and Team C would be trouble shooters, working with either of the first two teams which might find itself in difficulty. Team A was Marvin Marx and Walter Stone; Sid Zelinka and Leonard Stern were Team B; the trouble shooters were Andy Russell and Herb Finn. The average pay of these writers came to $750 a week each. The bill for writers came to $4,500 a week, and, for that money, Gleason expected good sketches.

The Fifty-second Street apartment was a jumble of writers, dead cigarettes, Gleason, Lee Meyers, Lee Reynolds, Bullets Durgom, yesterday's newspapers and a warm typewriter. There was one telephone, one bathroom. Gleason needed an office, and that was another item on his check list.

The insomnia was on Gleason. Often he got to bed at 3:00 A.M. and was up at 4:30 with a headful of ideas and no one to tell them to. Often he read the newspapers a second time in the lonely hours, or turned on the television set to see if, by chance, there might be a late, late, late show.

One morning he was tuned in on NBC at 7:00 A.M. and saw the "Dave Garroway Show." His one-time friend of the disk-jockey days, Jack Lescoulie, did the announcing for the show and Gleason watched him close and liked his diffident, almost boyish approach.

When the show was over, he phoned Lescoulie and said, "Little Abner, you want to go to work for me?"

"Jackie!" said Lescoulie.

"There's a job as announcer, if you want it."

"Of course I want it."

"Remember I told you that someday—"

"I remember. I'm glad that you did."

It wasn't quite that simple. Lescoulie was now working for NBC and if there was one thing which sparked no enthusiasm in the breasts of the National Broadcasting Company brass it was releasing a good announcer to the Columbia Broadcasting System. And that wasn't all. The Columbia Broadcasting System, with a full staff of competent announcers, could hardly have been more horrified if Gleason had yelled, "Sarnoff!" into a live microphone. They wrestled orally with Jackie, and they tried to sell him one of their staff men, but his answer was: "Look. I want Lescoulie. Nobody else. He's a pal of mine. So far as NBC is concerned, they have six weeks to go on the contract and that's when I intend to sign him."

"We think you owe it to us to audition our announcers."

"Fine," Jackie snarled. "If you want to pay for the camera time, and if you want to send them in here, I'll just sit and listen to each and every one of them, and when they're all through, Jack Lescoulie is the boy who's going to get the job."

Lescoulie got the job, but NBC could not find a suitable replacement for him, and for years afterward he was the only announcer who worked for Gleason on CBS and Garroway on NBC.

The dream team was being drawn together quickly and, in a very real sense, permanently, but an office was needed desperately. Jackie solved this quicker than the average woman can decide on a pair of dollar-forty-nine stockings. He walked into the Park Sheraton Hotel at Fifty-fifth Street and Seventh Avenue and found that they had a penthouse to lease. He leased it for $25,000 a year, and, looking down on Central Park from the terrace, he realized for the first time that he was really traveling first class.

The penthouse was not ideal—either as an office or as a home —but it was a plush start. There were a bamboo bar, with a gallon of brandy in a wooden cradle, some wrought-iron furniture and glass table tops, a living room with a Spanish-Moroccan motif, a fireplace, a bedroom, an up-the-curved-stairway office for Bullets and one for Lee Reynolds, a downstairs office for Gleason and Philbin, a kitchen, terrace, porch furniture and a girl receptionist. On the outer door, in small gold letters, was the information: "j.g. enterprises."

Here Gleason lived in the splendor to which he wanted to become accustomed. Here Tony Amico, in a white coat, made spaghetti and meatballs in the predawn hours, and here the leeches and free-loaders hung out, flattering the new king and wishing him a long reign.

One of the gifts was a talking parakeet which stood sullenly in a cage in the foyer and never even imitated a bird.

"Maybe," said Philbin, "he's holding out for a writer."

Jackie glared at the parakeet. "All I can say," he said loudly, "is that it's supposed to be a talking parakeet. Let the bird take it from there."

In July of 1952 Gleason and Company went off on the personal-appearance tour—Pittsburgh, Chicago, Detroit, Cleveland, Boston, etc. He and his troupe broke records everywhere. Whereas, only a short time before, the complaint was that "nobody ever heard of Jackie Gleason," now everyone seemed to know him and long lines of theatergoers attested to his popularity. George Clarke, veteran city editor and columnist, took a look at the swirling mobs in Boston and said that he had never seen anything like it.

Leaving Pittsburgh, the whole troupe had a "ball." They had worked four shows a day and they were tired and eager for laughter. A lot of Scotch sweetened a lot of good stories, and when the last story had been laughed into a vacuum, Pert Kelton, one-time motion-picture comic and now the life of "The Honeymooners" as Mrs. Ralph Kramden, picked her feet up slowly and set them down and leaned heavily against the walls of the swaying train en route to her roomette.

"She'll be okay in the morning," Jackie said.

"Sure she will," Lee Reynolds said. "Get some sleep yourself."

Pert Kelton wasn't all right in the morning. The train was standing in the terminal at Chicago and everybody was off the train except Pert. It required time and patience for Lee Reynolds to get her to unlock the door.

"Listen," Jackie said to Miss Reynolds, "she'll have to pull herself together. We've got a big show on our hands."

Rehearsal was at 11:00 A.M. Pert Kelton went on. She kept saying that she couldn't. There were four shows. Lee Reynolds stood in the wings holding a white basin. The thousands out front roaring with laughter thought that it was part of the act when Alice screamed at Ralph, then wheeled around toward the wings, disappeared through the bedroom door for a moment, and came out again for another funny line.

The people out front were wrong. So were some of the people on stage. Jackie felt no special concern because, as a drinking man, he knew that he had to be in shape for the show and, in all his recorded life, had missed a performance but once.

"I have a pain in my arm," Pert Kelton whispered more than once. "You're killing me."

In the fourth show that day, she collapsed. She was taken to a hospital and a doctor examined her, smiled a little, and said, "Nothing but a hang-over." Still, Bullets and Lee Reynolds were worried because they couldn't remember ever seeing a hang-over that became increasingly worse. Lee phoned Pert Kelton's husband in New York.

"Try an electrocardiogram," he said. "She didn't want anybody to know."

Pert Kelton had sustained a coronary thrombosis. She never played the part of Alice Kramden again.

The troupe returned to New York in late August, and the first order of business was to find a homely-looking actress who could work herself into a livid rage quickly. Many were auditioned, none of them was chosen.

One afternoon Val Irving, a handsome theatrical manager, was taking a walk when he met the Sorrowful Sam of the Gleason organization, Mr. Durgom.

"You got a minute?" said Irving. "I'm going up to see Audrey. Come on."

One of his clients was Audrey Meadows, the cute redhead who had spent almost all of one Christmas night out with Gleason. Durgom sat and the three began to discuss the problem of replacing Pert Kelton. Each one had names to suggest, and each time a name was suggested, the remaining two could think of a good reason why that person could not take the job.

"How about me?" said Miss Meadows.

Durgom gave her the forgiving smile.

"I can play it," she said, with spirit. They talked about it more, and the more they studied the girl's prettiness, the better they understood why she could never play the part. Alice Kramden should be a tough, flea-bitten shrew.

She argued. They shrugged and took her to see Jackie. The Greatest listened, looked again at Miss Meadows to make sure, and then said, "You guys nuts or something? This girl is pretty. Alice is round-shouldered and tough. She's a real mean broad."

Miss Meadows left in anger. She executes her angers with much realism. Durgom suggested that she go to a photographer, muss her flaming hair, pull it sideward until it became stringy, put on an old housedress, ancient shoes, lean on a mop, and look tired and nasty. When the photo was ready, she mailed it to Jackie Gleason.

"Who's this?" he asked. When he heard that it was Audrey Meadows, he could not believe it. Then he took another look and laughed. "Any dame who would have her picture taken like this deserves the job." She got it. Overnight, Audrey Meadows became Alice Kramden—without an audition.

Before the show opened in the autumn, Jackie still had work to do. He would need supporting actors and he had marked the name of Sammy Birch at the top of the list. Sammy had been good to him in the old Halsey Theatre days; now Jackie would be good to Sammy. The next item was girls. He wanted a good chorus line, and so he phoned June Taylor.

"You want to come over with me, honey?"

"I'd love it."

"You'll get everything you want."

"How about an arranger?"

"June, you'll get anything you want to make this show the way I want it."

The whole team met at Sands Point one summer week end to plot the format of the show, and here is where great ideas were thrown into the air only to be shot into fragments, like clay pigeons, by the rest of the company. Jackie, whale fat in trunks and robe, sat and listened, speaking only when he had made a decision, or could think of an objection. He thinks very fast and accurately, for the most part. Now and then he becomes stubborn and therefore stupid, but, as a rule, he is sharp and has a flair for getting at the nub of an idea quickly.

He introduced the newest member of the team, director Frank Satenstein, to the older ones. Satenstein, tall and slender and young, was a CBS director, the only man from the network to make the Gleason show. His family owns one of the biggest book binderies in America (Stratford Press), but Satenstein felt no fascination for it and, conversely, learned to love sitting in a sound booth and watching everything go to hell.

They talked for an hour, a lot of it in witty lines and friendly ribbing, and then Gleason said, "What do you say we put sixteen girls on this show?" Then, answering his own question, he said, "This will be great."

Hurdle looked at Durgom. Durgom looked at Philbin. Philbin looked at Herb Rosenthal. Rosenthal looked at Katz. Katz looked at Lee Reynolds. Miss Reynolds looked at her fingernails. Sol Lerner, who was not part of the team but was June Taylor's husband, announced that sixteen girls swinging their legs across a twenty-one-inch screen would be tiny and ridiculous.

"But Jack," said Durgom. "The cost."

"How much are you going to pay for girls who will be on the screen how long—two minutes?" said Rosenthal.

Gleason flicked the ashes from a cigarette. He toyed with an empty coffee cup and he saw each one get up the courage to say that the idea was dangerous, costly, without point, without benefit to the show. When they had finished, he put the cup down and said airily, "Okay, June. Let's go ahead and get sixteen girls. You take care of it."

"Yes," said the choreographer. "I'll take care of it."

Miss Taylor, from the first, seemed to have a better-than-average understanding of Gleason. She knew, for instance, that he seldom ever uttered an off-hand idea. The chances were that he had been thinking about the sixteen chorus girls for days, had weighed the matter pro and con and had come to the conclusion that the girls would be worth the money.

She knew also that he had an old-fashioned idea of chorus

girls. He thought, for instance, that all chorus girls should be able to tap-dance—at least enough to execute a time step. He also thought that they should be short. He was not aware that the trend in chorus girls had been away from short ones in favor of tall ones, and that tap was old hat and the style was now toward ballet. He wanted short, pretty tap dancers—girls who were fast on their feet—and that's just what June Taylor was going to get for him.

She sensed also that he was a moody man when it came to music. He felt all music deeply, but he could not explain in technical terms what he felt. He understood cadence and tempo and shades of musical feeling, but he could explain none of it. In time, June reached a stage where, by listening to a musical number and trying to think like Jackie, she could almost tell in advance whether he would okay it or not.

Now, for some reason which only Jackie could understand, he wanted to open the show with sixteen girls. When the meeting was over, Rosenthal of MCA and Durgom of Gleason turned their guns on Miss Taylor.

"Sixteen girls?" they said, with pained expressions. "*Sixteen girls?* How much is this going to cost?"

Miss Taylor looked up at the last of a summer sky. "Let me see," she said slowly, ticking dollars off on her fingers. "They will come to about a hundred and twenty-five apiece. That's two thousand dollars, I think. Then we'll need costumes, shoes, a choreographer, studio rehearsal time and my services. I think we ought to be able to do it for three thousand."

"How are you going to photograph them with a camera?" the two men asked. "The girls going to stand a block away?"

"Yes," June said, nodding her head. "Three thousand ought to see it through."

"Three thousand a week?" the two men said. They looked at each other. "Well, let it go. This thing will last two weeks and then we'll cut down to eight girls."

The show went on in late September and was an almost instantaneous hit. As Jackie came down the center of the stage of the old Hammerstein Theatre on Broadway, he was a big, good-looking man, with the widest grin, and he nodded left and right to the sixteen girls who had just finished the first opening number of the first show. From backstage, he had timed his entrance so that the applause for the girls was beginning to die off, and, as they parted ranks to permit him to come through, the theater audience gave him a welcome, so the show opened on a double round of applause.

When it died down, he looked up toward the gallery coyly and said, "Oh, but you you're a dan-dan-dandy group!" and he had them in his palm, not only in the theater, but across the nation as well. This man was always confident in his stage attitudes, and the audience sensed it and appreciated it. This was no quasi-comedian feeling his way and hoping that the people would think that he was funny. This actor knew that he was funny and expected the audience to be intelligent enough to understand that fact.

The first rating was Gleason 14; Jimmy Durante, on NBC's "All-Star Review," 28. The following week Jackie reached 15. Then 17. When he rose to within two points of the "All-Star Review," NBC began to worry. They drew up a gigantic show consisting of Milton Berle, Groucho Marx, Ethel Barrymore and Martha Raye and tried to beat him to death with high-priced talent. But more than 30,000,000 persons with television sets had already been inoculated with Ralph Kramden, Reggie Van Gleason III, The Poor Soul and Charley Bratton and, when the ratings came up on Monday morning, the latter four proved to be more popular than the million-dollar quartet.

In time, the audience of 30,000,000 grew to be 40,000,000 and later 50,000,000, and some say that it went almost to 60,000,000 Americans, but whether it did or not is, in itself, a statistic. What is provable is that Jackie Gleason, in a short time, became a great star of television. The results were felt in many ways. In some cities, the police noticed that there was less traffic than usual on the roads on Saturday evenings. Theater managers reported a drop in business on Saturday nights. Supermarkets had a decline in dollar volume on Saturdays.

And yet, behind the scenes, Jackie was not a serene star. When he was disappointed in his writers, the roars of rage could be

heard down the corridors of the twenty-third floor of the Park
Sheraton Hotel. Much of what he had to say will not appear in
any book. At the same time, he became less tractable. Durgom
and Philbin learned quickly that if Jackie did not relish a sug-
gestion, one might as well remain silent because he did not want
to listen to arguments in favor of something he had already decided against.

Sometimes, when he could not sleep, he paced his bedroom
until 9:00 A.M. and then came out into the office section and
roared, "Where the hell *is* everybody? I thought that this office
was run on a nine-to-five basis. Let's get it understood around
here once and for all time—if the people are due to be in here
at nine, make sure they get in at nine!"

This was not the popping of a swelled head. His egomania
was no worse, no better than it had been all along. This was the
result of too much work, too much frustration, the refusal, on his
part, to delegate some authority to the others on his team. Everything had to be okayed personally by Jackie. Everybody understood this, and so nobody but Gleason had any real authority
and nobody but Jackie did the real work.

From the start, he was his own producer, his own director, his
own business agent, his own star and his own pet peeve. In the
first few weeks, the Columbia Broadcasting System thought it
had a tiger by the tail. Jackie said that the scenery the network
built for his show was too expensive. Also, it didn't fit right. Also,
it arrived too late.

Hubbell Robinson, the vice-president, became so irritated that
he assigned a special man from his office to do nothing but
adjust matters between CBS and JG.

Gleason wanted a special telephone line direct to CBS and
got it. He wanted another direct line to MCA and got it. For a
time, whatever scorn he felt for his agents was channeled into
the ears of little Jerry Katz. The young man's face reddened,
whitened and sometimes blued. But he had the necessary iron
to do the job and he listed Gleason's complaints and got on the
direct telephone line and repeated the Gleason gripes, softening
some of the blunt words here and there.

The sponsors were fighting too. Each one claimed that he had the poorest spot on the program, and Gleason, in anger, rotated them. Another source of irritation, to him, was that they rehearsed their commercials at the last moment, the only time he wanted to rehearse his show. He put it to Hubbell Robinson bluntly, "If you don't get these commercials out of here, pal, we won't be able to go on tonight." And yet, to help the sponsors, he conceived the idea of having beautiful girls in portrait frames to hold the sponsors' products in view of millions at the start of the show. He called these showgirls his "Portrettes."

Everyone in show business understands temperament, which, in a loose translation, is bad manners in a big actor, but Hubbell Robinson reached the point of total absorption and sent a note to Gleason with a countercomplaint. In doing this, Robinson forgot for the moment that he was vulnerable, inasmuch as he had given Gleason only 75 television stations in the CBS network, whereas NBC's "All-Star Review" had 105 outlets. The return letter from Gleason came quick enough to snap Robinson's head.

DEAR HUBBELL:

As you can see, we are kicking everyone out of the Trendex where we have an equal chance in station against station. The reason we lose nationally is because we haven't nearly as many stations as these other shows you've mentioned.

I cannot understand your attitude, Hubbell. I thought we would get a great deal of encouragement from you, which this letter does not indicate. However, I am being paid to do the best job possible, which I am certainly trying to do. My only question to you is how can we get more stations?

Kindest regards,

JACKIE

P.S. Why don't you put Red Buttons opposite "All Star?" He's in the first ten!

Gleason always had a keen idea of his own rights and prerogatives, and no one was going to push him around. When they tried it at the old Club Miami, he invited them out in the alley.

This was a different league, a different world, where all the fighting was done with words, but if those were the rules he too could fight with words.

One Saturday at noon he was rehearsing the show and someone whispered to Jackie that, unknown to him, his rehearsal was being piped into the home of a CBS official. The star, interrupting the action, walked over to his director, Frank Satenstein, and asked if it were true. Satenstein began to limp through an explanation.

"All I want to know," said Jackie, "is whether this rehearsal is being run through a camera to somebody's house. That's all, and the answer is either yes or no."

"Yes," said Satenstein, "it is. But what I—"

"That's all!" Jackie shouted. He walked over to the nearest camera. "You want to watch television!" he shouted. "Pay for it!" and he stalked off stage. He went up to his dressing room and announced that under no circumstances would he go before the cameras that night. He didn't care what anybody said, or did, there would be no Gleason show that night. He dressed for the street.

On stage, everything was quiet. Deathly quiet. This was no temperament. No bluff. Jackie was outraged, and nothing could force him to do the show that night. Phones buzzed all over town. Agents were called and the word was passed. "No Gleason tonight. He quits." The word went to CBS. "No Gleason tonight. He refuses to go on." Within a few minutes cabs from several sectors of New York were converging on the Hammerstein Theatre, and pleading voices were trying to get Jackie to change his mind.

Not a chance, he said. This show was his show, his responsibility, and if Bill Paley himself walked into that theater and Jackie didn't want him to be there, the star had a perfect right to order him off the premises, even though he was president of the network. Therefore, by what right did CBS pipe his rehearsals, with all its mistakes and its roughness, into the home of an official? By no right whatever. It was a sneaky move, but he had found out about it. Now let them find another star in the next three hours to put the show on.

Matters reached the stage where CBS was running through some old kinescopes of other Gleason shows and was preparing to show them and to make an announcement that Jackie was indisposed, or something.

At the last moment someone got the ear of the star and explained to him that the reason the show had been secretly piped to the home of a CBS official was that the official's wife was a chronically ill shut-in, and the only laughs she seemed to get was watching Jackie cavort on the stage.

The face of The Greatest settled into the deep, shadowy, homely lines it assumes when he is touched. "Is that true?" he whispered. His informer nodded. Jackie stood for a moment, just looking at the floor and breathing.

"She's really sick?"

The man nodded. Jackie's voice was low. "Nobody told me. Why didn't somebody tell me this?" He did the show that night. And he asked that the show continue to be piped privately to the lady every Saturday afternoon.

For a time there was trouble with Audrey Meadows too. Among Miss Meadows weaknesses there is no trace of a congenital inferiority complex. She too understands her prerogatives, and one of them is the right to rehearse. Gleason said that he was sorry, but he didn't like to rehearse. Made him stale.

"I'm sorry, Jack," she said in the nasal, Alice Kramden tone. "I've got to rehearse."

"Okay," he said grudgingly. "We'll rehearse Friday."

On Friday Miss Meadows was present with a copy of the next evening's script. So was Art Carney. So too was Joyce Randolph. No Gleason. On Saturday Gleason showed up at 2:00 P.M.—six hours before showtime—and announced that there would be a short rehearsal, but only for the guest star, who, in this case, happened to be Jane Froman.

Audrey Meadows walked backstage to her manager and said, "Tell Jackie that I've quit."

"Don't be a fool, Audrey," Val Irving begged. "Don't leave now. You're leaving yourself wide open as an actress who walks out on a contract."

Miss Meadows did what any woman in like circumstances

would do. She burst into tears. She was so angry that when she saw Jackie she wiped her eyes and said, "You know what? You don't need me, Jackie. You don't need anybody. You're a very talented man. I'm just going out there tonight and listen to you."

Gleason, to whom all women are beyond comprehension, looked pained and said, "Now what did I do?" and walked on. Later in the day, when everyone was out for a pre-show rest, Jackie seemed to sense the propriety of Miss Meadows' anger. He phoned her at her apartment.

"This," he cooed, "is the world's greatest comedian."

"Who?" Audrey said.

"The World's Greatest."

On her end of the phone, Miss Meadows felt a smile coming on. "Well, this is the world's greatest straight woman to the world's greatest comedian."

"I'm throwing a party tonight at the Park Sheraton for you. You can bring your sister."

"I'll bring my dog."

"The pooch will be welcome."

The Greatest tossed charm, and in a short time Miss Meadows graciously assured him that rehearsals *were* a complete waste of time, and Jackie Gleason was indeed the World's Greatest Comedian.

On that show, Jane Froman, the guest star, had forgotten that once upon a long ago she had been kind to a rough kid in a show called *Keep Off the Grass*. Since that time she had been hurt in a plane accident and had suffered long and had fought hard to get back to the top.

Now, after rehearsal, she went to the dressing room assigned to her, and on the dressing table was a large package. She opened it, and inside was a silver mink stole. The card read: "Because you were so nice to me—Keep Off the Grass—Jackie."

Two women wept that day.

The very nature of the business is emotional. The pendulum of feeling swings farther to the left toward laughter and farther to the right toward tears than in any other occupation or profession. The very merchandise being sold is emotion. And so it should come as no surprise that the people in the business are more prone toward laughter and toward anger than normal people.

There were differences of opinion between Gleason and Durgom, and this sometimes led to funny notes being exchanged between the two. Once, when Bullets was in California, Jackie sent him a note complaining that he had been sued for a bill amounting to $350 and the court not only ordered him to pay the $350, but also $716 in court costs. Mr. J. made it plain, in the letter, that he regarded this as Durgom's bill.

. . . I, in no way, have any intention of paying this—his salary, I mean. Now I don't care how you do it, Bullets, but you had better straighten it out with him. I am sick of being the fall guy. I've been too easy about everything. Now get at it, Bullets; I don't want to receive any more letters from lawyers.

Kindly take care of this immediately. I have other things to think about.

jackie

This was followed by another love letter, advising Bullets that he owed $35 on the office telephone bill and inviting him, if he didn't like it, to make other arrangements. This letter was followed by remorse; followed so closely, in fact, that regret showed in the postscript.

P.S. Dear Bullets: This is not the way I would like to write. However, things are such that I find it necessary to play the part of a s—— h——. I also realize, Bullets, that you and I are the real Poor Souls.

Durgom, having been thoroughly aroused by the first letter, was in no mood to read twittering postscripts. He wrote one of his own, and it jarred Jackie's jaw for five pages. The opening sentence read: "I would like very much to have you sit right down, turn off the records, sit back, read this letter carefully, and before making any hasty decisions, read it again." Then he swung the editorial ax in all directions, hitting at bills from lawyers, phone bills and obligations which Gleason hadn't discussed.

"Before leaving New York I told you my financial situation was not such that I could pay it at this time. Then I brought up the fact that you owe me $1,000.00 cash, which you immediately questioned. I am now beginning to believe that you don't trust me. You also owe me $400 on a personal wager. . . .

". . . you mentioned that you had no one but me to look to for guidance. I must say that if sitting there all day, every day, listening to your ideas and demands is called guidance, then I have the wrong dictionary. Anytime I have any ideas or advice you override it with a shrug of your shoulders or top me with some very clever line. Naturally I can't get back to you on it or I would have my own show. . . .

"Just because of our close friendship I don't intend to forget about the money that is due me. I think you know how I admire you as a guy and the great respect I have for your talent, but let me say in closing that I have no intention of 'Going back to Newark.' "

These were not deep wounds. They were the superficial scratches of success—matters of momentary irritation to be forgotten tomorrow. Or the next day. On the other hand, there is no sudden runaway success without some real pain, some permanent damage, some regret. In Jackie's case, the permanent hurt was reserved for Genevieve.

Within three months after "The Jackie Gleason Show" was put on the big network, they had made their final adieus. It would have happened in any case, but it might have been delayed a little longer if Jackie had not, at that time, felt the bitterness of constant upbraiding at home so sharply compared to the sweetness of adulation that he was now getting everywhere else. He was becoming impatient with criticism from any source; in his wife it became intolerable.

His rebuttal, "You never had it so good," did not answer her questioning charge, "Why can't you come home like other men?

Who are these women you're seen with? What's going on in the
Park Sheraton? Is it an office or a hide-out?"

The split came in December 1952, and this one was permanent. It might be that, at the time, Gen counted it as one more
in a long list of separations, followed always by contrition and
love. It is possible that she did not know that this one would
wreck the marriage for good.

The separation would hurt both parties. Her hurt was the
deeper because Genevieve still loved Jack. His hurt was the
breaking of an old habit—she had been his woman for sixteen
years and, despite the turbulence of the relationship, there was
a severing of an old bond, a turning away from an object of
respect and one-time affection.

Geraldine was thirteen, at an age to understand part of the
loss to her mother. Linda was eleven, the gaiety momentarily
stilled in watching something painful happen. Under the laws
of God, the children were entitled to the love and services of a
mother and a father. They loved both. Like Jackie, at the disappearance of his father so many years before, the little girls were
learning that it is nearly intolerable to lose a parent to anything
except the finality of the cemetery.

There was no other woman in Gleason's life. His heart was
not involved anywhere. He made dates, and he kept them, but
these were "for kicks." Each of these women, he knew, would be
out with another man on the next night. He needed feminine
warmth and flattery just as he needed a crease in his trousers.
He could do without both, but it made him feel better to have
them.

When a man makes a decision to end his marriage, he sees a
lawyer. Years ago, old-fashioned Catholics did not do this. They
ran to the priest for advice. Gleason did not consult his attorney;
instead, he phoned the Archdiocese of New York. He was connected with Father Roberts and, in a lengthy conversation, told
his story. It is not an easy thing to do, especially when a man has
resolved neither to excuse himself nor to throw the blame for
the rupture on his wife.

The priest asked a lot of questions, and Jackie tried to answer
them. He asked for Jackie's address, and Gen's too, and asked

if it would be all right for the Archdiocese to get in touch with Mrs. Gleason.

This happened ten days before Christmas.

A few days later Gleason received a letter from the Assistant Chancellor of the Archdiocese of New York.

DEAR MR. GLEASON:

Father Roberts has informed me of your conversation with him last Friday.

I have written to your wife asking her to see me as soon as is convenient for her.

If there is anything further you wish to add to your conversation with Father Roberts I am always available on Wednesdays from 10:00 A.M. to 4:00 P.M. and on Saturdays from 10:00 A.M. to 12:30 P.M.

If I can be of any help to you and your wife I shall be happy to aid you. . . .

                                             CYRIL J. POTOCEK

A month later a second letter arrived.

DEAR MR. GLEASON:

Pursuant to our conversation on January 8 regarding your marital problems, Mrs. Gleason came to see me at the Chancery Office on January 10.

I explained to your wife your desire to arrive at an amicable settlement on finances, so that your mind can be set at rest regarding your obligations to her and your two daughters.

Mrs. Gleason assured me that she would co-operate and would see you to conclude a mutually acceptable agreement on a financial settlement which would care for her and your daughters.

I am very happy to have been of service to you and your wife. If there is any further aid I can render, please do not hesitate to call on me.

With every best wish for success in your career, I am

                              Very cordially in Christ,
                                             CYRIL J. POTOCEK

P.S. I am sending a copy of this letter to Mrs. Gleason.

The matter was attended to quietly. It took time, but eventually Supreme Court Justice William C. Hecht, Jr. granted a separation to Genevieve and custody of both children. Jackie agreed to give to his wife 12½ per cent of his gross earnings, with 1 per cent going to each of his daughters for their education. Over a period of time this would average better than $50,000 a year.

All of which lends an added poignancy to the letters a father gets from little girls who try hard to understand. At Christmas, Linda the irrepressible wrote to her father:

DEAR SANTA:

I, "Miss Linda Mae John Gleason" and family cordially invite you to spend Christmas Day at 40 Central Park South with yours truly. Please reply by phone.

The following items are the things I desire for Christmas:
1. A felt skirt size 14 childrens.
2. Capizo beaded party slippers to match skirt. Size 5¼.
3. A long long stocking cap.
4. Sterling silver charm bracelet with movable charms.
5. A surprise.

Yours truly,
THE GREATEST

P.S. Love and kisses, Linda.

Geraldine, two years older and more restrained, sent the following to her father:

DEAR DADDY:

Thank you so much for the puppy. He is so cute but he is in the hospital getting a shot.

These are the things that I want for Christmas. I hope they meet with your approval:
1. All of your records plus
You Brought Me Love—Four Aces
High Noon—Frankie Laine
Tiger Rag—Les Paul and Mary Ford
Slaughter on Tenth Avenue

2. A necklace and bracelet to match (to go with sweaters and skirts).

3. A long stocking hat.

4. Extra large sled (for both Linda and I)

5. A set of a full skirt and a little vest to match. Size 14.

6. And last a surprise.

Lots of love and Prayers,

Your Daughter,

GERALDINE

There were letters from Jack to Gen, and from Gen to Jack too. Gleason's letters have some of the flavor of Ralph Kramden screaming impotently at the world.

DEAR GEN:

I received your letter and the lovely prayer enclosed. Strangely enough I was glad to get both, although they made me sad and miserable. I don't know why you continually point out my failings as I am well aware of what they are, even more so than you.

Please do not make it any more difficult to lead my life than it already is. Sitting in a chair on a terrace of a penthouse office or a bench in a park are equally aggravating when problems arise that seem impossible to overcome. Television is a rat race, and remember this, even if you win you are still a rat.

In closing, I hope that you are enjoying your vacation as I wish I could have enjoyed mine. I am now back at work in what you call an ivory tower but what I call an irony tower.

Your pet (peeve)

JACKIE

Letters from Genevieve were terse and held an aloof hint of the hurt in the breast of an estranged wife.

DEAR JACK:

Received the check for $300, which paid the bill and left $65. I need more money so if you can arrange with your auditor I shall be very thankful to you.

GEN

Near the end of the first year a certain self-assurance began to pervade Jackie Gleason. This was not the cockiness of the braggart, but perhaps the quiet confidence of the successful organizer. He had little cash. Hundreds of thousands of dollars were pouring in, and rapidly out, of his organization, but the future was assured. He had a good taste of the business world and he liked it.

There were other ways of making money besides pretending to slam a window on a fat hand. One of the ways was to make a show work for you long after you finished with it. By kinescope or film, a show remained funny and had a degree of permanence. It could be sold, again and again, to small independent television stations—stations not on a network. Suggestions had been made that Gleason could make a fortune selling his likeness in dolls. There could be a Ralph the Bus Driver Doll and a Poor Soul Doll and a Reggie, and so forth. There was money to be made in the music-publishing business, and in recordings, if a man had notions of what kind of music the public wanted. Too, there was money to be made in bankrolling, or producing a feature motion picture, or a Broadway show, or in any one of a number of ways.

He liked the members of his team, even though they were all members of a mutual aggravation society, and he wanted to reward them. That included his valet, Tony Amico. One morning, in the most casual way, Gleason stuck his arms into the coat Tony was holding and said, "Things are going pretty good for me, pal. From now on, you get a hundred a week."

At rehearsal one Saturday afternoon Jack Lescoulie was walking up the aisle to get a ham sandwich as Gleason was coming down.

"You going to be with us next year, Little Abner?"

"Sure, Jack," said Lescoulie. "Why?"

"Would a hundred and a half raise be all right?"

"Would a—you bet your life it would!"

One day he reorganized jackie gleason enterprises and made Bullets president and Lee Reynolds secretary-treasurer. Miss Reynolds was earning more than $10,000 a year as his private secretary and now, as an officer of enterprises, she was eligible for an annual bonus if the corporation made money.

"It's a lot of work," Gleason said to Durgom one morning.

"What's a lot of work?"

"Your job, my friend. You have to guide the affairs of a corporation, as president, and you also have to take care of me, a big ham."

"It *is* a lot of work, come to think of it," said Bullets. "Janie says I never get home, and you know something? She's right."

"Of course she's right," said Jackie, smiling happily. "And that leads to another problem. You're going to need help. You can't do all this by yourself."

"Nothing doing!" Durgom shouted. "Philbin is more your man than mine."

"How much is he getting?"

"Three hundred."

"Tell you what I'll do, Bull. Let's give him two hundred more and that will make five hundred."

"I know how much it makes."

"Philbin has asked for five hundred and, let's be honest, he's worth it."

"Okay. I'm conned into it."

"Thanks, pal. Tell Jack to step inside. I want to see him."

Philbin went in, not knowing what was coming. When he emerged, he looked like a very happy man. He walked up to Bullets in the Durgom office and shook hands.

"Thanks, Bullets. I know that I owe this to you."

"What happened?"

"I'm getting a thousand a week."

When Philbin left the office, Durgom looked at his secretary, the beautiful Elizabeth Caldwell, and shook his head.

"Gleason," he murmured, "is a genius. A great talent. But about business he doesn't know his class from third base. He moans that money is flying all over the place and he isn't getting enough of it, so a guy comes along who is getting three hundred and wants five, and Jackie gives him a thousand."

In retrospect, it seems inevitable that Jackie would someday try to compose music, or conduct it, or record it. A long time before, he had written, "Musicians I dig the most." Music was almost a fetish, nearly a compulsion.

None of his kind of music was what can properly be called *good* music. He was not a devotee of Brahms, or the opera, or Toscanini. He didn't even like all kinds of toe-tapping music. What he liked was sexily sentimental melodies and Dixieland jazz. Beyond those two, he did not care to think.

Jackie composed a song called "Lovers' Rhapsody" by sitting at a piano and tapping it out on one finger exactly as he heard it in his head. Then he asked Pete King, a music arranger, to sit and listen to it and make suggestions and write it properly. King worked it out in thirds, or diminished fifths, and laughed heartily when he heard Jackie call a glissando a "pussy cat."

Jackie composed a second number, "Melancholy Serenade." Although both numbers were successful, they did not rock the musical world with huzzahs for a great new talent, and that's exactly what Gleason proposed to set his sights on. The sickening part of any great talent is that the world expects that it must be stupid in all other things. Although the comparison is startling, the world never recovered from its astonishment that the late great physicist, Dr. Einstein, could play a violin. It never occurred to anyone that Einstein the violinist might have been a little surprised to find that he was so clever at physics. Joe E. Lewis, gambler, has never recovered from his astonishment at finding out that he is also a monologist. Practically all great talents have an affinity for another art. It is a breath-taking truth that Ignace Paderewski, President of Poland, was also a concert pianist.

One morning the door to j.g. enterprises opened and Leo Talent stood outside. He wanted to see Philbin. (He really wanted to see Gleason, but he didn't have the nerve to ask for him.) Talent is a modest man of integrity and dignity. He knows music, but most of all he knows music publishing. He saw Philbin and he explained that he was tired of publishing song sheets and trying to plug things like "Me and My Teddy Bear." He needed a job with a weekly pay check. Philbin talked to Gleason, Jackie's eyes bugged with fresh ideas, and, in an hour, Leo Talent was general manager of Gleason's nonexistent music-publishing house.

Leo, who whispers and has tight wavy hair and will always appear to be about forty-five years of age, sat and listened to

Gleason pick out the tune of a new song on an old piano. It was painful and frustrating. Anyone could see that Jackie could hear the song inside, but he was betrayed by his fingers. An arranger listened, and now and then the arranger would sit at the piano and, with elaborate bass and treble, try to rap out what The Greatest seemed to have been playing.

Jackie would hold both hands against the sides of his head and moan, "No, no! That isn't it!" He would go back to the bench, plop on it, incline his head toward the keyboard and, with the utmost concentration, tap a key, then another, and another, and, by trying to hum it at the same time, make a crude effort to communicate what lay in his heart to someone else's head. Often this went on all afternoon until at last when all three were exhausted, Gleason would clap his hands and yell, "You got it! You got it!" and the arranger would play it again and again, becoming more sure of himself each time, and then he would start chording the music and reducing it to written eighths and quarters, with little rest signs in between.

Gleason organized two music companies. One is Songsmiths Inc. The other is Jaglea, a contraction of "Jackie Gleason." At the moment they had nothing to publish, but in a short while their function was going to be to make America sleepily sexy. The word sexy, under ordinary circumstances, would not need definition, but in this case it means sensually sentimental, not dirty.

According to the Gleason thesis, everybody is either hopelessly in love or about to fall in love. That being so, what the world needed was more love songs, especially earthy love songs, torch songs, songs of the moody hopelessness of love. They wanted something that told, in a higher language of strings and lutes and muted brass, how they felt about love.

He was ready, with a little ebony baton, but the musical world wasn't. Jackie sent the word out that he was going to record. No echo came back; at least no pleasant echo. The big recording companies yawned. No group of musicians rushed forward either. Okay, Gleason said. If that's the way it's going to be, that's the way it's going to be.

Some phone calls were made, and he learned that if he wanted to make a recording on his own, it would cost about $8,000 for a pickup orchestra, the rental of a recording studio, plus sound booth, engineers, sound mixers and a master platter. This was a considerable sum, so Gleason invited his personal physician, Dr. Seymour Zucker, to invest a couple of thousand. Zucker could hardly restrain his enthusiastic No. Who, he wanted to know, would buy music published by a clown? The doctor has since chewed and masticated these words down to split-letter size.

Jackie invited Bullets to come along for $4,000, in return for half the profits. The manager couldn't think of a graceful way of saying no at the moment, so he dealt himself in, although he, of all the team, had more experience with music and with orchestras and knew that this mad new notion of Gleason's was the laughingstock of Tin Pan Alley. So he dealt himself in, and, in the middle of the very next dispute with Jackie, dealt himself out. Durgom later figured that this decision cost him about $60,000 in profits.

The $8,000 was borrowed. On March 19, 1952, Jackie hired a recording studio from Decca, picked up a lopsided orchestra of twenty-four violins and one trumpet and, waving a baton while Durgom leaned against a soundproof door and shook his head sadly, heard music.

The songs were not new, but the violins dripping tears of love were. They recorded "I'm in the Mood for Love," "I Only Have Eyes for You," "Love Is Here to Stay," "Body and Soul," "My Funny Valentine," "Love, Your Magic Spell Is Everywhere," "Alone Together" and "But Not for Me." In the main, these were the songs which had done well for him back in the days when he had kicked the busted record player under the bed. And, carrying out his thinking, if they could work for him they could work for anybody.

He conducted in open-neck shirt, tie askew, standing in brazen white lights on a tiny lectern perspiring. When the phrasing wasn't exactly right, he rapped the baton on the wood and yelled, "Hold it, fellows!" and turned to the sound booth. After a conference, they began again and this went on all night. The bows scraped the gut, the fingers danced, the muted trumpet shrilled, and Durgom slipped out on tiptoe and made phone calls and came back and listened and mournfully watched his pride and joy and went out and made more phone calls.

At some hour of the morning the musicians got into their coats and went home. The lights in the studio went out, the chairs were empty, the place looked dirty and dark. In the sound booth, Jackie sat and listened to his album. It was bad. It did not sing anything like the music he had heard in his heart. Bitterly, he told the arranger that the whole thing would have to be done over again.

Decca announced crisply that doing it over would cost $4,000. This hurt more than $4,000 worth. More than $8,000 worth. The thing was a fiasco. This man ached to coax *his* kind of music out of a group of musicians, but what he was getting was an arranger's idea of what Gleason was thinking.

On March 24, Jackie had borrowed another $4,000 and had the musicians back again. He recorded four sides, and they were pleasing. On April 9, he recorded four more. They too were good. Happily, Jackie Gleason offered them to Decca Records for a $4,000 advance.

Decca said no. He was, they assured him, a great comedian indeed, but who in the record-buying public wanted to pay for a comic's idea of senitmental music? A fat funnyman selling an album entitled "For Lovers Only"? Oh, no. No, no, no.

The decision of Decca Records was supported by all the other big companies. Nobody wanted the album. Despite the enormous prestige of Gleason as a performer, he wasn't worth a $4,000 risk in the field of music. Nor, as he found out, $3,000. Or $2,000. As an act of pity, Bobby Brenner of MCA took the album around and asked $1,000 advance.

No.

Brenner handles bands for MCA and knows how to market the unmarketable. "Okay," he said to Capitol Records. "So Gleason won't sell music. All right. Why not take the album for $1,000 advance anyway, because Gleason is bound to exploit and publicize it on his program and you'll get $1,000 worth of free plugs. Besides, some of your artists are out of work, and Jackie may give some of them work on his program."

Yes.

Capitol took the records and decided to publish the album. This, as far as Jackie was concerned, was musical success. Not an album had been sold yet, but that part was automatic, he figured. So he drew plans to record a composition of his own: "Lovers' Rhapsody." It came in four sensual parts—Desire, Flirtation, Temptation, Enchantment—and The Greatest had no doubt that Capitol Records would jump at the chance to put it on wax. But they didn't. They seemed slightly irritated that he had the nerve to come back to them so quickly. When he told them further that he planned to use fifty musicians in the recording orchestra, they knew that they were not in the same world with Jackie, and that whichever one he had been in, he was now out of it.

Still, to keep the man amused, they agreed to a $1,000 advance. Gleason put up $3,500 more and rounded up his fifty musicians. He made the recording and was pleased with what he heard. Leo Talent, who was toting up Gleason's debts, figured that he would have to sell close to 60,000 copies of the first album, at 12½ cents royalty per album, just to break even. Sixty thousand copies is a sizable number.

The first one sold 500,000 copies.

Now he was a musical success, and all of the recording companies would have been delighted to have him work their musicians until their sharps were flat, but Jackie listened to nobody but Capitol. Now the Messrs. Durgom and Zucker would have been happy to underwrite Gleason if he proposed to sell canned bear meat, invent a portable bathroom or write novels, but he did not propose to write novels and he also did not propose to give anyone a second chance.

He was on a musical binge and Gleason recorded "Music to Remember Her," "Tawny" (his own symphonic creation), "Music to Make You Misty," "Melancholy Serenade," "Music, Martinis and Memories" and something called "And Awaaay We Go!" For this he earned a lot of money and won a lot of acclaim. He was acknowledged to be the band leader of the year, he was awarded a solid-gold record for selling one million albums of music, his office and his home held gold statuettes.

On a sale of a million albums, he would normally earn about

$125,000, but Jackie gave away percentages of his success to Bobby Hackett and Sammy Speer, two musicians who believed in him and who helped him when no one else would. In any case, during the first four years of successful music, Jackie took no money from the profits. As fast as the royalties rolled in, he sowed them into more recordings. Once he used a band composed chiefly of sixteen mandolin players. On another occasion, he wanted to use an oboe d'amour, but few musicians had ever heard of it and no one had one. Leo went out, found one in an old musical shop, and rented it by the day until Gleason finished a certain song.

He has a yearning to create new musical sounds and speaks eloquently about recording with a big orchestra in the Luray Caverns of Virginia, or on a boat in the middle of a mountain lake.

One of the happier moments in his dealings with Capitol Records occurred when he met Dick Jones, an executive of the company. Jones is small and dark and nervous and quick. At one time he played piano for Tommy Dorsey.

"Know why I like you?" Gleason said to Jones after the first recording. "When I give you an idea, you don't bust out laughing." That was true, but Jones worried about some of the stuff Gleason was doing. For example, when Jackie announced that the title of the first album would be "Music for Lovers Only," Jones shook his head dolefully. He could not imagine a man, bald and forty-five, walking up to a pretty clerk and saying, "Give me a copy of 'Music for Lovers Only.'"

Jones was wrong.

When the album called "And Awaaay We Go!" was published, it contained songs in which the lyrics referred to Jackie's antics on his show. One recording told about the old days in the Dennehy's flat, and Gleason, for old time's sake, sent a free album to Pop Dennehy.

Pop blew up all over the kitchen. "What in hell can I do with this?" he roared. "That dumb kid sent it and he knows damn well I got nothing to play it on!" Still, curiosity won out and Pop Dennehy went out and spent $38 on a record player. After he heard the record, he was twice as mad.

Still, Mr. Dennehy's reaction cannot be construed as common because, in the first three years of recording, the American people spent $2,705,795.60 for the "dumb kid's" music.

More and more people were asking Jackie to trim his weight. Even his listeners were writing to him about it. Durgom was so frantic that he often sneaked in on his man at Toots Shor's and begged, "Tell me the truth, Jack. Is that the first hot roast beef you're eating or is it the second?"

Dr. Zucker said that the best thing for Gleason to do—so long as he could not trust himself to stay on a diet—would be to check himself into Doctors Hospital in New York. Under medical supervision, he could be kept on a diet as low as 650 calories per day and, for some time, he could live off his own fat.

Jackie tried it. The doctors and nurses were agreeable to him, and, except that they starved him daily, he was permitted such luxuries as a television set, a private telephone and visitors of all kinds at all hours. After that, he was in and out of the hospital like a hysterical intern. Some weeks he lost fifteen pounds.

Jack E. Leonard, the fatter comedian, came in for a visit one day and said, "What a swanky dump. They even have monogrammed germs."

The Greatest checked himself in and out very much as though the hospital was a hotel. One night he checked out to see a fight at the Polo Grounds and lost all interest in the fight because a vendor kept walking up and down in front of him yelling, "Hot dogs! Hot dogs! Get 'em while they're red hot!"

By the time he checked back into the hospital it was after midnight and he was exhausted from resisting temptation. So he summoned a night orderly and said, "Here's five bucks. Go out and get me a dozen frankfurters with the sauerkraut on top and the relish and anything else they got to put on them. Bring them right back and keep the change." When the man got back, Jackie gave him one of the hot dogs and ate the remaining eleven in ten minutes.

One day Harry Crane, the man who developed the shoulder tic trying to write the Gleason show, arrived with an armload of flowers to see Jackie.

The nurse pointed to the empty bed. "He's not here," she said.
"He isn't," Crane said innocently. "Why?"
"He went home."
"But why?"
"He said he didn't feel well."
Crane dropped the flowers and left the hospital slapping the
side of his head with the palm of his hand.

Sometimes love is a thing to be resisted. There are cases where
it arrives unbidden, unwanted, a portent of danger, a source of
worry. Jackie Gleason had made a mockery of love because he
had been hurt by it over a long span of years. He wanted no
more of love—ever. Romance would be all right so long as he
could lie in the road and become a hit-and-run victim, but romance is a game—like Russian roulette. Love, on the other hand,
implies permanence, selflessness, service, sympathy, possessive-
ness, proprietorship.
Jackie fell in love.
The girl was Marilyn Ann Veronica Taylor, younger sister of
June. She was not beautiful; she was "cute"—a dark blonde with
a provocative smile, the pale eyes of an inscrutable kitten and
a surprising wealth of common sense.
The two sisters came from Chicago and were daughters of a
private chauffeur. June became a dancer, and after much hard
work fell seriously ill. The Taylors have a quietly indomitable
spirit, and by the time June had recovered she resolved that if she
could not longer dance she could at least become a choreographer
and thus direct other dancers.
One of the girls in the "June Taylor Line" was Marilyn. It is
fair to say that she was probably never the prettiest girl in the
line. Like June, she studied dancing and dancers, met boys, had
dates and, unhappily, found that most of the boys were pretty
dull.
The first time she saw Jackie Gleason was when she and her
mother bought tickets to *Follow the Girls*. Marilyn was eighteen
and thought that the fat boy was pretty funny. The next time
was two years later, at the Chanticleer in Baltimore, when June
and Jackie sat talking about how to work a fast chorus line

around a master of ceremonies. Marilyn was not introduced and
she observed that Gleason was more moody than funny.

The third time was when the June Taylor dancers began to
work with Gleason on DuMont. Jackie wanted to do a Charleston
with the chorus line, but he didn't know how to do a Charleston.
Marilyn was selected, along with one other girl, to teach him.
She was not attracted to him because she had already met Mrs.
Gleason and Geraldine and Linda. He was not attracted to her
because he had heard that this was June's "kid sister" and he
could hardly afford to risk the services of a top-flight choreographer for the momentary fun he might find in Marilyn.

In October, 1951, they met by telephone. Someone told the
star that Marilyn Taylor had a slipped disk and was in a hospital.
He sent flowers and he phoned.

"How do you feel? Your spirits up? Okay, honey. If there is
anything that you need . . . Okay. Good-by." On show night
he announced that "little Marilyn Taylor will not be with us
tonight. . . ."

At the turn of the year Marilyn went to the Copa with June
and her husband. When the floor show was almost done, Gleason
walked in with a party of friends. He waved to the Taylors. They
waved. He drank a lot of brandy and appeared to be having a
lot of fun. When the Taylor party left the Copa, Gleason stood
in the way and permitted June and her husband to pass, but
blocked the entrance to Marilyn.

"You know what?" he said. "I think you're awfully nice."

"Thank you," she said. "I think you're nice too."

"We should get together," Jackie said. "We could have a lot of
laughs."

"Sure. Sure we could."

She slipped under his arm and out.

A month later he celebrated his birthday in the Park Sheraton
penthouse. The whole cast of the show was present, and so was
a good part of Broadway. The place was jumping with noise.
Marilyn found a chair and a drink. Some of the guests were out
on the terrace looking at the cold blinking stars and some were
in the offices upstairs engaged in after-hours business deals.

Jackie, carrying a handful of drinks for guests, skidded past

Marilyn, stopped, and leaned close to her ear to be heard. "Now that you're here," he said, "you're my girl and I don't want you to be looking at anybody else."

Marilyn Taylor laughed and nodded her head. The thoughts of this young woman of twenty-seven are of some interest. Like most women, her primary concern is a wedding ring. She regarded this jocular statement of his about "my girl" as a manifestation of interest on his part, but she also detected overtones of the tease in it. As a member of the show cast, she had knowledge of Gleason's casual manner with women, and she also knew that he and Mrs. Gleason had split up and that the matter was before the courts. He was, she felt, going to be eligible in a short while, although he wasn't eligible yet. Jackie was ten years older, too.

He was a big star, going to be bigger. He was a Catholic. She was a Catholic. Their common bond of interest lay in the theater, the world of entertainment. He was a difficult man to tame, but what girl ever admitted to herself that she could not tame a man if only she could get him to the altar?

These were the major factors in her thinking. On his side, all Jackie knew was that Marilyn Taylor had a reputation, among the boys who make it their business to know, of being a good girl, a nice kid. She had character, common sense, and she was the antithesis of the hysteric—she could sit, sometimes for hours, with legs turned under her, smiling and purring and not talking.

Jackie was sure that he would not fall in love. He had had enough of that. He was much more interested in becoming a tycoon. Marilyn felt that love, the deeper emotion, was something that a girl could control. She had never been in love before, she was twenty-seven, and she had confidence in her ability to skirt danger. She too could play a game, and in a waiting game she had patience.

The day after the birthday party Jackie invited some of the guests back to a recuperation party. The hang-overs were monumental, and a little whisky jogged memories and everyone helped in a post-mortem of the night before.

"Well . . . hello!"

Everyone looked up. Mrs. Gleason was standing in the room. Linda was at her side.

Jackie looked sheepish. "Hello," he said. He got up and kissed Linda. Mrs. Gleason was smiling and nodding to those guests she knew. She nodded to Marilyn Taylor.

"You had a dinner date with us," Gen said, almost gaily.

"Oh, no," Jackie said grimly. "I wouldn't make two dates for one evening, Gen."

"No? I'm sure you said tonight. . . ."

"Will you have a drink, Gen?" one of the men asked.

"Thank you, no," she said. She turned on the brave smile of one who is defeated in public. "Well, let me excuse myself. If you don't mind, I'll leave Linda here—"

"Sure, sure," Gleason said. "Let Linda stay. Hell, you can stay, Gen, if you—"

"No, I have some things to do. I'll stop by a little later."

The party lacked spontaneity after that. They sat and talked, and Jackie poured the drinks, and the valet got the ice, and a few reverted silently to black coffee, for now there were certain stories which could not be told because little Linda was there.

"Gen heard about the party," said Jackie with bitterness. "So she came over. What can I do?"

No one tried to answer. Food was ordered, and some ate and some didn't. The tables were being rolled out of the penthouse when Gen returned. One of the guests suggested that the party adjourn to Jimmy Ryan's club on Fifty-second Street. Everybody left except Jack, Gen and Linda.

Much later, Gleason arrived at Jimmy Ryan's place and he looked troubled. He apologized to Marilyn for the mix-up. She wanted to argue, to tell him that she felt hurt and a little bit humiliated, but she couldn't because she had not been his date at the party—just another guest.

That night, as she undressed for bed, Marilyn Taylor had a long talk with her sister June. She did not want advice as much as she wanted to listen to herself debate the situation, and thus clarify it in her own mind.

"I don't think I'll see him any more," Marilyn said.

"Maybe you're smart, honey."

"The trouble is, I like him."

"How much?"

"Enough."

"You're a big girl."

"Somebody said they were getting divorced."

"Separation."

"Why a separation?"

"Because Gen doesn't want a divorce, I guess."

"Well, I'm not going to be the other woman."

"Why don't you get a good night's sleep? We can talk in the morning."

"If a man is working at his marriage . . ."

"He isn't."

"Then please tell me how come she can walk in just like that? She walked right in and said, 'Hello,' just like that. Would you walk in if you and Sol—"

"I don't know what I'd do. Put the light out."

"If he calls from now on, I'm busy."

"Okay."

He phoned. Marilyn was busy. He tried several times, and she was not abrupt with him, but she was "busy." Jackie understood.

One night, after a dance-routine rehearsal, costumes had to be photographed in color. Marilyn was ordered to stay and to pose. She was under hot lights for an hour and fifteen minutes. When the ordeal was over, Jackie said, "Come on. We'll buy you a drink."

He took her to the dark little bar next door to the Hammerstein Theatre and they had a drink or two and he wasn't talking much.

"Let's go over to Shor's for dinner," he said. This was a big question and he knew it was a big question, because if she said yes to this proposal, then she wasn't busy any more.

"All right," she said. "I'm kind of hungry."

Of a sudden, he was witty and bright. He told stories, made her laugh, although she never thought of dropping twenty-five cents into his hand and saying, "Make me laugh twice." For nothing at all he made her laugh many times, and after dinner they went to the Copa, and after that to the Embers for some good music. A little after 3:00 A.M. he stepped out of a cab and said good night. Going upstairs in the elevator, Marilyn could hear every important word he had said throughout the evening, "You're beautiful, Mah" . . . "You're for me" . . . "Sure I've been with lots of girls, but not this way" . . . "I didn't want it this way. I wasn't angling for it. It just happens" . . . "I hope you feel the same way I do, Mah" . . . "Don't worry. Everything will work out."

June was sleeping when Marilyn pounded on the door of the bedroom. She had to tell someone, and it could not wait until morning. June yawned through some of it, listened intently at other parts, and finally stood up and shrugged.

"You know what I told you, Marilyn. You're grown up. So is he. You both know what you're doing—I hope."

"Think I ought to call mamma tomorrow?"

"Why not? It's better than waiting until she reads about it."

The calendar flipped its pages around to April, 1953. At 3:00 A.M. one frosty morning Marilyn Taylor was sleeping when the phone rang. It was Gleason.

"Do me a favor?" he begged. "Meet me at the Hofbrau."

"When?"

"Now."

"Jack, I was sleeping when the phone—"

"That's great. I wish that I could sleep. Will you meet me?"

"All right. It's going to take a little time."

"I'll be waiting."

There was a little German place on the East Side. A three-piece orchestra, composed of tired Germans, played *lieber* music. Gleason sat at the same table—next to the violinist—that he always used when Marilyn was with him. When Miss Taylor arrived, the orchestra played the same number they always played for her—"Our Love Is Here to Stay."

Gleason was beyond containment. He had been hooked again by love, and he had been hooked good. He couldn't sleep. He couldn't think. He smoked cigarette after cigarette, and a drink no longer tasted like anything but rusty anchor chains. There

had to be an understanding, some sort of an understanding. His
feet hurt from pacing his own bedroom floor.

"Here it is, Mah. I love you."

"I love you too."

"You do?"

"Of course I do. I've known it for some time."

"I'll be frank. It's got me nuts."

"I know."

"I mean completely. I don't want to hurt you, and I don't want
you to get mixed up in newspaper stories with me—and, damn
it, I don't want to let you go either!"

Two people lost. In a situation such as this one, the girl stands
to lose heavily. She will even lose so long as she does not fall in
love, but, once having slipped into the plush-lined pit, there is
no way out.

"I've read some newspaper stories about you and Gen."

"I know."

"They say that you'll never get a divorce, Jack."

"I never thought I'd fall in love again."

"But what about us?"

Jackie was desperate. In a ridiculous way, his heart was standing on one side of his being and his soul on the other. Can a
man trade one for the other? He most certainly can. Few men
are equipped with a more articulate conscience than Jackie
Gleason. It warns him loud and plain every time he tries to do
something wrong.

"About Gen," he said softly, "that will work itself out someday.
Don't worry, Mah. We'll have a home on top of the hill, and
we'll have kids too." He sighed. "It's going to be a long struggle,
Mah, and a tough one. But we'll make it, Love." He patted her
hand. "We'll make it."

They talked and talked, until the three-piece orchestra quit
and the manager began to douse the lights one by one. They
didn't look like a romantic couple eager to peek at the future.
They looked troubled, worried, like nervous plotters who feel
sure that there is a solution to their problem, but are unified on
only one thing—that neither has thought of one.

They dated and waited. Nothing happened. Geneviéve was

sitting in the marital driver's seat, and it seemed pretty certain that she would not contemplate a divorce even if *she* fell in love with someone else, so there was no chance that she would permit such a thing to cross her mind just because Jackie had fallen in love. Besides, she never gave any of her friends, or Jackie's, the feeling that she regarded this separation as a permanent thing.

Thus the observer is left with a picture of the old triangle: two women, one man. One of the women can have him, if she wants, but she can't marry him. The other can remain married to him, if she chooses, but she can't have him. Three puppets in a state of suspended animation.

The last scene of the January 30, 1954, show lacked greatness. It induced chuckles from the audience in the Hammerstein Theatre, but no one was ever going to tick it off on his fingers as one of the ten best that Gleason ever did. The scene was a parody on the kid comedies of the old silent motion pictures. The setting was a drawing room and the cast, in 1910 apparel, danced and jerked its arms and legs convulsively in the manner of the early film illusions.

Art Carney, as the father of the bride, wore a cutaway and goatee and passed out champagne to his friends and drank a toast. Jackie Gleason, as an overgrown Katzenjammer kid in Buster Brown suit, came on stage with a box plainly labeled BEES under his arm, and winked wisely at the camera. He opened the box and ran off stage through a doorway to the right.

The bees stung the dancers, the guests jumped and slapped, the ladies made facial contortions as though screaming, and father went off stage and dragged Jackie back by the ear. There was a silent parental lecture, with wagging of jerky finger. The kid left and returned a moment later and stooped to open the valves of all the radiators in the room. Steam engulfed the lower part of the room and the silent dancers jumped and howled mutely.

The pet cocks on the three radiators were supposed to have been aimed upward. Unknown to anyone, a stagehand had them turned down so that the steam (in reality a fire-extinguishing product) hit the floor and condensed into puddles. The radiators were still jetting "steam" when Jackie returned to the stage with an electric fan and a pillow full of feathers. Again he winked broadly at the camera and turned to skip off stage. As he passed the radiator near the door at stage right, both of his legs suddenly skidded to the left. He crashed hard on his right side and right leg, and for the first time the audience roared.

Art Carney knew that it was not part of the act and he edged toward the door to help Jackie get off stage. Out of view, two stagehands took his arms and dragged him off. The wedding party, still dancing, began to leave the set. Too late, somebody turned the fan on and, instead of feathers, talcum was blown up the stage at Art Carney, the only player left in view. The curtain came down.

Backstage, everyone sensed that Gleason had been hurt, but no one guessed how badly. Stanley Poss, assistant producer, pushed Jack Lescoulie in front of the curtain with whispered instructions to close the show. He saw Carney and pushed him out too. "Say good night to the people in Jackie's place," he said.

Gleason, in the little boy's suit, was lying on his side moaning that he had been hurt. He tried to get up, but couldn't. Someone ran to phone Dr. Zucker. "My leg hurts," he said several times. Two big stagehands lifted him onto a chair. Three men carried the chair across the back of the stage, through the maze of ropes, into a knot of worried faces, up the back stairs and into Gleason's dressing room, with its scarred old table, its Coca-Cola machine, its couch and shower.

The pain was going good now and it ran from the foot up most of the leg. One of the chorus girls sent her husband, a doctor, in and he tried to examine the foot, but Gleason kept saying, "Thanks, pal. I'll wait for my own doctor. Thanks. Thanks." Someone else came in with two pillows and one was placed under the ankle, the other under the knee.

"Whatever is broke, it's right under the kneecap," Gleason said. "That's where it hurts most."

Out front, in the theater, Tony Amico sat with Geraldine and Linda. They seldom laugh at their daddy on stage; they stare fascinated, but if they laugh it is usually at Carney or someone else. On this night, when he fell, they laughed because they thought it was part of the act and they had seen their father do hundreds of these falls.

Tony wasn't fooled. "Sit right here," he said. "I'll be back. Your daddy's hurt."

When Dr. Zucker arrived, he probed manually and found a broken ankle. It was so swollen that he had to take shears and cut the shoe and sock off. It was obvious that Jackie Gleason would not star in his show for at least two months.

He was taken to his old room at Doctors Hospital and, always traveling in class, ordered flowers, a big television set, lounge chairs, whisky, ice, soda and glasses. He still wanted to supervise the show, okay the scripts, the sets, the dances, camera angles and actors. He ran it from his hospital room. Messages came from fans everywhere, and practically all of Broadway made the pilgrimage to the hospital.

On a Sunday afternoon Jackie and Marilyn were alone. The leg, in a cast, was propped up. She sat in a chair beside the bed. They were not holding a conversation at the time because Gleason was watching a show called "Life with Father." He knew most of the members of the cast and was commenting, now and then, on their techniques when Genevieve walked into the room.

One man, two women.

Gen looked from one to the other. She knew all about his casual romances, but this one had been going on a long time and was now passing out of the casual status. A woman wins nothing by exposing the hurt in her heart, but that fact never stopped one, nor even slowed one down.

Mrs. Gleason, unable to hide her emotion, began her indictment of Jackie and she opened it by saying that he was taking advantage of an innocent girl and should be ashamed of himself. She was in mid-flight when Gleason picked up the phone, called Dr. Zucker, and said, "Doc, you better get right over here. I'm in trouble. Gen is here and so is Marilyn."

Genevieve railed against her husband, and most of what she had to say was justified by the facts. If anything, it was astonishing how much she knew about her man. When she finished, for the moment, she turned on Marilyn Taylor (who tried to keep her

eyes fixed on the television screen) and referred to the dancer in
terms one might reserve for a hard-boiled, broken-down chorus
girl.

Zucker arrived in the midst of an icy silence and asked Genevieve to step out into the hall with him. "I'd like to talk to you
a minute," he said, "privately."

When they were outside the door, he talked swiftly. "What
are you trying to prove?" he said. "Will you please tell me what
you're trying to prove? You're an intelligent person. This is your
husband—granted. But you're smart enough to see what the
situation is, Gen. You can't win him back with threats.

"Why don't you accept this one fact? Everybody sees this
thing and now you see it. Please don't make a fuss here, Gen.
It's not good for him and it isn't any good for you. Be a good
girl. Go home."

She thought about it a moment, decided to say something,
decided not to, and turned and walked out. There is an overtone
of minor-league tragedy in a wife walking off the field of battle,
but Zucker was right. There was nothing that could be won by
remaining. She walked down the corridor, purse under arm,
chin held a little bit extra high, her lips set and unquivering.

Inside the room Marilyn sat looking at the floor. She hadn't
wanted to be the Other Woman. She had dreaded it, hated it,
and now, out of millions of men, she had to fall in love with a
man who was married, father of two children, and who could
not find a solution to his own problem. She did not like Gen
nor what Gen had done to her, and yet, somewhere inside, she
respected Gen as she herself hoped to be respected. She had
felt like standing up, a few minutes ago, and yelling, "I didn't
want him. I didn't chase him. Now I'm in love with him and I
don't know which way to turn. You had him and you lost him.
Why hang on?"

But she had said nothing. She had sat, dying inside, pretending to look at a television show she no longer saw. She was
learning, the hard way, that an item of importance to women
is the respect of other women.

A few days later a newspaper published a few paragraphs
about the scene in the hospital. Jackie Gleason read it in bed and

he flung the paper from him. Years before, he had said in Newark, "If I could only get my name in the New York papers—boy, I'd be made!" Now he had his mention and it hurt. It sparked a whole train of newspaper stories about Jackie Gleason and his dancer girl friend. The reporters had a field day.

In the early summer of 1954 The Greatest finally tired. The super-duper energy suddenly ran out; the flashing feet in the eighty-five-dollar shoes were full of lead; the back of the trousers hung heavy; the eyes pouched; the show was over and, in its place, Gleason had produced a summer show with the Dorsey Brothers. Now he had time, and nothing to do, and the exhaustion was so deep that the bones ached.

Everybody talked vacation to Jackie. You need a rest, my boy. You've been working too hard. After all, you're pushing close to forty. Bermuda is only three hours away. Have you ever stayed at the Reforma in Mexico City? Believe me, if it was me, I'd get on a tramp steamer and just go somewhere. For a real rest, try Guatemala—you're five thousand feet up when you're walking on the street, and those volcanoes are big and purple. Jackie, Europe. I'm not going to say another word except Europe because if you've never been to Europe you don't even know what life is all about. Kid, the Laurentians in the summertime, with a little old side trip to Lake Louise, and the first thing you know you've got muscles on your muscles. What's the matter with Hawaii? Have you ever given a thought to how lonesome those brown chicks get while their men are out on those surfboards? They got a drink out there made of hot coffee and rum, and I'm telling you, my boy . . ."

He decided to go to Europe. One of the factors in the decision was that he still had intestinal adhesions from the appendectomy of years before, and Dr. Zucker had recommended a Swiss surgeon to correct it.

"Tone," said Jackie to Amico one morning, "we're going to Europe."

"Fine," said Tony. That exhausted the topic.

Telling Marilyn was rough. He wanted her to go with him—couldn't bear the thought of leaving her home—and he knew

that she would be thrilled at the thought of such a trip. But he
had to tell her that they could not leave together; they could
not be on the same plane; they would have to sneak out of New
York in spurious innocence.

He told her, and Marilyn tried to understand. It wasn't easy.
She had become edgy and irritable because she felt that they
were "hiding" all the time; they could not be seen at the same
night-club table together; they could not be seen in a restaurant together unless they were part of a big, heterogeneous
group; they couldn't even stroll in the park alone. Someone
might see. Someone might tell. Someone might print it in the
paper.

On the other hand, both of them realized that the world
automatically took the side of the wife, and that meant that
Jackie and Marilyn were condemned without a hearing. So far
as the world was concerned, on one side stood a brave wife and
two children; on the other was a husband and an alien woman.
No amount of sentiment could alter the picture.

Mutely, she agreed to take a plane the day after Jackie and
wait for him in Zurich. She was beginning to learn how to be a
loser. Some people say that this is something only champions
ever master.

All the tickets were bought and paid for before Jackie got
ready to leave. Still, he had a pretty loud argument with Lee
Reynolds about the amount of money he proposed to take with
him. He wanted $10,000 in cash, plus the tickets. She said that
he wouldn't need more than $5,000. He said that if she didn't
mind he would determine how much he would need and her job
was solely to get the dough and give it to him. Miss Reynolds
said that it would be dangerous carrying $10,000 on his person
just to drive up and down and around Alps. In the end, he
took $5,000 on her promise that, at the first cry for help, she
would cable him an additional $5,000.

So that secrecy could be maintained, Jackie and Tony planned
to make the trip to Washington to acquire passports. Gleason
might have got them in New York, but he was afraid that the
story of his trip would "leak" to the newspapers. The following

letter was written to the Department of Health in Brooklyn on June 4, 1953:

GENTLEMEN:

Enclosed herewith is my check for One Dollar ($1.00) for the purchase of my birth certificate.

I was born February 26, 1916, on Herkimer Street to Mae Kelly Gleason and Herbert Gleason.

Will you kindly forward the certificate to me as soon as possible as I'm trying to get a passport.

Thank you,
JOHN CLEMENS GLEASON

That brought about a mix-up in names which could be oriented only by a psychologist. Jackie Gleason was not christened Jackie or John. He was named after his father, Herbert, although his mother always referred to him as "Jack" or "Jackie." The name "Clemens" did not belong to Jackie at all; Clemence was his older brother's name. The Department of Health checked its records and sent a birth certificate made out to Herbert Gleason, and Jackie, irritated at what he thought was bureaucratic bungling, returned it at once.

GENTLEMEN:

I am returning herewith a birth certificate sent in error in the name of Herbert Gleason. Strangly enough, Herbert Gleason was born to Mae Kelly Gleason and Herbert W. Gleason, but not on that date. He was born about five years earlier than 1916. The certificate I had requested was for John C. Gleason, born to Herbert W. Gleason and Mae Kelly Gleason on February 26, 1916. It appears that the wrong name was registered on this certificate.

It is quite imperative that I have a corrected birth certificate in the name of John C. Gleason as I am planning to go abroad and must have the proper credentials in order to get a passport.

Will you kindly handle this matter for me as soon as possible.

Cordially,
JACKIE GLEASON

It took a little time to straighten out the matter of the name, but he was christened Herbert John, and it came as a shock to learn that he had been named after his father.

There was no farewell party. There was no announcement in the newspapers that Jackie Gleason was off on a tour of Europe on a well-earned vacation. What there was, was silence. At the last moment Gleason got aboard a Swiss Air Constellation and was in the hospital when Marilyn and Tony arrived in Zurich.

Switzerland was undergoing several days of rain and fog when the patient left the hospital. Only Tony was happy. He got into his car, with the luggage, and said, "Jackie, I'll follow you."

"It's a funny thing," Jackie said to Marilyn, "but I couldn't relax in that hospital. Every time I picked the phone up, I had to wait ten minutes to get the operator. Then it turned out she didn't understand a word of English. This must be a great place, if you're a Swiss."

He got into the car, consulted maps, and took off to see Europe. They drove down through the passes to Stresa, Italy. Tony talked Italian to the people and had a wonderful time. Gleason didn't like Stresa.

"Let's scoot this place," he said. They drove to Venice. He didn't like that either. Three in a gondola in sunlight isn't quite romantic. The gondolier spoke English. He said, "Beautiful, hey? Clean city, never no dust."

Gleason, in a bad mood, watched a piece of grapefruit float by. "Maybe so," he said, "but you ought to strain these canals once a week."

In Rome, he sat brooding in a hotel, or shopping, while Tony Amico went around town shopping for girls and finally found a girl who was just right for him. He took her to lunch, built up the history of his noble ancestors, and made a date with her for that evening at 7:00 P.M. They would meet at a certain fountain. The girl liked Tony, and his heart was singing as he went back to the hotel.

There he found Jackie packing.

"What's up?" asked Tony, as though he couldn't guess.

"Let's blow," said Gleason.

"Right now?"

Jackie nodded. "Right now. I spent eight days here and I got nothing to show for it except a set of dishes and some shoes. Maybe London will be different."

"London?"

"Yeah. You've heard of it, I'm sure."

"How about Paris?"

"We make Paris on the way."

When they got on the train, Jackie shook his head in disbelief. "I wouldn't like to spread this around," he said, "but they don't know how to make spaghetti or pizza in Rome. For that you got to go to New York."

Tony sat through the night looking out at the countryside and wondering how long the girl would wait at the fountain.

When they arrived in Paris, Jackie and Marilyn and Tony remained in the big railroad terminal.

"Aren't we going to see Paris?" asked Marilyn.

"What's to see?" said Gleason in exasperation. "A big tower, a couple of art museums, a bunch of Frenchmen who can't even talk English? Let's wait for the boat train right here."

They wandered around the station for three hours. Then they got aboard another train, then the boat across the Channel. London was in fog. He phoned Lee Reynolds in New York. "I'm telling you," he said, "if I wasn't so afraid to fly I'd be back home tonight."

"You need some more money, Jackie?"

"No. No, I'm set. I'm going to stick around a while and see some people."

Gleason spent two weeks at the Savoy Hotel. Most of this time was spent visiting entertainers backstage, or having them over to his suite for a party. Here, for the first time, there were people who had heard of Jackie Gleason. Here there was some newspaper notice of his arrival. And here too were many American performers who felt a special warmth when they met another American performer far from home.

Tony Amico was out by day cultivating a London brunette. She was twenty-two; but she had no idea that time was running out for Tony, and so she cultivated slowly. After three or four hit shows, and three or four intimate suppers, she agreed to meet

Tony one evening in front of the lions at Piccadilly Circus. The time: 7:00 P.M.

At 6:00 P.M. Gleason was packing. Tony was horror-stricken. "We going home, Jack?"

"Sure we're going home," Gleason said. "Let's scoot this place."

"When?"

"Right now. Mah is packing in her room. We got tickets on the *United States* and we have to get to Southampton in a hurry."

Tony, a barrel-shaped little man, looked heavenward for guidance and started to pack.

Aboard the liner *United States*, Jackie was delighted to find producer Lou Walters of the Latin Quarter. This gave him someone to talk to all the way home and gave Tony Amico a little time to himself. He found a friendly ship's officer who gave him a key to the second-class quarters. There he met a lonely Italian girl, and on their third meeting they were having a drink in her cabin before going upstairs to a dance.

"What makes you smile like that?" the girl asked in Italian.

"Well," said Tony, "I don't know how to say it in Italian, but I know a certain guy who can't say, 'Let's scoot *this* place.'"

When they returned, Gleason again was a great star. Marilyn again was a chorus girl. On Saturdays in the autumn the old Hammerstein Theatre was dark and dismal, except for the stage. An old-time burlesque runway split the middle of the orchestra, but instead of a shapely dolly dancing up and down it to the delight of bald-headed customers, a shapeless steel camera dollied back and forth, taking long shots of the actors on the stage, or medium close-ups.

In the seats were the thirty-two dancers Jackie decided he needed for the 1954 season, in brief red velvet panties and white blouses and opera-length net stockings. They knitted and chatted, waiting to be called on stage. Jack Goldstein, of CBS public relations, sat talking about a new book to Art Carney, who chewed gum and nodded.

Farther back, Phil Silvers and Jack E. Leonard talked about whatever two top-flight comics talk about when both want to

talk and neither wants to listen. In the rear of the orchestra, a
man carved roast beef and ham on a table as Audrey Meadows
and Val Irving waited for coffee. Down front, a second camera
and a third moved back on the sides of the stage to photograph
small placards about coffee and razors and, on stage, Jack Lescoulie squinted in the bright lights to read a large printed sign
held by the side of the camera. Up in a booth to the left, Frank
Satenstein used a stage microphone to tell camera three that he
was back too far, "move in a little." On stage, men in slacks were
putting together a familiar kitchen set, with ice box and drip
pan, with old sink and sideboard. They tested the two doors to
see if they were working properly.

Down front, Jackie Gleason sat on a high stool and leaned on
the footlight shields as he watched the camera views in a monitor
set to his left. Jack Philbin, at his side, yelled something up to
Hurdle, on stage, and, off to the far right, Ray Bloch removed a
pipe from his mouth, held his baton up, waited for his musicians
to get ready, and started the music for the opening of "The
Jackie Gleason Show."

It was 4:00 P.M. and the show would go on in four hours. Back-
stage, Stanley Poss blinked through his glasses at a stop watch
hanging around his neck. He would time the dancers, "The
Honeymooners," the commercials, the music, down to the second.
The show should add up to fifty-four minutes of entertainment.
The remaining six minutes would be for the commercials.

Myron Kirk came in, nodded happily to Gleason—they had
been to Detroit together the time Jackie pressed a button for the
community fund drive—and Kirk looked around.

"Where's Philbin?" he asked.

"Up there," said somebody, pointing to the middle of the
theater.

Kirk, known as Mike, looks like what he is: an advertising tycoon with Homburg and matching accessories. His agency,
Kudner, had handled the Buick automobile account for years,
and Buick had employed Milton Berle, the king of television.
Part of his sepulchral job is to know the state of health of the king
and to have a pleasant relationship with the crown prince.

Philbin was now chatting with Herb Rosenthal, of MCA. Kirk sat down in the row before them and turned half around so that he could talk.

"I got a hell of an idea," he said, "that could make Jackie a fortune." Rosenthal and Philbin began to listen, with an ear apiece. They had heard many ideas calculated to make a fortune for Gleason, and there was always something unpalatable about it, so the fortune never materialized. "It involves doing 'The Honeymooners' on film," said Mike. "The residuals alone could make him rich." (*Author's note:* residuals are the secondary rights to film and amounts to selling the film to non-network stations after the first big showing.)

"Who would sponsor it—Buick?"

"Could be," said Kirk. "I haven't talked to anybody about it yet. It's just an idea."

Without further discussion, Philbin and Rosenthal knew that Kirk would not be there discussing a hell of an idea unless Berle was on the way out at Buick and Gleason was being considered as the new king. Rosenthal, who sits higher than anybody else, looked over Kirk and saw that Gleason had left his stool.

"It sounds interesting," he said. "Let's go up and tell it to Jackie."

In the second-floor dressing room, Jackie lounged on the settee and listened and smoked. He too understood what it meant, but he was not going to be caught enthusing about it and then have nothing happen.

"Well," he said, "you fellows go ahead and talk about it."

Gleason went downstairs again and the three called Durgom in. In the Gleason entourage, when an idea is broached, the newest man at the conference always asks the same question, "What does Jackie say?" When Bullets asked the question and heard that permission had been granted to explore the idea, the men sat around trying to think of what was wrong with the idea. This is sound, because it prevents an impossible idea from commanding too much valuable time before anyone finds out that it is unworkable.

The more they talked about it, the better it sounded. "There's a lot of money and prestige in a thing like this," Bullets said.

"If it's a half-hour show on film," Rosenthal said, "it could mean more money for Jackie and less work."

"Maybe Jackie won't like film," said Philbin.

"Why?" everybody said.

"He never had a good word to say for a filmed show," said Philbin.

"Well," said Bullets, "that may be a hang-over from Hollywood. This is different."

"I haven't discussed it with Ivan Wile yet," said Kirk.

"Who's that?"

"Vice-president of General Motors, President of Buick."

"Oh."

Kirk was in a sensitive position. It was his idea, but once he told it MCA could go out and peddle it elsewhere. He was aware of this and he asked for a period of thirty days to use his own idea. If he could not sell it in that time, the gentlemen around the table would be free to use it any way they saw fit. They agreed.

The first conferences were called between Kirk, Ivan Wile and Herb Rosenthal. The Columbia Broadcasting System was not called in because they had Gleason to a contract to put on a show for Schick, Schaefer and Nescafé. Robert Schulman, Gleason's lawyer, was called in, and the negotiations began to spell themselves out into dollars and clauses.

The road blocks were the normal ones for this kind of a deal: MCA wanted more money and a longer contract than Buick was willing to grant. MCA wanted three years—from September 1955 until September 1958. The matter was compromised with a two-year contract and an option for Buick on a possible third year.

Moneywise, the average half-hour film show costs between $25,000 and $30,000. Buick was willing to pay Gleason Enterprises $65,000 for every half-hour can of film he delivered and would return it to him for any use he might want to make of it after three years. In the second year they would pay $70,000; the third year $75,000. In sum, it could sell the same film again and again, anywhere that the corporation might find a purchaser.

Out of the $65,000 each week, Gleason Enterprises would, as usual, pay all salaries for stars, actors, technicians, film, cameras,

cameramen, sets, directors, producers—the package. If Gleason
Enterprises paid the star $10,000, and the cost of a given show
was $55,000, the corporation would make $10,000 of corporation
profits. And, as the sponsors insisted on buying "The Honeymooners" sketch, and nothing but "The Honeymooners," Jack
Hurdle kept asking himself, "How much can the same kitchen
cost?"

Once the agency and the automobile company were in agreement, they called CBS in. The network could hardly help but be
pleased. Milton Berle and Buick had been on NBC for years.
Now the automobile company was about to drop Berle for
Gleason, and drop NBC for CBS. Cordiality was dripping all
over the conference floor.

The only unhappy people were the old sponsors—Nescafé,
Schick and Schaefer—but in this case Gleason, who had remained outside the negotiations, came through with an idea.

"What are you going to do with the extra half hour?" he asked.

"What half hour?" asked CBS.

"I'm doing an hour show now. Next year I'll be doing a half
hour. Suppose, for the sake of argument, I go on from eight-
thirty to nine, Eastern Time. What are you people going to do
with the eight to eight-thirty spot?"

"Oh, we'll sell it. Don't worry about it."

"That's what I don't want you to do. We can put on a live show
—bands, the June Taylor dancers, a good variety show. Enterprises can produce it—I'll put Philbin in that spot—and, if our
present sponsors like it, why can't they sponsor it?"

That's the way it was done. They put on a full-hour show split
in halves, with Jackie on film in the latter half and his old
sponsors paying the bill for the live half. When the contract was
drawn up in its final form, it was the biggest ever negotiated for
a performer in the history of show business.

It will take years to find out how much it means in countable
dollars, but the gross earnings of the corporation will probably
be: $11,000,000 for the Buick show for three years; $3,000,000 in
residual film rights in the years ahead; $500,000 to jackie gleason
enterprises for producing the live half hour; $1,170,000 to Gleason
as a performer; all in addition to another $500,000 on musical

recordings and other earnings. What will stick to Jackie Gleason's fingers, after taxes, in the first three years will be around $350,-000, and in addition his corporation will have about $600,000.

To some, the most interesting part of the deal was a secondary contract, supplementing the first, which was drawn up between CBS and Gleason. This guaranteed to the network Jackie's exclusive services for fifteen years, until 1970, in return for which the network would pay him $100,000 a year for any year in which he did not work, or the difference between that sum and what he earned if he made less.

Almost overnight Jackie Gleason was at the top of his profession, the new king, the new millionaire. He had said, twenty-five years before, that someday he would pass "Milton Berle and all them guys" and he *had* passed Milton Berle and all them guys. He was on top. There was only one direction left to go.

He raised salaries and kept his old team. Philbin became executive producer over everything. Hurdle produced "The Honeymooners." Art Carney was now getting $3,500 a week; Audrey Meadows $2,000; Joyce Randoph $500.

The day before the contract was signed Jackie went out at 4:00 P.M. with Johnny Ray and Salvador Dali, the painter, and they drank all evening and all night. At 5:00 A.M. Gleason was in bed. The signing was to take place at a luncheon in President William Paley's office at noon.

At 11:00 A.M. Jackie was on the phone with Dr. Zucker.

"Doc," he said. "Please rush right over here. I'm awful sick. I've got the world's greatest hang-over and I can't stand up."

When the doctor arrived, Jackie said contritely, "I'll never make it."

Zucker examined him and said, "For once, you have not exaggerated. You have the world's greatest hang-over. Tell you what I'm going to do. I'm going to give you an injection of something new. It's not a narcotic. It's excellent for nausea and vomiting."

"What are you going to give me—Thorizine?"

The doctor shrugged resignedly. He was always amazed at Jackie's knowledge of what was new in the field of medicine. "That's exactly what I'm going to give you," he said.

In fifteen minutes the patient was feeling well enough to live.

He had to dress, so he put on old slacks, a flaming wool shirt, soft slippers, bright red socks, loud sports jacket, and then he said, "Doc, will you drive me over to CBS. I haven't got any money."

Zucker drove him, and at the big conference Gleason drank tomato juice and fell asleep.

Hubbell Robinson, of CBS, looked at the snoring figure and said to the assemblage, "How relaxed can you get?"

As his fortieth birthday passed, with no more attention paid to it than gunfire in the White House, a new and more sober Gleason began to emerge. More and more he was interested in business other than Ralph Kramden and The Honeymooners. More and more he was interested in off-beat ideas. He wanted to build a chain of night clubs, for example. They would not be replicas of the Miami Club. In fact, as he saw his chain, the clubs would be the antithesis of the old Bucket of Blood.

There would be no master of ceremonies; no eccentric dancers; no Latins tossing darts at spread-eagled girls. Just music. Soft, romantic music with a riff of Dixieland. The clubs would be built in a chain of hotels from coast to coast, and each one would be called the Music for Lovers Only Room. Under Gleason, Bobby Hackett would be in charge. Before the deal was negotiated, Jackie had called in a decorator and had laid out the color motif of these clubs.

In the mornings at his office, Jackie was busy with Joe Bigelow on another matter called Audible Literature. People by the millions, Jackie decided, are neglecting the classics. If they won't read, let them listen. He is going to record the classics. Not just excerpts, mind you. The whole story, including every last comma. At the turn of the year, he had no deal with any record company to market these records, but, with his sublime faith in his ability to make a success of anything, he had set up recording dates for actors to do the first book.

He wanted to begin with Charles Dickens' *A Tale of Two Cities*. Bigelow estimated that it would require an album of twenty records spinning for twenty hours to tell the story right, and Jackie insists that everything be done "right." The first record will open with an introduction by Gleason. He will be followed by a story narrator, who will read all parts of the book which do not require actors. The remainder will be done by characters who will play the various parts. Behind this will be mood music of the era in which the action takes place; in the case of *A Tale of Two Cities*, there will be no piano, just a harpsichord. The cost of listening to the book may run to thirty-five or forty dollars per album.

While these matters are discussed daily, and move forward, Jackie has been receiving fabulous offers from Hollywood to star in a feature picture. Like a patient hound-dog, he has been sitting and licking his paws while waiting for this. Sooner or later (sublime faith in self) he knew that they would come to him, and, by 1956, they had not only come but they were groveling. The president of a big studio phoned one afternoon and put his proposition on the line: "Tell you what I'll do. If you'll come out here, Jackie, I'll throw everybody off the lot. You pick your own story, set up your own production unit and make a picture for me."

Gleason said no. He had been ready in 1941, but he wasn't ready now. This too had to be done "right." First, he wanted a story. A top-flight story into which he could throw all his energies. As spring came along, he was still looking. He was certain that he would find one before summer, and then, on vacation, he would go to Hollywood with it and name his own producer, his own director, have his own picture staff and production unit, and the first Jackie Gleason Production would be ready to roll. Ironically, most of the moneymen around Broadway who had failed him when he needed cash years ago now begged permission to invest in anything Gleason wanted to do.

He had come a long way. A very long way.

Times were abnormally good for the kid from Brooklyn. He leased a duplex penthouse on Fifth Avenue while still maintaining the other one as an office. Buick promised to build a car for him to Gleason's specifications and they did. He wanted solid-gold wallpaper in one of his bathrooms and he got it. He pretended that Central Park, below his apartment, was his garden and it felt good to pretend. Everywhere he went people looked

and gasped and said, "There goes Jackie Gleason!" If he wanted
to make a personal appearance on somebody else's program, he
could command a fortune for it or, if he chose, he could appear
at a church communion breakfast for nothing, as he did for
Monsignor LeRoy McWilliams. He could be waited on hand and
foot; he could give away thousands of dollars (as he did, without publicity); he could travel anywhere in the world; build a
yacht, own a private railway car; go to Hollywood and star in a
picture of his own choosing; star on Broadway in a play; win a
smile from almost any girl; quit working when he was in the
mood; control the welfare of a couple of hundred high-priced
employees; have a drink; skip a drink; gamble; stay out until
dawn; read whatever he chose; ignore the things which dis-
pleased him; see an ad and say, "Send me ten"; help the poor;
have steak for breakfast; he was the king!

As the middle years opened to Jackie Gleason, he began to
work harder. Every morning at eight he left the penthouse on
Fifth Avenue for the penthouse office on Fifty-sixth Street. He
was sorting mail before the receptionist and the secretaries arrived. Everything in the huge office was new—even the names
in gold on the doors. On Gleason's door the legend is simple:
"Elephant Room."

He was in a perpetual morning fever to get things done because these were the big years and he wanted to keep them big
as long as possible. Jackie realized that there was only one direction in which he could now go—down. There was no further up;
there were no more Berles ahead. Somewhere, he knew, there
was a hungry young comedian with a new style whose goal was
to take Gleason.

It had to be.

A white-coated man named Roberts made coffee all day on an
electric range and brought cups of it, black, to Jackie with a little
lump of sugar lying on the saucer. Jackie Miles, one of the finest
stand-up comics in America, dropped in to talk about an appearance on Gleason's Stage Show. They did not trade jokes because what they had to discuss was serious: how much and for
how long?

Gleason's office is big—a combination of his old bedroom and his old office—and everything, including the huge two-legged desk, looks expensive. From a record player in a clothes closet jazz whispers in muted notes. Everyone with a problem files in and out: Durgom, Talent, Hurdle, Philbin, the writers, Reynolds, Satenstein, Poss. Jackie listens gravely, head held low over the blotter, the jowls hanging loose and heavy, and he shakes his head no, or he shakes his head yes.

He thinks he knows the people, and maybe he does. Gleason feels that the average American is smarter than the average newspaper editor rates him. "Don't try to fool the people," he says. "They won't go for the hoke. In my case, for instance, they sense what I am and it's foolish to try to con them into believing anything else."

The phone rings. It's Marilyn on the private extension. He gets to the point quickly, without asking how she feels or what she is doing. "I got two tickets for the fight tonight. . . . The fight. Yeah. . . . Well, if you want to go . . . Uh-huh. Oh, no. I thought maybe you'd eat first because CBS has a press party upstairs and I have to show. . . . Yes. . . . Well, why don't you do it this way? Pick me up here about a quarter to nine. . . . Hah? I'll hire a car. We'll go up to see the fights and then get something to eat. . . . Sure. Sure. . . . Quarter of nine. . . . Here. . . ."

He leaves his desk, balancing the most recent cup of coffee, and goes into Stanley's office to look at the newest film show of "The Honeymooners." It is shown on a screen in his one-time Spanish living room and he makes comments as it unwinds. He puffs and sips as Ralph Kramden comes in from a day's work and starts to fight with Alice. Afterward, he goes into another room and looks at the film in a machine akin to the old penny-arcade movies. Here he decides which camera angle to use in a given scene.

Between noon and 3:00 P.M. the executives of j.g. enterprises are eating in their respective offices—some eat early, some eat late. The Park Sheraton waiters seem to be always wheeling snowy tables into the office, or out.

Jackie makes two film shows a week—one on Tuesday night and one on Friday. At 2:00 P.M. he walks a block to the Adelphi

Theatre, where he got his start in television, and the cast runs through the sketch. At 7:15 P.M. ticket-holders are admitted to the theater and are entertained by a six-piece Dixieland Band.

At 7:45 P.M. Gleason puts on a bus driver's uniform, Audrey Meadows and Joyce Randolph don housedresses and aprons and old slippers, Carney dresses in sweat shirt, ancient vest and slacks, and a battered hat with upturned brim. They chat in the wings in whispers, and then, after a fanfare from the band, Jack Lescoulie steps on stage under raw white lights and introduces the members of the cast—Gleason last. The announcer explains why the three big cameras are spotted on stage and how the three will grind film simultaneously, so that the best angle can be selected from each clip. The curtains part, and the audience applauds as it sees the familiar kitchen, in color, for the first time. In thirty-seven minutes the show is over, locked in nine big cans of film, and Jackie goes back to his dressing room, pouring perspiration, to sit in a bathrobe and smoke a cigarette, while the well-wishers parade in and out to tell him how great he is, and how they have invoked God's blessing on his work for being such a wonderful man. Some try to tell funny stories to him, and he smiles tiredly as he listens, the hair on his chest black and curly in the V of the bathrobe.

He showers, dresses, and, when he leaves, there is a knot of people outside the stage door with autograph pads and pencils. They press close, and he quips feebly with them, "Oh, you're a dan-dan-dandy group!" and he edges slowly toward the curb and the open door of the car. He gets in, sometimes alone, sometimes with Bullets, and the chauffeur clicks it shut and the car hisses off up Fifty-third Street toward Seventh Avenue. If there is no fight to go to, and no hunger for food or a drink, he goes directly home and plays records or gets on the phone with Philbin or Marilyn or Toots. Then he wanders around, appearing to be in a great hurry, jotting ideas on pads or sitting and reading books about religion or metaphysics.

Jackie can turn on any one of his many television sets, or all of them. He can pop a sleeping pill into his mouth and take a gamble that something good will happen, or he can read and doze, sleeping pretty well in a chair but badly in bed, or he can phone someone who might have nothing to do and might want to kill an hour or two playing gin rummy at a cent a point. He can jump aboard the liner *United States* or charter a Constellation to Tokyo, or even run over to Proce's saloon in Brooklyn.

But he won't. He'll read and watch the clock until it gets around to 8:00 A.M. again.

One afternoon, in the new penthouse, Jackie was bouncing around in pajamas, playing records, making notes, putting phone calls through, and he walked into a room and saw Tony hanging suits and talking to himself.

"Jeez, we got to do something about you, pal," said Gleason.

Tony grinned apologetically.

"I mean," said Jackie, "when you start that stuff—"

"I've been busy," said Tony. "Sometimes three days go by and I don't even get to ride in the elevator."

"I know. I know. From now on, it's not good enough that you're hanging out with me all the time. From now on, you got to take a day off on your own. Alone. I'm just used to the two of us together."

"Okay, Jackie. Whatever you say."

"All right. Mondays. You take the new Buick."

"No. I couldn't do that."

"Don't give me that stuff, pal. You're taking the car."

"What will you use?"

"I'll hire a car on Mondays."

"Okay."

"One of us ought to get some fun out of all this."

He had everything but happiness. He could not sleep and he could not marry the girl he loved. Everything else was his. He did too much lonely thinking in too many lonely hours. He could phone Marilyn at any hour—her apartment was exactly fifteen blocks away from his penthouse—but when she said, "What's new?" he had to admit that there was nothing new. Not a thing.

"The house on the hill was such a lovely idea," she said once.

"It still is," he said.

"Yes. It still is," she said, "almost three years later."

"Mah, I swear I'll work it out."

"I love you, Jackie."

"I love you too. I tell you we're going to have our house on the hill and I mean we're going to have that house."

"I know."

"Promise you'll be patient with me."

"I promise."

"And I promise I'll work it out. I don't know how, yet, but I'll work it out."

"I believe you."

"Those three words you just said are worth all the gold in the world."

Today, the old neighborhood in Brooklyn looks tired. The flats lean against each other for mutual support and the boys that Jackie Gleason once dazzled with a pool cue are now paunchy and middle-aged. Practically all of them have moved from Chauncey and Herkimer and Saratoga. The little Proce tavern is still on the corner. It still has two television sets—one for those who prefer the fights; one for those who want Gleason.

In the record player are some of Jackie's records, but these are so old that they are unreliable and sometimes stick in the groove. Someone up front yells, "Ah, shut the damn thing off!" In the back is a picture of a young and gay Jackie Gleason hanging on a wall. Underneath is a legend: "Not responsible for personal property."

Orange hasn't been seen in many years. John Cocoman became a fireman. Charlie Cretter was a disk jockey in an A&P. Marty Dyer became a detective. The Healys drove trucks. Jimmy O'Hare ran an elevator. Jimmy Kiernan became a police sergeant. Harold Kroell was head of the bureau of unemployment in Brooklyn. Tommy Dennehy was a beer salesman in Jersey. Teddy Gilanza was an office assistant to Gleason. Primo Ippolito died. Adolf Signorelli was killed in World War II. Heinzy died of tuberculosis. Bookshelf Robinson became a professor at New York University. Buster Sands was a store clerk. Two became drug addicts. One served time for robbery. One is a priest. Almost all of the girls married and could be seen, with their noses high in the air, pushing perambulators past Proce's saloon.

All of them knew about Jackie's success and nobody envied

him. "He had it," they said. "He had it all along. Give him
credit." Sometimes—though not often—one of the gang would
stop backstage to see Jackie. The name would be sent in and
there would be a little nervousness. "Maybe the guy's busy. We
don't want to bother Jackie." Not long ago Julie Dennehy and
her husband hired a baby sitter and took Julie's sister with them
to see Gleason. After the show they sent their names in to his
dressing room and waited anxiously.

The door swung open, Gleason bounced out bright and happy
in a blue robe with arms wide apart. "Gotzie!" he roared and took
them both in his arms and shooed the producers and directors
outside and ordered drinks sent up to the dressing room and
talked old times.

Joe Tolle, tall and bald and quietly independent, wanted to see
a Gleason show. He knew that he could not stand a refusal from
Jackie, so he didn't ask. He wrote to the network for tickets, but
none came. He saw Jimmy Proce one day and asked for tickets,
and Jimmy said, "You know Jackie as well as I do. Ask him." So
Joe gave up. Later, he learned that his sister-in-law was a member of a Jackie Gleason fan club. Through her, he got two tickets
and sat shiny-eyed watching the neighborhood kid wow 50,000,-
000 people through cameras. Afterward, he went home without
sending his name up.

Pop Dennehy is old and he sits in front of his television screen
watching the kid he knew so well and he can't, for the life of him,
see what's funny about Jackie Gleason. "He's a crazy kid," he
says, "and that's all there is to that."

Mrs. Dennehy, who often lent a dollar to Jackie, walked into
an A&P on Broadway, Brooklyn, one morning and saw a dark,
handsome man talking into a microphone. She squinted her eyes
for a better look and then she ran up to the microphone and
screamed, "Charlie Cretter, you old son of a bee, what are you
doing here?" She could be heard all over the store and down a
few sidewalks. Charlie, now a disk jockey, covered the microphone with his hands and figured that he was fired for sure,
especially because Mrs. Dennehy forgot to use the word "bee."
Still, it was a voice from home, and he shut off the apparatus
and they talked for half an hour.

"Do you ever see Jackie, God bless him?"

"No, Mrs. Dennehy, I don't. I've been so darn busy, and he's busy; I just don't get the time. But he hasn't forgotten, Mrs. Dennehy. You got to hand it to Jackie. When he sees you, he stops cold. I haven't seen him—well, what's the use of lying to you— he's a big man today, Mrs. Dennehy. You've got to respect him and when you walk up to him you don't feel the same any more. Yet you know he's the same guy and he wants to be the same guy—oh, I don't know."

Mrs. Dennehy decided to go over to see Jackie, and after the show she stood on the backstage stairway in company with all the grand ladies in their minks and sables, and all the notable men waiting to shake his hand. Jackie came out and practically carried Mrs. Dennehy inside and he held her face in his hands and almost cried. The two of them talked so loud that neither one could hear what the other was saying, and when Mrs. Dennehy left she told Jackie that poor old St. Benedict's had a leak in the roof and could he do something about it.

He sent a check for $1,000.

At 40 Central Park South, Genevieve Halford Gleason sat with Linda and Geraldine studying the lush view below. It was a cold night and, under the swinging lights on the paths of Central Park, the trees seemed to be hung with rock candy and the meadows were smooth with vanilla icing. Cabs and hansoms moved slowly along the curving roads, and the three sat in silence, just watching.

One mile to the north Jackie Gleason stood alone on the terrace of his penthouse, looking below at the same view. He saw the yellow lights of the cabs moving through the dead trees and he saw the mystical beauty of a winter night over Central Park. He pulled a muffler tighter around his neck, puffed on a cigarette, and yelled, "Tone!"

He waited. There was no answer. Then he remembered. This was Monday—Tony's day off. Jackie was alone.

About the Author

JIM BISHOP *began his literary career as copy boy for the New* York Daily News. *Then in 1930 Mark Hellinger went to the* Daily Mirror *and took Mr. Bishop as his assistant very shortly after that. From such beginnings Jim Bishop went on to hold almost every job there is to be done in the business. He has been a reporter, a rewrite man, a feature writer, a magazine editor, a literary agent and a free-lance author. He is at present executive editor of* Catholic Digest, *and he did the writing of* The Golden Ham *on week ends and in the evening after his editorial chores had been completed.*

Mr. Jim Bishop
Hotel Excelsior
Rome, Italy

DEAR JIM:

Well, I have read the book!

Am I supposed to indignantly shout "libel-fable" in offense, or meekly murmur "circumstance-adversity" in defense?

It is too late in life for me to feign either attitude. I have allowed my egoism to carefully manufacture two luxury items; a dignity opposed to denial, and a pride disturbed by pity.

To admit the truth of most if not all you report gives me no heroic glow. The heroism of confession is satisfying only to a fool. Besides, the clarity and evidence of my indiscretions insulate me from the warmth of any such emotional deceit.

I have no legitimate argument for my conduct There have been times that I have tried philosophy and liquor to justify my behavior and pacify my conscience. The experiments failed—wisdom and whisky make promises they can't keep.

I have never been a modest man and I have always been suspicious of an actor's modesty It is usually counterfeit and is actually commercial naivete. The cause and *effect* contradict the virtue. So, please believe me when I tell you I don't want my success to be admired—just the incongruity of it.

Sincerely,

JACKIE GLEASON

P.S. Giving it all one last thought, Jim, it has occurred to me that an actor's security and the eye of a hurricane have a great deal in common.

jg

Mr. Jackie Gleason
Park Sheraton Hotel
7th Avenue at 55th Street
New York, N. Y.

DEAR JACK:

Here is the manuscript. It's a little bit bulky, but then so are you.
Read it carefully and, if you find any inaccuracies, please draw lines
in the margin and we will discuss them. . . .

Under the agreement between us, you have no right to change or
omit anything in this book. It is facetious on my part to remind
you of this because, throughout the writing of it, you have been
reminding me that this is Jim Bishop's book, Jim Bishop's idea of
Gleason. . . .

A good part of the book is unflattering. Some of it would shake a
sinner. It is all here—all on the record. You were, at times, a boaster,
a braggart There are scenes of drunkenness and despair. Others
describe, in some detail, your affinity for blondes. There is one—a
heartbreaker to write—of your mother dying while you sat jobless.
As a Roman Catholic, you staggered, skidded, slipped and fell all
over the ecclesiastical landscape. As a husband, you failed, and you
failed a good woman. Later in life you fell in love with a fine girl,
but even in this, with the best of intentions, you were blocked by
forces spiritual, emotional and legal.

There are few men I've met who have tried harder to be "good."
To some, I am sure, it comes easily. Not to you. Everything you have
done—personally and professionally—has been done the hard way.
This, if you can stand one opinion, makes you a bigger and better
man than you think. Conscience and contrition are brothers—and,
brother, you have both in king size! . . .

This biography—unless I have missed the target entirely—is a
complete recitation of the great and awful things in a man's life. It
has no "slant," either in your favor or opposed to you. I think that
the life of every man is a balance of good and evil, of courage and
cowardice, of racing toward the stars while creeping toward the
grave.

Good luck in the next forty, my friend. . . .

JIM BISHOP

CPSIA information can be obtained
at www.ICGtesting.com
Printed in the USA
BVHW040240091220
595252BV00022B/1445